THE LIBERAL ANGLICAN
IDEA OF HISTORY

Prince Consort Prize Essay

1950

THE
LIBERAL ANGLICAN
IDEA OF HISTORY

BY

DUNCAN FORBES

CAMBRIDGE
AT THE UNIVERSITY PRESS
1952

PUBLISHED BY

THE SYNDICS OF THE CAMBRIDGE UNIVERSITY PRESS

London Office: Bentley House, N.W.I
American Branch: New York

Agents for Canada, India, and Pakistan: Macmillan

Printed in Great Britain by The Carlyle Press, Birmingham, 6

CONTENTS

CONTENTS

NOTE

Figures in brackets in the text and footnotes refer
the reader to further notes at the end of the book

FOREWORD

HISTORIANS have often observed and commented on the strength of the tradition of 18th century Rationalism in England in the first half of the 19th century, and it is not surprising that the outlook of the 'philosophic' century still generally prevailed in historical theory and practice. Hallam, James Mill, Grote, Macaulay and Scott belonged to the tradition of the Rationalist historians of the 18th century. The presuppositions of their historical thinking were Rationalist presuppositions. They believed, for example, that men are everywhere and at all times mentally the same, though this did not prevent them from believing also, paradoxically enough, that history reveals the moral and intellectual progress of the race, the 'March of Mind'. The belief in the uniformity of human nature was the great stumbling-block which prevented the Rationalists from reaching a truly historical outlook.

No intellectual epoch is homogeneous, and even during the Triumvirate of Hume, Robertson and Gibbon there had been dissenters, and signs of new attitudes in historical thinking.[1] But these signs of change—primitivism, pietism, medievalism, nationalism—cannot be said to represent a decisive break with the Rationalist tradition, which was able to accommodate the new modes, as the Roman Empire accommodated the barbarian tribes, without fundamentally altering the laws of its intellectual existence. Enthusiasm for the Middle Ages, for instance, could exist in Scott alongside the belief in the essential sameness of human nature in all ages. A considerable amount of scene-shifting had already taken place on the Rationalist stage to accommodate the idea of progress, and the conception of the vital contribution of the Medieval Church to civilization. But in spite of these movements, the grounds of the historical thinking of Voltaire, Turgot and

---

[1] See T. P. Peardon, *The Transition in English Historical Writing*, 1760-1830 (1933).

Condorcet, of Hume, Gibbon, Hallam, James Mill and Scott, remained unshaken.

Because Rationalist philosophy and history were so closely allied, there had to be a new philosophy, a new *Weltanschauung*, before there could be a new history. In Germany the new historical outlook was established by the end of the 18th century, when, significantly enough, Vico began to be appreciated and Vichian ideas to circulate; but in England it was not until the decade 1820-30, or thereabouts, that the attempted construction by Coleridge of a new system, opposed to everything which the Rationalists held most vital, brought about of necessity a real revolution in historical thinking. The history of both Rationalists and Romantics, of the 18th century and the revolt against it, was fundamentally practical, and therefore fundamentally different, because inseparable from contrasting views of man and nature.

It was because their history was essentially practical, therefore, and because they challenged the Rationalist tradition at all the vital points, that the disciples and followers of Coleridge, the men who looked to Germany and to Vico for inspiration, the 'Germano-Coleridgeans', Thomas Arnold and his friends, played the vital role in England in the development of an attitude to history opposed to that of the Rationalists: one which was in many ways more truly historical, especially in its substitution for the uniformity of human nature of what may be called the Vichian or Romantic philosophy of mind.

The Liberal Anglicans, as this group of people [1] may be called, have hitherto been neglected [2] because the history of history in England has tended to deal only with the 'great historians', the Carlyles, Grotes and Macaulays, and also because it has not taken sufficient account of the practical character of the historical thinking of the age, which is the real clue to interpretation. It has studied the Liberal Anglicans in compartments of 'classical' and 'ecclesiastical' history, and neglected their idea of history as a whole. It has tended to confine itself to formal 'Histories' and Lectures, which, studied in isolation, may give a misleading impression. The Liberal Anglicans, as will be seen, used the term 'ecclesiastical history' for academic purposes, though they firmly believed (and it was a belief involving practical consequences of fundamental importance for their whole outlook on Church and State) that there was no such thing in the academic sense of the word: that secular and ecclesiastical history were one and indivisible. Thomas Arnold, too, in his lectures at Oxford, deliberately modified his conception of history to fit the prevailing academic divisions of 'Ancient' and 'Modern', though all the other evidence shows that these divisions had no real meaning for him. The history of history must break through the artificial crust of historical narrative and the cake of academic custom to the living thought beneath.

In the first half of the 19th century, then, one sees the development in England of an attitude to the past more truly historical than that of the Rationalists—at least one sees this development carried so much further, so much more systematically and consciously, as to constitute an intellectual revolution. It is the object of this study to examine the Liberal Anglican share in the unfolding of the new historical outlook, to try to find out how far the Liberal Anglicans may be said to have brought about a revolution in historical thinking in England, to examine the relation between their ideas and their practice, and to estimate how far these ideas may be said to be truly historical from the critical point of view of the modern observer. It is so easy to misinterpret the written word that I have tried to let Thomas Arnold and his friends speak for themselves as much as possible.

My thanks are due to the editor of *The Quarterly Review* for answering my queries as to the authorship of articles in the early numbers, and to Mr A. J. Hunt for showing me MSS of Arnold and Stanley in the possession of Rugby School.

I am grateful to Professor Butterfield for his interest and encouragement.

Also, I would like to thank the Cambridge University Press for helping to prepare the MS for publication; in particular, for carrying out a surgical operation of some delicacy in severing the notes from the references. Essential references in footnotes have been cut to the minimum, and notes (marked in the text by square brackets), which support and, it is hoped, enrich the argument have been relegated to the end of the volume.

The work which is now published is substantially the same as a Prize Essay which was awarded a Prince Consort Prize in 1950.

DUNCAN FORBES

CAMBRIDGE
November 1950

CHAPTER I

THE LIBERAL ANGLICANS AND THE PROBLEM OF THE NATURE OF PROGRESS

THE years in which the Liberal Anglican idea of history took shape were critical in the social history of modern England. This background of social crisis in the first half of the 19th century, which hardly affected Macaulay's attitude to the past, made a deep impression on the Liberal Anglicans and is a vital factor in the interpretation of their historical thought, as it is also in the historical thought of Carlyle. This means that the search for the origins of Liberal Anglican thought must begin on the plane of ideas and temperament, because the social matrix of Thomas Arnold and his friends was that of Macaulay. Why was the historical outlook of the Liberal Anglicans not typical of the prosperous, rising middle class?

The Liberal Anglicans were in revolt against the 18th century, against that world of optimism, of utilitarianism and individualism which, in the words of Cobban,[1] came finally into its own in England in the 19th century. All the signs of the Romantic revolt against the 18th century are present in the ideas of the Liberal Anglicans: their political thought was in the direct line of descent from Burke and Coleridge; their philosophy was Coleridgean, opposed to the mechanical, materialistic epistemology of the Lockian tradition; they looked to the historians and philosophers of the 'German Movement', rather than to the French liberal thinkers, for inspiration; their religion was not an external form, an affair of 'evidences' and rational proofs, but an inward conviction and belief in God's providential government of the world. In short, they belonged to the 'Germano-Coleridgean' school, as John Mill called it.

It is the Romantic strain in their minds which is significant for the history of history. Whately, it is true, the 'typical Noetic',[2]

---

[1] A. Cobban, *Edmund Burke and the Revolt against the 18th Century.*

[2] V. F. Storr, *The Development of English Theology in the 19th Century* (1913), p. 96. Whately 'appreciated the logic rather than the poetry of life'.

can hardly be called a Romantic; he, too, alone of the group, remained ignorant of German. He was nevertheless the friend and mentor of Arnold, and he claimed that he was the first to stress the importance of the imagination in the study of history.[1] In Milman also there are obvious marks of the 18th century. His piety was 'rational, articulate, objective, confident, robust . . . neither sensitive nor subtle'.[2] Alone among the Liberal Anglicans he admired Gibbon greatly, in the *History of the Jews* there are traces of what Milman himself called Gibbon's 'covert sneer', [3] and the edition of the *Decline and Fall* which he prepared remained the standard edition until that of Bury. He has been called 'a survivor from the Age of Reason, a kind of Christian Gibbon, without the indecency and without the fun'.[3] But in his poetic youth Milman was compared with Byron.[4] Later, under the influence of the Schlegels, he was attracted to the poetry of India and published a translation of the Mahabharata. What is more to the point, he admired Vico and possessed a copy of the *Scienza Nuova*.

Julius Hare and Thirlwall were the champions of Wordsworth and Coleridge, and translators not only of Niebuhr's *History of Rome*, but of tales by Tieck and Fouqué. Tieck's object, wrote Carlyle, was 'to penetrate into the inmost shrines of Imagination', to seize and adapt to the feelings of modern minds 'the true tone of that ancient time when man was in his childhood, when the universe within was divided by no walls of adamant from the universe without'.

Thomas Arnold was the friend of Wordsworth (politics notwithstanding) and made his home, the beloved Fox How, among the mountains of Cumberland. He was, in a sense, a Lakist, an aspect of the man which has lately received attention.[5] He used to take pupils from Rugby to Fox How, because mountains and dales were, he said, 'a great point in education'. A. P. Stanley was Arnold's pupil and intellectual heir, and his thought is dominated by that of the master. He was a romantic in biblical interpretation,

[1] *Life and Correspondence of R. Whately*, vol. II, p. 211.
[2] Charles Smyth, *Dean Milman* (1949), p. 19.
[3] Smyth, *Dean Milman*, p. 19.
[4] C. H. Herford, *The Age of Wordsworth*, p. 46.
[5] See Basil Willey, *Studies in Nineteenth Century Thought*, p. 68. [4]

bringing the Bible to life by the power of his historical sympathy and pictorial imagination,[1] following, in this, the Coleridgean reaction against the abstractions of Rationalist history. For Coleridge had written:

In nothing is Scriptural history more strongly contrasted with the histories of highest note in the present age, than in its freedom from the hollowness of abstractions. While the latter present a shadow-fight of Things and Quantities, the former gives us the history of men, and balances the important influence of individual Minds with the previous state of the national morals and manners. . . . How should it be otherwise? The histories and political economy of the present and preceding century partake in the general contagion of its mechanic philosophy, and are the *product* of an unenlivened generalizing Understanding.[2]

It was the concrete, the pictorial in ecclesiastical history which appealed particularly to Stanley; his delight was in the recreation of the atmosphere of historical scenes. One does not go to Milman, either, for the history of dogma and doctrine. What one gets, in both historians, is rather the climate of opinion, the living atmosphere, in Stanley, of particular scenes, in Milman of whole centuries. Dislike of party-spirit and party-warfare reinforced this romantic method of historical reconstruction, for dogma and doctrine for the Liberal Anglicans meant controversy over inessentials.

The Liberal Anglicans, like Carlyle, did not escape the experience of the Everlasting No. Early in their biographies one meets spiritual crisis, doubt, scepticism, pessimism, irony. Stanley in his *Life of Arnold* talks of 'the morbid state of mind into which he was thrown, from various causes, at his entrance on life'.[3] The years spent at Laleham (1819-28) seem to represent in Arnold's life a withdrawal in which he finally overcame all his early doubts, restlessness, and lack of purpose. Thirlwall was described by Carlyle as 'the massive Cantabrigian Scholar and Sceptic',[4] and his biographer talks of his habitual tone of irony. Thirlwall, in fact, made a famous study of irony, in which he distinguished a practical as

---

[1] Storr, *Development of English Theology*, p. 399.
[2] *Statesman's Manual* (1816), pp. 34-5.
[3] *Life of Thomas Arnold*, pp. 15-16, 340n.
[4] J. C. Thirlwall, *Connop Thirlwall*, p. 116; cf. p. 23.

opposed to a purely verbal irony, an irony of Providence which evolves good out of apparent evil. It was this irony, inherent in the events, which lent, in Thirlwall's eyes, 'the highest degree of interest to the conflicts of religious and political parties'.[1] In Hare, a certain puritanical, Old Testament strain, like that of Carlyle, was very strong; he denounced the ease in Zion and luxury of too much civilization, pointed sternly to the inevitable end of all non-Christian nations, and appears sometimes in the guise of a prophet alone in the moral wilderness of civilization, with its sophisticated fear of ridicule, its painted ladies, and pickpockets. 'Excitement' was, for Arnold and his friends, the great spiritual danger in what Stanley called an 'overheated' civilization. The growing popularity of novels and other symptoms were viewed as sure signs of decadence.

One result of this hostile atttitude to the world which was being created by the industrial revolution and modern science was that the Liberal Anglicans were readier than those who, like Macaulay, gloried in the march of material civilization to feel the full weight of the misery and squalor of the critical years in which their historical thought was taking shape. Their awareness of crisis was as sharp as that of any of their contemporaries, and deeper than most. Even during his phase of youthful Toryism, in 1815, Arnold apparently expressed real feeling about the social state of England.[2] It was to be a perpetual source of anxiety to him in later life. In 1848 Milman wrote of 'the wilderness of our manufacturing world', and of the probability, nay the certainty, that 'the fatal cycle will continue to revolve with more intense force and rapidity—speculation, prosperity, over-production, glut, distress'.[3] Thirlwall, described by his biographer as in the vanguard of social thought, was the only bishop to vote for the repeal of the Corn Laws. The crisis was, for the Liberal Anglicans, not only economic and social, but, as for Coleridge, moral and intellectual also, and this alone would have made for a deeper and wider conception of history than that of their contemporaries, at a time when history was still generally thought of as essentially practical, a conscious relation of past and

---

[1] *Remains: Literary and Theological*, vol. III, p. 8 ('The Irony of Sophocles').
[2] Stanley, *Life*, p. 14.   [3] *Quarterly Review*, vol. 78, pp. 385-6.

present. That their interpretation of the present was not confined to the level of potential legislative remedy, to the plane of institutions and mere political machinery, as was that of the Utilitarians, of Grote, for example, but plumbed depths of experience hardly recognized to exist by the Utilitarians and their allies, was part cause and part consequence of a deeper understanding of the past. As has been seen, the history of history cannot separate past and present, and it is especially true of the Liberal Anglicans that their attitude to contemporary problems is a clue to their historical thought. Arnold said of his anxiety about the state of the nation: 'Perhaps it comes from my fondness for History, that political things have as great a reality to my mind, as things of private life, and the life of the nation becomes distinct as that of an individual.'[1] The study of the past intensified Arnold's awareness of the present, and vice versa.

Underlying and subtly influencing the approach of their Rationalist adversaries to these contemporary problems, as it seemed to the Liberal Anglicans, was the idea of progress, and to view the Liberal Anglican idea of history as an enquiry into the true nature of progress—somewhat artificial as this proceeding may be—is useful not only for purposes of exposition—because it introduces a unifying principle into the whole—but also because it emphasizes the practical character, as well as the depth and dimensions of their thought, while at the same time illuminating more fully its emotional background.

Progress in 1815 was the faith of Radicals and atheists, a belief still tainted with Jacobinism, with violent revolution and godlessness. Hatred of the Radicals was reinforced by the fear of imminent social conflict. These emotions the Liberal Anglicans shared with the majority of the 'respectable' classes, but the Liberal Anglican dislike of the Radical solution was not grounded on fear and prejudice alone, but on a philosophy of life which was one facet of the great post-war religious movement, whose 'lunatic fringe' looked for the coming of the millennium, and which led ultimately either to Oxford, or to Rome or to the Broad Church. The Liberal Anglicans hated Radicalism as a symptom of the materialism

[1] Letter of 10 May 1839.

of the age, of the philosophical vacuum which that materialism represented, of the shameful intellectual backwardness of England as compared with France or Germany,[1] and as the heir to the Rationalism of the 18th century, which had learnt nothing from the French Revolution, being still grounded on abstract theory and not on historical experience. They organized themselves intellectually against the Benthamites in the tradition of Burke and Coleridge, and by the time that the unreasoning fear of 'perfectibility' had died away and the idea of progress had become respectable, they had entrenched themselves against it in the study of history, reinforced from the great arsenal (which they had discovered) of German historical speculation. Progress became the *credo* of triumphant Victorianism with the development of the purely material side of civilization, a development which the Liberal Anglicans distrusted in itself, and progress, in becoming respectable, became from the Liberal Anglican point of view more dangerous intrinsically, as well as more widespread, than the revolutionary doctrine of perfectibility had been. The latter was an avowed belief in man to the exclusion of God, the clearly defined faith of a small militant party, while the former could afford to neglect God while still outwardly conforming to a belief in His Providence.

The Liberal Anglican enquiry into the nature of true progress, which had its beginnings in the dislike of Utilitarianism and fear of Jacobinism, was not seriously modified, therefore, when the 'Jacobinical' idea of progress developed in the course of the century into a widespread belief in the inevitable onward march of civilization. By this time, the Liberal Anglicans had arrived at a conception of history which gave the lie to the popular idea of progress as an unbroken course of inevitable material improvement,[5] and which emphasized not the material and exclusively intellectual, but the moral and spiritual aspect of civilization, or, in Coleridge's words, 'cultivation', rather than 'civilization.' Their emotional pessimism of 1815-30 became a 'scientific' pessimism, based on a 'science of history'.

[2] Cf. Thirlwall's letters to Bunsen (1821) in *Letters*, ed. Perowne and Stokes, pp. 60, 65-6.

Progress, being for the Liberal Anglicans, not an unquestioned assumption, but a challenge to their deepest beliefs, provides the logical starting point for an examination of the Liberal Anglican idea of history, because it is a presupposition, but not the absolute presupposition, of their thought. [6] Their absolute presupposition was God's Providence; it is this which they took for granted and which they never questioned or doubted.

That progress was not a Liberal Anglican assumption is a distinguishing mark of their historical thinking, representing, historically, a decisive and fundamental break with the whole spirit of Rationalist history in England. The 'philosophical history' of the Rationalists, as represented, for example, by Condorcet, took progress for granted. Its task was to describe the stages in the inevitable process of the 'March of Mind'. Progress in this sense was the presupposition of the Scottish school of 'conjectural history', as Dugald Stewart called it, the 'natural history of society' as studied by Millar, Adam Ferguson and others. James Mill, as an historian, belonged to this tradition. His primary object in the famous second book of his *History of British India* was not to describe the culture of India, but to fix it in the scale of progressive civilization. In other words, for these historians, civilization was a question of degree. Such a view assumes that 'civilization' is inevitable and a good thing in itself, and begs the whole question of its value and of its inevitability. The Liberal Anglicans refused to think of progress as 'civilization' in this sense, and were repelled by the spiritual and imaginative poverty of the conception of the 'March of Mind'. 'How baseless and delusive is the vulgar notion of the march of mind as necessarily exhibiting a steady regular advance within the same nation in all things', said Hare.[1]

'O trust not in the efficacy of Civilization! there is no baser, more senseless idolatry. If things are at all better to-day, it is not Civilization that has bettered them. As for any charm in Civilization to preserve us from cruelty there is none such: if Civilization of itself could anywise soften the heart, it would only be by weakening and unmanning it. . . . When Civilization is severed from moral principle and religious doctrine, there is no power in it to make the heart gentle.[2]

'What', he asked, 'is the great blessing of a very general state of

[1] *Guesses ai Truth* (2nd ed., 2nd series), p. 15.   [2] *Ibid.* (1827 ed.), vol. II, pp. 306-9.

civilization? That there are no highwaymen and . . . plenty of pickpockets,'[1] and he pointed to the fact that effective resistance to Napoleon was found on the fringes of civilization, in Spain and Russia.[2] 'Civilization' and the 'March of Mind' were assumptions which the Liberal Anglicans could not accept, because they dispensed with God's Providence. Progress in the Rationalist sense, too, was part of a conception of history (*histoire raisonné*) which from the point of view of Romanticism was lacking in fulness and depth. The Rationalists held, in words used by Gibbon and quoted with approval by James Mill, that 'aux yeux d'un philosophe, les faits composent la partie la moins interressante de l'histoire'.[3] Such an idea of progress as that of the Rationalist historians, related, as it was, to an individualistic conception of society, was unsatisfactory to men whose interest was stirred by the contemplation of the concrete and particular, and for whom the state was a growing organism, not a collection of atomistic individuals.

On the other hand, such history as was written by Romantics in the first three decades of the 19th century in England could not have seemed satisfactory to men for whom history was nothing if not practical. It was not philosophical enough. It conformed too closely to Aristotle's definition, almost wholly immersed in the particular, as it was, and not rising to any kind of useful generalization about the development of society, nor making any contribution to the critical problems of the social condition of England. Lingard, for example, in whom, according to Fueter, the opposition to the historiography of Rationalism in England is first clearly seen, rejected the 'philosophical' history of the 18th century, but sought to transform the historian into a mere reporter of events.[4] And it is worth noting that Scott, as a philosophical historian—a title to which he may justly lay claim—wrote altogether in the tradition of the Rationalist historians.[5] The chapter in the *Tales of a Grandfather*, for instance, which treats of the progress of society, is pure 'conjectural' history (Scott had been a pupil of Dugald

---

[1] *Ibid.* p. 18. [7]   [2] *Ibid.* p. 307.
[3] *History of British India* (1817), vol. I, p. xix n.
[4] Fueter, *Histoire de l'Historiographie Moderne* (1914), p. 640; Gooch, *History and Historians*, p. 290; Peardon, *Transition in English Historical Writing*, pp. 282-3.
[5] A. W. Benn, *History of English Rationalism in the 19th Century*, vol. I, p. 310.

Stewart),[1] and Master Little John, for whom the book was written, showed himself more of a Romantic than Scott in this respect by heartily disliking this chapter.

For men like Arnold, urgently seeking a science of society which could be applied effectively, but repudiating the Rationalist route to the same end, the great fault of this Romantic view of history in England was that it was too close to mere antiquarianism or too imaginative to be brought to bear with weight on present problems. It gloried too much in the past for its own sake. Arnold attacked this sort of history, which Taine described as 'poetical history', as unpractical, and because it tended to bring the serious study of history into disrepute with practical men, a disastrous development from his point of view.

The pictures thus produced, [he wrote] were striking and beautiful indeed, but nothing practical could be learnt from them since they displayed a world as unreal as the fantastic creations of romance. Indeed if their brilliancy ever excited a wish to imitate them the result was . . . mischievous, when attempts were made to force the character and practice of modern nations from their proper growth and course, in the vain hope of making them resemble a pattern purely imaginary. . . . We may hope that the folly is gone by of painting the manners, institutions and events of ancient times in colours most strongly contrasted with everything which we know from our own experience.[2]

Moreover although its national outlook (Turner's desire to arouse by his History a 'patriotic curiosity' about the Anglo-Saxons is an example)[3] was an improvement on the soul-destroying cosmopolitanism of the Rationalist historians, which was bad because 'unnatural' in Romantic eyes, this was, from a practical point of view, from the point of view of a science of history, a narrowing outlook, and to be deplored if it buttressed the sort of chauvinistic patriotism which the Liberal Anglicans denounced whenever it raised its head. Liberal Anglican thought, indeed, represents a reaction against parochialism in the form either of Romantic nationalism or in that of Rationalist Europocentricism

---

[1] See Lockhart's *Life of Scott* (1837), vol. I, pp. 171-4. In an essay on the feudal system submitted to Dugald Stewart, Scott 'endeavoured to prove that it proceeds upon principles common to all nations when placed in a certain situation'.

[2] *Quarterly Review*, vol. 32, pp. 77-8.

[3] Peardon, *Transition in English Historical Writing*, p. 224.

—for Rationalist history, which had begun with Voltaire's protest against the theological Europocentricism of Bossuet, had substituted a Europocentricism based on the idea of progress—and this is seen, for instance, in F. D. Maurice's *Religions of the World*, which was for Stanley the sign of a new era in the relations of Christianity with the whole world.[1]

Rationalist history was practical; it related past and present; was concerned with causes and general laws; but although claiming to be universal in outlook, its conception of history was limited and superficial. Romantic history delighted in the fulness and complexity of the past, but even when it traversed many ages and many societies (as in Southey) was not universal in outlook, at least in England, nor practical in nature, being content to describe the particular, and not attempting to argue from the particular to the general.

What the Liberal Anglicans, concerned as they were with the practical problems of the condition of England, and loyal to the tradition of Wordsworth and Coleridge, required, therefore, was the practical character of Rationalist history in alliance with history seen in all its fulness and depth; a philosophical history concerned with general laws, but based on the concrete individuality of the nation's life-course; the subjection of the idea of progress to the test of the real facts of history, that is, the facts of history seen in their wholeness.

A conception of history which was practical, yet not Rationalist, which was philosophical, but not in the 18th-century sense of 'philosophical' history, which was Romantic, yet concerned with general laws and based on critical scholarship, which was related to an organic conception of the state, and which was deeply religious, the Liberal Anglicans discovered in the German historical movement, and in Vico who stood behind it.

The nature of the revolution which this discovery worked in their minds is revealed by a remark of Sterling, the pupil and friend of Hare, who said that Niebuhr's *History of Rome* 'was the first help I had in getting out of the slough of Benthamism'.[2] It

---

[1] See Stanley's *Essay on the Theology of the 19th Century*.

[2] In a letter to Hare (1829), Hare's 'Life of the Author', *Essays and Tales of John Sterling*, vol. I, p. xxix.

was not long before Niebuhr, who at first appeared to the Liberal Anglicans as an oasis in the desert of Rationalism, was seen to be only one region of a vast new intellectual continent, hitherto almost totally unexplored by Englishmen. It is easy to say, therefore, that the revolutionary character of the Liberal Anglican idea of history in the England of the early 19th century is due to the the fact that they were the first to enter this new continent. The imprint of German thought is an obvious distinguishing mark, and this, at a time when the number of those who could read German, let alone those who had any real acquaintance with the thought of Germany, was infinitesimal in England, gives this intellectual revolution, at first glance, a precise beginning, such as few movements in the history of ideas possess. But no 'influence' is a simple gift, the filling of a vacuum, though this seems to be a presupposition of many studies of 'influences', and to trace any revolution in thought to an 'influence' or influences is to proceed mechanically, and not historically, for what is given is straightway transformed and made part of a whole which has its own individuality, and its peculiar conditions of development. [8] Not until the Liberal Anglican idea of history has been presented in its totality, therefore, can there be any discussion as to the nature of the revolution which it represented in the history of history in England.

CHAPTER II

THE LIBERAL ANGLICAN
SCIENCE OF HISTORY

(a) The Progress of Nations: Social and Political

(i) Arnold, Niebuhr and Vico

It is not the primary object of this study to examine the influence of the German historical movement, to discuss the problem of the development of *Historismus* in England; so that it is not necessary, in sketching the main outlines of the Liberal Anglican idea of history, to trace back each separate strand of thought to its origin. Niebuhr was the spearhead of *Altertumwissenschaft* in England (Thirlwall and Hare had read Niebuhr by 1818), but *Altertumwissenschaft* is only a part of the whole 'German Movement'. Certain assumptions of Niebuhr's method, and the whole atmosphere in which he moved, are important for the Liberal Anglican idea of history, rather than any specific contributions which he may have made to it. Behind the German Movement, moreover, stands Vico; a fact of which the Liberal Anglicans were aware[9]. The Liberal Anglican science of history arose out of the application of ideas which belong to this tradition; there is not the evidence to enable one to unravel the complex pedigree of these ideas; to attempt to trace each back to its origin, and to assess the force of each particular impact, would be as barren a task as it would be difficult. It is the force and nature of the impact of the whole tradition which is relevant here.

It was Thomas Arnold who pursued the possibility of a science of history most ardently, and who alone gave his ideas on the subject any formal shape. This was because Arnold was more concerned with practical problems of social and political history than any of the other Liberal Anglicans [10]. The interests of Hare and Milman were more philosophical and literary. By the time Arnold's pupil, Stanley, took over the notion from him, its main outlines had been fixed, and Stanley's was not the mind to elaborate a speculative system. [11]

The impact of 'the new intellectual world which dawned upon' Arnold (to use the words of his biographer, Stanley) was in its first stage almost solely and completely the impact of Niebuhr's *History of Rome*. In 1824 Arnold learned German to read this book, which Hare had recommended to him. But although he read Niebuhr with the purely technical aim of writing a history of Rome himself,[1] though his immediate problems were therefore intellectual problems only, and though the aspect of Arnold's discovery which is best known is the merely technical one, and the revolution in method which Niebuhr effected continued to work in him until his death, so that he is known in the history of historiography as the exponent of Niebuhr's critical method in England, much more important for Arnold was the larger revolution of ideas which took place in him almost as rapidly, and which must therefore have satisfied deep-seated needs, showing that the ground was prepared for it; a revolution which represents for Arnold what John Stuart Mill's crisis represented in the Utilitarian world, the inrush of a 19th century outlook. This was, however, much less of a 'conversion' for Arnold, because he had rejected Jacobinism, Utilitarianism and Toryism, and was already seeking, in history, solutions to contemporary problems. Arnold had been convinced before 1824 that history should be didactic, but it was perhaps only the special intensity with which he held this conviction —an intensity due to the state of England in the post-1815 years— which distinguished it in any way from the normal 18th-century belief in the usefulness of history. He was deeply concerned for the possible real harmfulness of wrong-headed history.[2] He was sure that ancient history was not an intellectual luxury, but a potential force in modern political thinking and practice, that the parallels constantly present to him between ancient and modern history were not merely interesting curiosities, useful in striking solemn literary attitudes or in imparting a flourish of gentlemanly learning

---

[1] Letter of 30 Sept. 1824.

[2] See letter of 5 April 1825. Cobbett's *History of the Reformation* writes Arnold, 'can do nothing but harm'.

to political speeches and writings, but had some real meaning and significance. 'I think daily', he said, speaking of the disturbances of 1819, 'of Thucydides and the Corcyrean sedition, and of the story of the French Revolution, and of the Cassandra-like fate of history, whose lessons are read in vain even to the very next generation.'[1] Coleridge had voiced a similar complaint a few years before: 'there will never be wanting answers and explanations and specious flatteries of hope to persuade a people and its government that the history of the past is inapplicable to *their* case.'[2]

Thucydides spoke to Arnold across the centuries as a contemporary, as he meant to speak and has spoken to many, but until 1824 Thucydides was for Arnold the timeless teacher that, with the Greek lack of feeling for historical relativity, he claimed to be, and the lessons of history were isolated and timeless, historical examples in the 18th-century Rationalist sense. By 1827 his attitude had changed, as the following entry in his book of themes shows: 'of the Use of Examples in Argument and the Cautions to be used in taking them from the history of other Times and Countries.'[3] But in 1825 Niebuhr was classed in Arnold's mind with Mitford, who had been one of Arnold's favourite historians in his phase of youthful Toryism. Niebuhr and Mitford, wrote Arnold, were 'the first modern discoverers in Grecian and Roman history . . . the giants who first cut through the rocks'.[4]

Mitford's pragmatical purpose (his aim was to defend the British Constitution from the inroads of Jacobinism by revealing Greek history as an example of the natural excesses of democracy), his relation of past and present, was forged in the heat of his immediate political passions and based on no scientific historical principle. Greece, in his hands, goes through the 'stages of society' of 18th-century philosophical history, and there is no revelation of an inner development in the history of Greece itself. The classes are fixed categories of 'the rich and the poor, the nobles and the Commons, the few and the many'.[5] Another example of Arnold's historical thinking before 1825 is provided by his abuse of feudal aristocracies

[1] Stanley, *Life*, p. 26. [2] *Statesman's Manual*, p. 14.
[3] This 'book of themes' is a MS at Rugby School.
[4] *Quarterly Review*, vol. 32, p. 72. [5] *History of Greece*, vol. IV, p. 330.

because 'the original tenure was founded on wrong'.[1] This was Hallam's view, and remained so. The remark in Hallam's *Middle Ages*[2]—'We know that a nobility is always insolent' and 'may safely presume' that it began by injustice and the abuse of power— was not altered in later editions of the work. Arnold's modification of his attitude towards feudal aristocracy is, we shall see, an instance of the revolution worked by Niebuhr on his thought.

The presuppositions of Niebuhr's critical method altered Arnold's whole conception of history, and pointed to a possible science which would render the application of history more certain, and make the scientific historian a real force in practical thinking, and in the solution of social and political problems.[3] This quest for a science of history may be called a legacy of the 18th to the 19th century. It was the great object of the historical speculation of the Utilitarians, and Hallam, too, among others, was seeking a more certain application of history [12], but almost wholly confined as he was within the Rationalist framework, he never arrived at the conception of a science of history which Arnold reached by way of Niebuhr and Vico. In spite of John Mill's lip-service to the ideals of the Germano-Coleridgeans and his flirtation with Carlyle, the Utilitarians reached their goal by an altogether different road from that of the Liberal Anglicans, and eventually found what they were seeking in Comte, whose ideas, like theirs, were in the direct line of descent from Condorcet and Turgot. These two routes are indicative of two worlds of thought in England, Rationalist and Romantic, and this dichotomy is the key to the pattern of the historical thought of the period. But the Liberal Anglican road did not end, as the Utilitarian road did, at the final stage of a science of history, but transcended it, as will be seen.

Niebuhr's critical principle was based on the assumption that all nations go through similar stages of development. But these were not the 'stages of society' of 18th-century philosophical history (on which he poured a scorn which Arnold thought excessive and too far-reaching),[4] because they were determined by

---

[1] Letter of 22 Feb. 1824.
[2] *View of the State of Europe during the Middle Ages* (1855 ed.), vol. I, p. 399.
[3] *Quarterly Review*, vol. 32, pp. 77-8.   [4] *Ibid.* vol. 32, p. 85 [13].

an inner dynamic of the nation's life: the struggle between classes for political power. It was this development, this evolution from within, of a particular nation which determined the features of a nation's life: its military organization, its constitution, its law. According to this principle, history is one in the sense that all nations go through this natural development; it is a unity of process, a uniformitarianism, not however, to be confused with the geological uniformitarianism of Lamarck, Hutton, Playfair and Lyell, because the course of events in the political and social world to-day was not taken as the clue to all history, but only to stages of development similar to our own reached by other nations in the past, whereas in geological uniformitarianism the geological processes of to-day were taken as the clue to the geological story of the whole past.

Nevertheless the presupposition of Niebuhr's critical method is that history is governed by law like the world of nature.[1] Otherwise the historian would not be able to use the history of one nation to throw light on the dark corners of the history of another. There are thus no lessons in history which are timeless, in the sense that they can be extracted arbitrarily from their context and applied to the present. The lessons of history must be used according to the same principle which governs the use of the critical method. Examples torn from their proper context are not only meaningless, but may, if applied, be misleading and harmful. The lessons and examples of history are not valid universally, but only for particular phases of development in the life of nations. To be aware of the clue which reveals the nature of this development is thus the special responsibility of the historian. If history when faulty and wrong-headed is dangerous and harmful [15] this is all the more reason for the historian to find the proper clue to its understanding.

The teaching of Thucydides therefore did not apply universally, that is, for every stage of national development, but Arnold came to see that it did apply to his own age. Not only did Thucydides now speak with all the knowledge and sophistication of an advanced age, an experienced age, but also as a contemporary in a new and

[1] Cf. Acton, 'German Schools of History', *Historical Essays and Studies*, p. 349 [14].

special sense. It is easy to appreciate the self-confidence which this revelation produced in Arnold, a very ambitious and an intensely practical man,[1] who had a special love for Thucydides and certainly a greater knowledge of his History than any other Englishman of his day.

Arnold's knowledge of Aristotle and Thucydides and his practical interest in the condition of England, his work on Greek and Roman history and his interest in modern history (unsatisfied by anything which he had so far read in English)[2] were now illuminated by Niebuhr, and recast between 1825 and 1830 in a new conception of history. The implications of Niebuhr's method alone form a sufficient foundation for a science of history as envisaged by Arnold. But by 1830 Arnold was acquainted with Vico's *Scienza Nuova* [16]. Whether Arnold worked out these implications to arrive at the idea of a science of history before reading Vico, or whether he worked them out at all, in which case Vico precipitated the whole idea in Arnold's mind, there is no evidence to show. But it is an exaggeration to say that the whole conception of Arnold's essay on 'The Social Progress of States' (which is the most complete formal expression of the Liberal Anglican science of history) is adapted from Vico.[3] The article of 1825 on Niebuhr in the *Quarterly Review* disproves this. [17]

Niebuhr, however, did not stress the idea of a possible science of history. He makes use of its assumptions in his critical method, but his aim was not to work out principles of historical development of a general nature. He was concerned first and foremost with resurrecting the history of Rome, especially the early history of Rome (a field in which Arnold was at his weakest [18]) and with analogies which could throw light on that, and not with universal history as such. He touched universal history only in so far as he made use of the laws which govern all history, but he was concerned primarily with the concrete facts of the organic life of one particular nation. [19]

He was practical in so far as he related the history of Rome to

---

[1] Stanley, *Life*, p. 18.
[2] *Ibid.* p. 90: 'We have no good history of any modern nation except our own.'
[3] Fisch and Bergin, *The Autobiography of G. Vico*, p. 86.

the needs of Germany (Rome was to be an inspiration of patriotism and civic virtue) and to the contemporary European scene. As a conscious relation of past and present his history was eminently practical, a characteristic which made a special appeal to Arnold (and one which Niebuhr shared with Mitford); but if it was scientific internally, it was not governed in its wider bearings, in its application to the present, by any science of history, but rather by prejudice and preconceived ideas. The practical aspects of Niebuhr's history were strongly criticized by Milman, who thought that 'the secret of some of what, in our more hopeful way of viewing human affairs, we consider his hallucinations' arose from his ability to behold history as if it were the present time, and read the present time as if it were history. Niebuhr, Milman said, lived in a kind of ideal world among his ancient Romans, and he went on to point out 'without in the slightest degree disparaging the sober application of history to modern events,' the caution that is necessary in the practical application of history.[1] Niebuhr's political outlook was not based on the law of social progress as Arnold saw it, and to Arnold there must have been an apparent contradiction between Niebuhr's history and his historical position. Niebuhr apparently either allowed his prejudices to cloud his vision, or did not see the whole of history clearly enough to see his way forward. In other words his political liberalism was not thoroughgoing enough for Arnold and the Liberal Anglicans, and in this respect the latter were on the same ground as Macaulay, who went so far as to suspect Niebuhr's judgement in Roman history because of 'the abject nonsense' which he scribbled 'about events which are passing under our eyes'.[2] This referred to the July Revolution in France, which Arnold welcomed whole-heartedly,[3] but which caused the death of Niebuhr, who saw in it another 1789, and looked forward to 'a period of destruction similar to that which the Roman world experienced about the middle of the third century'. Seeley said of Niebuhr that the strongest passion of his life was his hatred of the French Revolution. He regarded 19th-century liberal stirrings as its offspring, and he

[1] *Quarterly Review*, vol. 66 (1840), pp. 557-8.
[2] G. O. Trevelyan, *Life and Letters of Macaulay*, p. 317.   [3] Letter of 24 Aug. 1830.

did not like 'middle class liberalism'. He had, says Guilland, a liberal mind without being a liberal in politics.[1]

In Niebuhr it is not Rome as an example of a law of historical development which is emphasized, but Rome as an example of political success; he holds up the life of Republican Rome as a Plutarchian life, a pattern of virtue, a noble example, not as a type of development (though this is implied in the critical principle which he uses to resurrect that life), not as the life of an organism in the scientific sense as revealing the workings of other organisms. His starting point is his Germany, the Germany of post-Jena, but he stops at Rome, and his abilities are concentrated on these two poles. He does not, like Vico, begin with Roman history and work outwards from that to universal history. National individuality came before the science of history.

Moreover, the idea of progress, a presupposition of Liberal Anglican thinking, is foreign to Niebuhr. He died in an atmosphere of unrelieved pessimism. To Arnold there seemed something un-Christian, something almost pagan about his veneration for a remote antiquity, the Golden Age of Republican Rome.[2] If, however, Arnold's suspicion of Niebuhr's lack of belief was soon quieted, [21] it was not until 1830 that his doubts were completely laid to rest, and it was not until later still that Niebuhr received Arnold's applause for grounding his history on the idea of Providence. For Hare and Thirlwall the translation of Niebuhr was 'scarcely less valuable as a moral than as an intellectual discipline'.[3]

What Niebuhr, embroiled in public affairs and the stirring events of his time, lacked, namely, a calm, objective, all-embracing outlook on universal history, Vico was able to supply; that is, principles, examples, types, the idea of a science of history. Vico, though his knowledge was largely confined to the history of Rome and his examples drawn from it, touches universal history at all points, because Greece and Rome are for him merely illustrations of the laws of historical development. History in its universal aspect, as governed by law, is his main concern. For this reason, Vico, the philosopher of the study, a Teufelsdröckh in comparison

[1] Guilland, *Modern Germany*, pp. 55-6. [2] *Quarterly Review*, vol. 32, p. 85 [20].
[3] Hare, *Vindication of Luther*, p. 201.

with Niebuhr, was for Arnold the truly practical historian, and although Vico himself did not stress the practical application of his science, it was this aspect of it which appealed to Arnold, all the more so because he discovered it as the Reform Bill crisis was approaching its dénouement. Under the pressure of this crisis, Arnold put forward the theory of the Social Progress of States,[1] which thus represents the historical ideas of Niebuhr and Vico fused with Arnold's practical desires and aspirations.

(ii) 'The Social Progress of States'

Arnold's theory of the social progress of states starts from the analogy between the life-course of the nation and that of the individual, part of the Romantic background to Niebuhr and the historical school of law, though the analogy is almost as old as history itself. The philosophical history of the 18th century abounds in such phrases as 'infancy of nations', 'infancy of society', 'infancy of Mankind', where 'nations' and 'society' have a general and not a particular bearing, and where the Rationalist idea of progress is an absolute presupposition. The difference between the 'social progress of states' of Arnold and the 'progress of society' of the philosophical historians of the 18th century and their 19th-century disciples is a measure of the difference between the Enlightenment and the revolt against it. Arnold's 'social progress of states' is a conception of historical development seen from inside the nation, based on the idea of national history working itself out internally, on the facts of the class-struggle, which binds the stages of national development into one progress. The nation's life is a unity in so far as it is bound together by the dynamic, internal social process which is governed by law and therefore inevitable.

The course of a nation's history, then, resembled the life of an individual, or a plant, or the astronomical progress of a day or a year. It had its boyhood and manhood, its intermediate stages and transition periods, its dawn, high-noon and dusk, its spring, summer, autumn and winter, its blossom and seed-time. When Arnold uses these phrases, as for example when in *The History of Rome* he talks of the autumn of the Greek city-states,[2] of the

---

[1] Appendix I to vol. I of Arnold's *Thucydides* (1830). [2] *History of Rome*, vol. II, p. 545.

springtime of the Roman people,[1] and of wealth, power and dominion bringing on 'the ripened Summer with more vigour indeed, but less of freshness',[2] he is referring to a special conception of history and not merely making use of a literary device, or assuming what he has not investigated and proved—the nature of progress.

Just as the individual is subject to the natural laws of childhood, youth, manhood and old age, with their characteristic features of tutelage, animal vigour ripening into thoughtful maturity and finally lapsing into decay, just as the individual goes through periods corresponding to spring, summer, autumn and winter in accordance with an inevitable and natural law of his being, and finally dies, so also the history of any nation consists of 'natural periods' which mark the development of that nation from 'what I may call a state of childhood to manhood'.[3] The nation is subject to the natural laws obeyed by individuals, plants, the days and seasons, and inevitably passes through phases of growth and decay. This is the law of a nation's being, but, as also in the case of an individual, it is liable to modification and to interruption from without, childhood may be unnaturally prolonged, death may intervene, maturity may never be reached, old age and decay drag on, but the ultimate end is in both cases the same. As Hare said, 'The natural life of nations as well as of individuals, has its fixed course and term. It springs forth, grows up, reaches its maturity, decays, perishes.'[4] 'States like individuals, go through certain changes in a certain order', the only difference being in the duration of the periods. In the history of the nation the length of the periods is not fixed by any law, as it is for the individual, though in both cases their order is perfectly regular, like the order of the seasons. 'One state may have existed a thousand years and its history may be full of striking events, and yet it may be still in its childhood: another may not be a century old and its history may contain nothing remarkable to a careless reader, and yet it may be verging to old age.'[5]

This analogy between states and individuals, the fact that nations

[1] *Ibid.* vol. II, p. 194.   [2] *Ibid.* vol. II, p. 545.
[3] *Thucydides*, vol. I, p. 615.   [4] *Guesses at Truth* (2nd ed., 2nd series), p. 21.
[5] *Thucydides*, vol. I, p. 615.

are subject to laws which are as natural and inevitable as the laws which govern a man's life or the order of the seasons, and pass through periods corresponding to the natural periods in the life of the individual or the course of the astronomical year, is the clue to the understanding of the complicated pattern of history. 'Knowledge of these periods', says Arnold, 'furnishesus with a clue to the study of history which the continuous succession of events in chronological order seems particularly to require.'[1]

The first period in the history of any nation is that of youth. In this we meet, as we should expect, all the characteristics common to the boyhood of the individual, and of these the most significant, for Arnold, is the necessity of tutelage. It is this necessity which justifies the social system of the period, and the ascendancy of the nobility. In the history of Greece this was the period of the so-called Homeric monarchies. These 'kings' constituted an initial difficulty. Apparently

the very first case to which I apply my theorem disproves its truth. But the old Homeric monarchies were in fact an instance of power depending on blood, and therefore of the ascendancy of the nobility. They were like the feudal monarchies of modern Europe, essentially aristocracies, in which the separation of all the chiefs or nobles from the inferior people was far more strongly marked than the elevation of the king above his nobles.

The so-called 'kings' of Greece in fact resemble the feudal vassals of France and Germany, each supreme over a dominion as extensive as the Greek kingdoms, forming together a body widely separated from the commons and whose members were felt to belong to the same class.[2]

It was virtually then the ascendancy of nobility, when all power and distinction were confined to the class of nobles, whether there was one individual elevated above the rest of his class with still higher power and distinction, or whether all the members of it exercised the sovereignty jointly or alternately.[3]

This Vichian view of the 'kings' of Greece was accepted also by Thirlwall. [23]

There have been many variations in history of this state of society, as, for example, when chief and priest were united in the same

---

[1] Ibid.   [2] Ibid. p. 616.   [3] Ibid. p. 617. [22]

persons, as in the heroic times in Greece, or in the person of
Melchisedek.[1] This first form of aristocracy, in which civil and
military command were united with the office of priest, existed
also in Rome and Etruria. Another and later form is when the
office of chief and priest are distinct. A third form is an aristocracy
of conquest.[2] Nevertheless, though

in other countries the same state of society has varied more or less in
its subordinate relations . . . yet if carefully examined it will be found
everywhere to retain its essential character, and to mark the first period,
or youth, of political existence. . . . The principle of the ascendancy of
noble blood necessarily marks the infancy of mankind.

One reason for this state of affairs, Arnold had shown in his
article on Niebuhr of 1825, is that in almost all rude societies the
principal military force has consisted of cavalry or chariots. Horse-
men were necessarily the wealthier members of the community,
who thus became also the most powerful. 'Exactly in the same
manner, when society was in its second infancy in the Middle
Ages, similar causes produced a similar result.'[3]

The general character of this first period, therefore, is of a
'state of bondage'. In a barbarous age of internecine warfare and
of unbridled passions, protection is the great need of society, and
it is provided by the feudal client-lord relationship. The nobles act
as the parents and guardians of society, and it is their duty and
privilege, the duty and privilege of aristocracy as such, to educate
society, to train it and make it fit to govern, because it must
inevitably come to govern some day, and then, when society is
educated and ready to govern itself, the nobles must cease to
exercise the authority of guardians. There is nothing intrinsically
bad (or, for that matter, intrinsically good) about aristocracies as
such.

The guilt of all aristocracies has consisted not so much in their original
acquisition of power as in their perseverance in retaining it: so that
what was innocent or even reasonable at the beginning has become in
later times atrocious injustice; as if a parent in his dotage should claim
the same authority over his son in the vigour of manhood, which
formerly in the maturity of his own faculties he had exercised naturally
and profitably over the infancy of his child.[4]

[1] *Ibid.* [24]   [2] *Ibid.* pp. 618-20, 622.   [3] *Quarterly Review*, vol. 32, p. 78. [25]
[4] *Thucydides*, vol. I, p. 622. [26]

Towards the end of this childhood period in the life of nations there begins, inevitably, a struggle between the nobility and the commons, between the guardian and his ward. By the 'commons', Arnold does not mean the whole of the rest of the population. Originally, 'all but the chiefs, that is, all who were not of noble blood, were alike comprised under the denomination of "commons"'. The earliest form of the existence of the 'commons' appears to be as the slaves of the chiefs or nobles. This form appears in the numerous households of the heads of the pastoral tribes, almost before anything deserving the name of a state was to be met with. The commons who struggle with the nobility in this first phase of social history are those of the political outcasts who managed to accumulate wealth, for, although they were treated with contempt by the nobility, and were not allowed to intermarry with them, or to hold any office in the state, or to minister at the altars of the gods, or even to take any part in the discussion of public affairs, though they were both politically and in private life liable to constant oppression, still, if they could acquire property, it remained their own, and they were able in time to reach a position of social and economic, if not yet of political, importance, by engaging in commerce, and even occasionally through the acquisition of land granted to them by the nobles. They thus obtained consideration and began to feel their own power and rights, and to be courted as auxiliaries in the civil contests of the aristocracy, before they were able to assert their own claims, and their own cause.[1] Moreover, as they acquired a certain amount of wealth, they were able to buy armour and weapons, and increase their efficiency as soldiers, 'and becoming of more importance as soldiers, gradually rose also in political consideration and weight'.[2] As all free citizens served at their own expense, the men of moderate fortunes could afford armour, and they also had leisure for drill, and this gave them a twofold advantage over the poorer classes.

Hence the popular party in the earliest times has consisted always of those citizens who were rich without nobility, as opposed to those who possessed at once nobility, riches and power; and the first steps towards liberty have been the result of a contest not between the rich and the mass of the community, but between the rich and the noble.[3]

[1] *Thucydides*, p. 626.   [2] *Quarterly Review*, vol. 32, p. 79.   [3] *Ibid.*

When the Commons feel themselves fit for independence, they begin to demand their share in political power, and there ensues the critical period of a nation's history, the transition from childhood to manhood, critical in the life of nations as in that of individuals, or of plants in Spring. The longer the period of childhood is prolonged, the more dangerous is the transition likely to be, because the long-continued period of infancy in a nation's history is a sign that it has been exploited by the 'selfish policy or criminal neglect of those who ought rather to have gradually trained it up to the independence of manhood'. If such a period is prolonged in this way, it is prolonged 'unnaturally', and the transition to the next stage will be unusually explosive. Sometimes, in fact, the dominion of the aristocracy has been overthrown chaotically; in other cases, 'the purposes of God for the progress of the human race have been better answered and the moral and political constitution, when recovered from the shock of its crisis, has gone on healthfully towards the full perfection of its being'.[1]

Arnold used the example of the history of Augsburg down to 1548 to show the manner in which the aristocracy of blood is naturally overthrown by the ordinary progress of a people in wealth and civilization; and to show too with how little difficulty and danger the change may be effected where no disturbing causes exist, and where the effort of the political constitution is neither hurried forwards nor violently checked. About the beginning of the 14th century the commons of Augsburg found themselves sufficiently advanced in wealth and power to lay claim to their share of the rights of citizenship. They seem first to have been admitted into the great council, as the plebeians at Rome voted in the comitia before being admitted to the Senate. Finally, in 1368, the commons secured not only equality of rights, but an absolute ascendancy. The subsequent revolution in Augsburg in 1548, when the aristocracy regained their power, was due to foreign violence, to a force, that is, external to the natural internal progress of states.[2]

'Spring is ever a critical period', and 'in the political Spring also there are peculiar dangers'. According to Arnold there are

___

[1] *Thucydides*, vol. I, p. 622.   [2] *Ibid.* pp. 626–8.

three principal dangers in the transition from the childhood to the manhood of nations, in the struggle between the aristocracy of blood and the aristocracy of property.[1] Firstly, the union of property, under peculiar local circumstances, with nobility is a check upon the growth of liberty which is found particularly in aristocracies of conquest, or where, for example in a landlocked feudal state, the commons are unable to acquire commercial wealth. Secondly, where the increasing influence of wealth leads to absolute monarchy instead of towards free government. This is a danger which arises out of the very crisis of the transition from the ascendancy of blood to that of property. Sometimes this despotism has been only transient, and after having been the instrument of good in plucking up by the roots the old aristocracy, has yielded in its turn to a free and liberal government. In other cases a worse and more enduring tyranny has been the result. 'The history of Europe affords but too many examples' of this.

Happy the people who have not suffered their liberties to be merely transferred from one spoiler to another, but have asserted their right to share in the victory of the crown. But in modern Europe the size of the kingdoms and the much more monarchical spirit of the people allowed the kings to consolidate their work . . . it has been an aggravation of the evil in modern times that the king, after he had once established his power, seemed to make common cause with the aristocracy against the people, and lent his support to maintain them in their many exemptions and prerogatives. At the same time the means by which he has maintained his own despotism, a mercenary standing army, has rendered finance a most important subject of attention, and has marked that second stage in society, in which money rather than birth confers the ascendancy.

Thirdly, an unfavourable state of foreign relations is a danger to the natural advance of society towards liberty, whether in the shape of foreign wars, which England in her critical period escaped, but France did not, or the 'accumulation of dominion', that is, empire.

During the course of this struggle between nobility and wealth there may be a 'false Spring', a premature acquisition of power by the commons.[2] In the history of Greece the reign of Theseus

[1] *Thucydides*, pp. 628-32. [2] *Ibid.* appendix III, pp. 665-6.

represents the false Spring; it was succeeded by the degradation of the Athenian commons and the corruption of the 'democratic' institutions of Theseus, which took place between that reign and the revolution of Cleisthenes. In the history of Rome the false Spring is represented by the reforms of Servius Tullius. These reforms were, as Niebuhr had shown, of a popular nature, concessions in favour of the property-owning commons, 'and it was then as liberal and as popular a principle to set property on a level with birth, as it was afterwards to confer a superiority on numbers over property'.[1] They were, however, succeeded by a period of aristocratical tyranny lasting until the passing of the Licinian and Publilian laws. The same thing happened in English history. The period of the Lancastrians was the false Spring, and it was succeeded by the Tudor despotism. In the political, as in the natural world, says Arnold, 'the blossoms that are brought forward by the deceitful warmth of a few fine days in the midst of winter, are sure to be checked, if not cut off altogether, by a long return of ungenial winter'.[2]

If a nation comes successfully through the false Spring and the dangers of the critical period either originally or finally (and many nations do not, many never pass through the transition to manhood, but have either 'gone on in protracted infancy', or 'received a shock at the moment of transition' which has condemned them to a 'long living death'),[3] it enters upon its state of manhood, the 'second stage of society'. In this stage money rather than birth confers the ascendancy. Here, also, one meets the characteristics of manhood, a greater earnestness, and sense of purpose, for example.

In this manhood stage of a nation's life-course, the struggle is between property and numbers. The popular party of the childhood period is now an anti-popular oligarchy of wealth. It was 'popular' before, because originally 'no more extensive idea could be formed of the term "popular" than as denoting those who presumed to claim a share in the government without the long established qualification of noble blood'.[4] The struggle between

---

[1] *Quarterly Review*, vol. 32, p. 80. [2] *Thucydides*, vol. I, appendix III, p. 665.
[3] *Ibid.* appendix I, p. 637. [4] *Quarterly Review*, vol. 32, p. 79.

property and numbers is far more ferocious than the struggle between nobility and wealth, because, for one thing, the passions of manhood are naturally more violent and more dangerous than those of childhood.[1] Secondly, the distinction between nobility and commons, originally a real one, that is, grounded upon the real physical and moral superiority of the nobility, has no existence at the moment of struggle between the two orders, whereas in the contest between property and numbers the course of things is exactly the opposite—the struggle here only takes place when the real differences have reached the widest point of separation, where the intermediate gradations of society are dissolved in one or other of the two extremes, and the state is divided between the two irreconcilable opposites of luxury and beggary. This is no contest between men really equal, to do away with a fictitious distinction; it is a struggle between utter contraries, with no sympathy between them, no knowledge of one by the other.[2]

The position of parties in the later conflict must be traced to causes connected with the conflict which preceded it. For example, the enormous inequality of property at Rome against which the Agrarian laws were particularly directed arose out of the exclusive claim to the rights of citizenship formerly asserted by the patricians. In modern times,

how much of the actual situation of our aristocracy of property is derived from our old aristocracy of conquest: the enormous landed estates of many of our nobility—the great political influence conferred by land above all other kinds of property—the law of primogeniture and the law of entails. Above all the existence of an order of nobility communicated by descent gives to the aristocracy of modern Europe much more of the character of the older aristocracy of blood than was retained after the corresponding revolution in Greece and Rome.[3]

The history of England since 1688 represents this phase of history and corresponds to the period of Thucydides in Greece, and in Rome to the period from the passing of the Publilian laws to the end of the Commonwealth.[4] Thus, the House of Commons, which was the popular part of our constitution so long as the struggle was between the nation and the Crown, has been regarded since the accession of George III as a body predominantly aristocratical,

[1] *Thucydides*, vol. I, pp. 633-4. [2] *Ibid.* p. 634. [3] *Ibid.* pp. 635-6. [4] *Ibid.* p. 633.

because the parties in the state have resolved themselves into the advocates of property on one side, and of general intelligence and numbers on the other.[1] Wherever the contest between property and numbers has come to a crisis, 'I know not', said Arnold, 'that it has in any instance terminated favourably.'[2]

(b) The Progress of Nations: Intellectual and Moral [28]

Arnold's theory of the social progress of states was engendered, as has been seen, by the problem of the social condition of England, and emphasizes the social and political development of nations. But the final Liberal Anglican theory of national development was much broader than this. Following Coleridge and Burke in the Romantic revolt against the atomistic political theories dominant in the 18th century, the Liberal Anglicans found political salvation in emphasizing the unity of all aspects of the nation's life. The nation for them was a whole, with its own characteristic inner life and personality, not a collection of individual units, nor divided into lay and clerical departments. The nation was one in another sense, therefore, to that implied in the dynamic inner evolution of its social history: it was a person in the fullest sense of the word, an intellectual and moral whole, and it grew, intellectually and morally, passing from childhood to manhood and expressing its inner life, its intellectual and spiritual desires and needs, in the manner characteristic of these stages of growth. This historical philosophy of mind, which applies both to individuals and to nations, and is opposed to the mechanical psychology which reached its complete expression in Condillac, and the March of Mind of Condorcet which is based on that psychology, represents the fundamental gulf that separates the Liberal Anglicans and the Utilitarians, the Romantics and the Enlightenment. For Condorcet, man is the same mental machine at all times, only more or less efficient, that is, more or less enlightened. For the Romantics, if man is everywhere the same, it is not because his mind is a machine; for them, the difference between childhood and manhood is not a question of degree, a difference of more or less reason, of more or

[1] *Ibid.* p. 633. [2] *Ibid.* p. 636. [27]

less experience, but a substantial difference between imagination and reason. The imaginative childhood passes away; it is superseded by reason and reflection. Wordsworth's 'Immortality Ode' may be taken as epitomizing this historical-biographical aspect of Romantic theory as it applies to the individual. The poem, as Basil Willey points out, derives its passionate quality from a sense of loss and alienation. The philosophic mind is but poor consolation for the glory and the dream of childhood experience.[1] It is significant that Stanley should quote this phrase: 'the glory and the dream', in connection with the mental history of nations.[2] This change, which is natural in man, is natural also in nations. In the psychology of the Lockian tradition, the transition is simply the increasing efficiency of the child's mind, the filling up of a blank through the machinery of the association of ideas; thus, when Condorcet speaks of the 'infancy of nations', he has in mind a mental blank, a phase of the march of mind, and any value this stage of history may possess lies in the grains of reason contained therein, destined to blossom into the fulness of enlightenment. Its historical significance lies in the potential development of that which it conspicuously lacked. For Vico and the Romantics the childhood of a nation, its imaginative and poetical phase, had its own value in itself, its own historical significance as great as that of its manhood. [30] The question of historical significance in fact does not arise when all phases of the national life are considered equally significant and valuable, though the Romantics, reacting violently against the 18th-century outlook, tended to prefer the childhood to the manhood periods, the ages of imagination to those of reason. (This romantic reaction, in so far as it represented a complete swing of the pendulum, was not approved by Arnold.) The Romantic historical philosophy of mind, which derives ultimately from Vico, [31] is the background of the ballad theories of Wolf and Niebuhr, and there are many ways by which the Liberal Anglicans may have been led to it; through the Homeric controversy, that is, by realizing the fundamental assumptions of the ballad theories, or through Vico, in this or in other connections, or through

[1] Basil Willey, *The Eighteenth Century Background*, pp. 285-7. [29]
[2] See below, p. 36.

grasping the philosophical foundation of German philology and studies in comparative literature, mythology, law and language, or through some other aspect of the Romantic movement in England or Germany. It was, after all, a commonplace of Romantic thought. [32]

This conception of the moral and intellectual development of nations concerned Arnold in three closely related ways: firstly, in the theory of the social progress of states, as a link between the political and the intellectual development of nations; secondly, at Rugby, where he was concerned with the intellectual and moral development of boys (he was appointed headmaster in 1827); thirdly, in his work on the interpretation of scripture, the clue to which was a progressive revelation adapted to the prevailing psychology at any given stage of historical development. Being concerned with these three problems, Arnold emphasized not the imaginative character of childhood, but its helplessness, its need for intellectual and moral tutelage. It is a state of bondage, the individual's bondage to the passions, and the consequent (and justified) social bondage of the weak to the strong, of the less to the more enlightened.

The period of childhood, in nations as in men, is one of ignorance and credulity. Feeling, as opposed to reflection, is in the ascendant. As Arnold wrote of the boys at Rugby, 'when the intellect is low, the animal part will predominate.'[1] It is therefore a period of spiritual and intellectual, as well as social, bondage. Ignorant men, like children, must be taught, for they will not learn by themselves. This teaching comes from God, is God's Providence in the guise of instructor. It is a direct interposition in the first place, because man could not have civilized himself; later, it is through the priesthood that God's commands are delivered to men. This is the justification of a priesthood; it forms a spiritual aristocracy. When men were in general children, as Milman said, the clergy only were men.[2] The priests are the tutors of a morally and intellectually obtuse age, just as the nobles are the parents and guardians in a crude and intrinsically anarchical society. But the priests obey God, and men obey the priests, from fear rather than from love.

[1] Letter to J. T. Coleridge, 12 Oct. 1835.   [2] *Savonarola and other essays*, p. 388.

'The condition of men in the old times who had a knowledge of God and his will is well compared to that of slaves under a master, or that of children learning their first rudiments at school; both obey from fear rather than from love.'[1] Preaching at Rugby, Arnold took as his text 'the Law was our schoolmaster to bring us unto Christ', and said, 'the words of the apostle are for ever useful and apply to the successive stages of our individual growth no less than to the successive periods in the existence of the world.'[2]

The link between intellectual and social history at this point lies in the phrase a 'state of bondage'. The childhood of the mind justifies the social arrangements characteristic of the nation's childhood; an aristocracy of power and intellect is necessary when society is weak and ignorant. To this extent the history of mental development explains social history, and according to Arnold is 'the most valuable part of history'. [33] The duty of aristocracy, its privilege from the point of view of history, is to instruct: where it does not, society is condemned to prolonged infancy and there is no progress. Where it does, it is working for its own abdication, and in the nature of things, it must eventually abdicate or be overthrown or rendered harmless. Intellectual independence then succeeds intellectual bondage, as at the time of the Reformation.

This bondage argument, an argument from the inevitable historical evolution of the nation, was used by Arnold in his pamphlet *The Christian Duty of Granting the claims of the Roman Catholics* (1829). Government, he says, is either a matter of agreement or arises out of a natural superiority, either temporary, as that of men over children, or perpetual, as that of men over beasts. Ireland was a nation in its manhood, in bondage to another nation, which was unnatural and intolerable.[3] The same argument, that bondage of any sort was fitted only to the childhood of nations, was much used by liberals in support of *laissez-faire*. Whately, for instance, said that over-governing was a kind of puerility which prevails in the earlier stages of civilization.[4] Macaulay, Buckle and Harriet Martineau[5] used the same argument.

---

[1] Arnold, *Sermons*, vol. II, pp. 359-60. [2] *Ibid.* p. 119.
[3] See *Catholic Claims*, pp. 38-43. [4] Whately's edition of Bacon's *Essays*, p. 131.
[5] *History of the Thirty Years Peace*, vol. I, p. 54.

This question of bondage was thus of practical importance for the Liberal Anglicans, which no doubt explains the prominence it assumed in Arnold's view of the childhood state, because Arnold was concerned with practical problems rather than with more exclusively intellectual problems of cultural development in history. He points, therefore, to the scepticism of late periods, which was for Arnold another practical problem, but he does not explain how or when intellectual vigour, which is presumably characteristic of manhood periods, passes into the barren intellectualism and uncreative scepticism characteristic of these late periods. 'The great transition from ancient history to modern', that is, from a childhood to a manhood period in the history of any nation, is 'the transition from an age of feeling to one of reflection, from a period of ignorance and credulity to one of enquiry and scepticism'.[1] In the history of Greece, this is the transition marked by Thucydides, when 'in his reflections on the bloody dissensions of Corcyra, he notices the decay and extinction of the simplicity of old times'.[2] 'The advance of civilization', says Arnold, 'destroys much that is noble, and throws over the mass of human society an atmosphere somewhat dull and hard,'[3] but he nowhere examines this development in any greater detail. Though the analogy between the development of states and individuals was constantly in his mind, and though he had written ballad poetry in his boyhood[4] and the spring had later dried up, he did not see in this fact of autobiography any urge to investigate more closely either the imaginative character of the state of childhood in nations, or the inevitable mental progress to an age of reflection. He was not at his best in dealing with childhood periods; his presentation of the legends of Ancient Rome in the style of the Bible and of Herodotus—'a style characteristic of a particular state of cultivation, which all people pass through at a certain stage in their progress'[5]—does not give the insight into the childhood mind of nations which was intended (Milman thought it 'singularly unfortunate'), and it is well known that his interest at Rugby was centred largely in the Sixth Form and in his more mature and intelligent pupils. [34] The

[1] Preface to *Thucydides*, vol. III, p. xix.   [2] *Ibid.*   [3] *Ibid.* p. xxi.
[4] Stanley, *Life*, p. 2.   [5] Letter of 20 Dec. 1837.

practical problems of his time, in which he rejoiced, were problems of a manhood stage of society. His feeling for the literature of his own time was based rather on sympathy and antipathy than on a critical appreciation, though he could always point to his theory of history to support his feelings. Novels, for example, were for him a sign of the 'excitement' of a late age, as well as being personally distasteful. He was, in fact, obviously reluctant to lay down laws where the things of the mind were concerned, in the same detail, and with the same confidence, as he did for the facts of social and political history.

Hare, the disciple of Coleridge, less concerned than Arnold with immediate social and political problems than with the philosophical roots of these problems, and more deeply versed in the thought and literature of Germany, was interested primarily in the intellectual and literary expression of national life. Milman, poet and Professor of Poetry at Oxford (1821-31), also stressed the intellectual and cultural aspects of the nation's development rather than the social and political factors. Reviewing Hallam's *European Literature*, Milman said he could not 'but yield to the temptation of inquiring whether we can trace any primary and simple laws of the intellectual development of man'. He saluted Hallam's work as the first great general map or chart of the intellectual world attempted in this country,[1] and he was also among the first to recognize the value of Lecky's *History of Rationalism*. In contrast with Arnold, Milman's interest was largely confined to early periods (his magnum opus, the *History of Latin Christianity*, deals entirely with a childhood period, the Middle Ages); he was more of a Romantic in this respect. For Arnold, the Middle Ages were a 'noisome cavern' even as late as 1841. One century, he said, will show fully its nature and details.[2] The impact of Niebuhr and Vico on Milman was primarily the impact of the ballad theory and the Homeric controversy;[3] the law of intellectual development presupposed by them is the assumption underlying the *History of the Jews* (1829): that all nations pass from an imaginative to a reflective state, and that

[1] *Quarterly Review*, vol. 65 (March 1840), pp. 341, 383.
[2] Letter to A. P. Stanley, 29 Sept. 1841.
[3] See Milman's review 'Origin of the Homeric Poems' in *Quarterly Review*, vol. 44 (Jan. 1831), pp. 128 *et seq.*

this is the fundamental law of their intellectual progress. [35] The framework of the history of the Jews is this natural development, to which the Jewish people conformed, like any other nation. Much more comprehensively than Arnold, he worked from the mind outwards; the leitmotiv of his *History of Latin Christianity* is the imaginative character of the age; it is this fundamental fact of mental development which, for Milman, supplies the key to the whole period, and is the explanation of its patterns of thought and action.

From the point of view of intellectual development, then, the childhood of nations is an imaginative age, an age, in Thirlwall's words, of 'vigorous but undefined imagination',[1] a mythic and heroic time, 'when history, law and religion are alike poetry,' in the Vichian words of Milman.[2] Mythic poetry, Milman explains, begins as the imaginative expression of the religious belief of the age. It is almost purely creative (that is, not built on historical fact) and not popular, because 'popular poetry would never be purely creative'.[3] It is of value to the historian as the expression of a particular society at a particular stage of development. Gradually more and more historical fact creeps into the fables. To quote Milman:

There must have been a border-land where the religious myth—the impersonation of the conception—ceased; and what we may call, in contradistinction, the poetic myth—that which aggrandized, altered and embellished real events and personages—began; where poetry and history were in some sort blended. . . . The myth, as it approached history, became, if we may so say, less and less mythic. It was by slow, yet dimly perceptible degrees that the haze cleared away and men began to see each other as men.[4]

In the nature of things, he concludes, we conceive that there must have been this semi-historic state or period at the dawn of all history. That society goes through this mythic stage is an 'almost unerring law of our intellectual development'.[5] It can be seen in the history of India, no less plainly than in the histories of Greece and Rome.[6]

[1] Thirlwall, *Remains*, vol. III, p. 12. [2] *Quarterly Review*, vol. 49, p. 287.
[3] *Ibid.* vol. 71, p. 456. [36]
[4] *Ibid.* vol. 78, p. 121. Review of Grote's *History of Greece*, vols. I and II (June 1846).
[5] *Ibid.* vol. 71, p. 457. [6] *Ibid.* vol. 68, p. 392. [37]

As nations go through the natural stages of the process of civilization, the imaginative elements recede, 'material and dimly mental man'[1] develops into spiritual and intellectual man, and a state of intellectual independence succeeds a state of intellectual bondage. The Romantic theory of mental development is expressed neatly and comprehensively in an essay by Hare in the 1838 edition of the *Guesses at Truth*, on the course of poetry. For Hare, true poetry is the expression of the national life; he reviews the development of poetry from childhood, when its character is objective and the poet loses himself in the object of his song (hence its forms are the epic and the ballad), when poetry is rather 'a natural growth of the mind than a work of art'; through the stage of youth and the awakening of consciousness, when 'self puts forth its horns' in feelings, desires and passions (hence the lyrical form); to manhood, and the control of the passions, and action (hence drama: 'the manhood of poetry is the drama').[2] Of epic, lyric and dramatic poetry, Milman said that each of these successive forms of the art had as it were spontaneously adapted itself to the changes in Grecian society. The epic was that of the heroic age . . . the lyric, and religious, that of the temple and the public games; the dramatic, that of the republican polity.[3]

The same idea underlies a prize-essay by Stanley (1840). [39] Periods of manhood, says Stanley, such as the age of the Sophists, of the Roman Empire, of the Reformation, are 'periods of Inquiry, of Reflection, of Science'. The craving for truth and reality is common to all three. 'The civilized mind finds its chief delight in that very exercise of thought which inflicts on the barbarian mind greater pain than bodily torture.' Induction takes the place of speculation and fancy. Scientific researches into the realities of past times become for the first time the basis of history. A philosophical phraseology, reflective and descriptive poetry, have been the peculiar growth of ages called 'to see into the life' of a world whose early freshness has long since passed away. 'The glory and the dream' of primitive fancy has gone, and with it the manly and

---

[1] Milman, *Christianity*, vol. 1, p. 132.
[2] *Guesses at Truth* (2nd ed., 2nd series), pp. 159 *et seq.*
[3] *Quarterly Review*, vol. 62, p. 301. [38]

classical vigour of the nation's rising energies. Imaginative poetry is succeeded in the manhood stage by philosophical poetry, the epic poets are succeeded by the civilized poets, such as Lucretius and Wordsworth.[1]

This manhood period, the height of moral perfection and greatness in a state (which is Milman's definition of 'civilization') tends to degenerate towards that 'worst barbarism, a worn out civilization'.[2] 'The ultimate tendency of civilization is towards barbarism', said Hare.[3] The refinement characteristic of civilization becomes luxury and complacency. A period of high civilization, Milman declared, is a period verging towards ease, luxury and mental discontent.[41] Intellectual vigour develops into scepticism, a barren theorizing.[42] Stanley talked of 'the false pride, the false knowledge, the false liberality, the false freedom, the false display, the false philosophy to which an intellectual age, especially in a declining nation, is constantly liable', and of 'a degenerate state of society, such as that which existed in the capital of Greece at that time [Corinth]—with a worn-out creed... a worn-out philosophy ... a worn-out character. ...'[4] 'The manners of a savage state', Thirlwall said, 'may be as far removed from the simplicity of a rational nature as the last stage of luxurious corruption, and that man utterly uncultivated may be almost as wretched and worthless as he can become by artificial depravity.'[5] A morbid self-consciousness, as in the later ages of Greece and Rome, destroys poetry by criticism and philosophy by 'false display'. Manly independence degenerates into a disregard for due authority and a vain desire to become impartial spectators of life. There is a danger of the richness of life being reduced to uniformity and mediocrity.[6] Hare said, 'In the wake of the human intellect, in proportion as it is more genial, more vigorous, more refined, there will be a greater variety, while here also, when genius is extinct, when imagination is feeble, the understanding comes forward with its rules of uniformity.'[7]

---

[1] Stanley, *Prize Essay*, pp. 16-18.

[2] Milman, *Latin Christianity*, vol. I, p. 4. The Greek clergy of the Byzantine Empire, he says, yielded to 'that worst barbarism', etc.

[3] *Guesses at Truth* (2nd ed., 2nd series), p. 234. The same phrase is found in the 1827 edition. [40]

[4] *Corinthians*, vol. I, pp. 5, 14.   [5] *Greece*, vol. II, p. 196.

[6] Stanley, *Prize Essay*, pp. 32-4.   [7] *Mission of the Comforter*, vol. I, p. 225.

Division of labour and 'variety' tend to become mere specialization and professionalism, 'co-operation' degenerates into a barren cosmopolitanism and excessive centralization. Mercenary troops, the cessation of national buildings, the rhetorical subtleties of Ovid and Tibullus, circuses, all these characteristics of the late period in Roman history have their counterpart in the period of full-grown luxury and grandeur of any civilized people.[1]

To all outward appearance these late periods are splendid and prosperous, but in reality the nation is inwardly in decay. Thirlwall calls this 'an universal law which manifests itself no less in the moral world than in the physical, according to which the period of inward languor, corruption and decay, which follows that of maturity, presents an aspect more dazzling and commanding, and to those who look only at the surface inspires greater confidence and respect, than the season of youthful health, of growing but unripened strength'. He instances Sparta after Leuctra, Persia under Xerxes. 'The moment of the highest prosperity is often that which immediately precedes the most ruinous disaster. . . .'[2] For Hare, the culminating point in the history of every nation was the period when it has reached the greatest height, not perhaps of outward force and sensual refinement, but of moral wisdom and dignity.[3]

Thus the Romantic onslaught against the dominant characteristics of the 18th century is linked, in the Liberal Anglican idea of history, to a fully-fledged philosophy of civilization, according to which all nations go through cycles of progress according to the law of their nature, passing inevitably from childhood to manhood and old age, from bondage, intellectual, moral and social, to independence, from credulity to incredulity, from feeling to reflection, from imaginative states, dimly mental, in the bosom of Nature, [43] through stages of intellectual clarity and vigour, to the final scepticism and barren theorizing, the second barbarism, of late periods. Such a conception had a two-fold importance:

(1) As an answer to the Rationalist March of Mind, and the Middle-class, Liberal idea of progress of the 19th century. The Liberal Anglican appeal to history, as expressed in the *Scienza*

---

[1] Stanley, *Prize Essay*, p. 29.   [2] Thirlwall, *Remains*, vol. III, pp. 6-8.
[3] *Mission of the Comforter*, vol. I, p. 194.

Nuova, implicit in the theory of Romanticism, and developed in Germany, revealed the March of Mind as a mere cycle. History, understood on Rationalist and Utilitarian levels, social, political and nakedly intellectual history, was an endless circle; the nation, on this plane of experience, simply travelled from one form of barbarism to another, the ultimate barbarism of reason. Thus there could be no confidence in any theory of progress which was based on a Rationalist reading of history.

(2) As the foundation for a possible science of history.

(c) History as a Science

It has already been pointed out that the presupposition of Niebuhr's critical method is a world of law, of orderly sequence. To build a past by the use of analogy is to foreshadow a possible science of history; that is, a science whose aim is the discovery and formulation of the laws which govern historical movement. This was Vico's prime purpose, and Arnold, Milman and Stanley were acquainted with the *Scienza Nuova*. Of the two main influences which went towards the creation of the Liberal Anglican science of history, that of Niebuhr was the earlier, but indirect, that of Vico was later, but direct.

A science of history, in the Vichian sense, is impossible from the Rationalist standpoint of the March of Mind, because in order to discover 'laws' of historical movement, it is necessary to possess more than one example of historical movement, a scientific law being, in its very nature, statistical. Where progress, as in the March of Mind, is conceived as a unilinear development of Mankind, a scientific 'law of progress', strictly speaking, is impossible. Such a 'law' is at most a graph-curve, or sign-post, or measuring-rod to be applied to nations. It is not a scientific 'law' of progress, because it is not discovered by an examination of examples of progress; it is the application of an arbitrary standard to the Past. Such progress can only be conjectured, not deduced scientifically. Where there was no historical evidence, the line of the graph of progress was simply extended backwards, as in Condorcet's sketch of the progress of the human mind, and in 'conjectural history' generally. It was assumed that the early history of mankind consisted of a progressive sequence of 'states of society', the hunting state, the pastoral state and so on. Since a comparative survey of primitive peoples could be made in the 18th century, the 'law' governing the development of these 'states of society' could claim to be scientific. But the higher stages of the process, represented by the history of Europe, were unique. The idea of progress of the Rationalist historians was thus like an inverted pyramid, because the greater part of the evidence for a progressive development of society was to be found at the bottom of the scale of progress, in the early ages of the world and among primitive peoples. The greater the enlightenment, the weaker the scientific foundation for the belief in its continuance or further development.

Any science of history, properly considered, can have nothing to do with progress as a unilinear development which applies to mankind or 'Society', but must deal with examples of movement supplied by societies, nations, cultures or civilizations; its presupposition must be a rhythmical movement, a periodicity of some sort, a *corso* and *ricorso*, which is intrinsic in history itself, not applied externally as a pattern or division into distinct stages, as it is, for example, by Condorcet or Fourier. [44] The Liberal Anglican science of history rests on the analogy between nations and individuals, in contrast with the March of Mind, in which all mankind or 'Society' has its childhood, boyhood, youth and manhood, as it does, for instance, in Lessing's *Education of the Human Race*.

The conception of the natural course of the life of the nation, with its successive stages of development, provided the Liberal Anglicans with the examples from which to shape a science of historical movement, the stages of national growth forming the common basis necessary for historical comparisons, and universal history, seen from the view-point of a science of history, was composed of such cycles of national development, presenting the appearance of an orderly rhythmical process like the world of Nature. In this natural historical world there is therefore a single process which applies to all nations, and the understanding of this is the key to historical movement in all its complexity. It has been seen that this uniformity of history, the presupposition of the Liberal Anglican science of history, does not correspond to the uniformitarianism of geology (later, of biology), because the historical processes of the present were not the key to all the historical processes of the past, even on the level of social history. A more decisive difference lies in the fact that for the Liberal Anglicans the processes of history were mental processes, governed by the intellectual and moral development of nations, so that it was a solecism to attempt to understand the working of the imaginative mind by extending to it one's knowledge of the rational mind of maturity. The uniformitarianism of 19th-century natural science has its true analogy in that 18th-century conception of history according to which the same law operated in childhood as in manhood periods, and not in the ideas of history of the 19th century except in so far as the Utilitarians, for example, or the Positivists carried on the Rationalist tradition. It is the March of Mind which is uniformitarian.

It is a presupposition of a science of history that 'man is the same . . . in every part of the world and in every period'. This was the basis of the 18th-century science of man and of Rationalist philosophical history. History was one, and a science of history possible, because man's mental development is uniform, so that he will express himself under the same circumstances in the same way. 'The same social arrangements grow out of the human mind under the same circumstances, without any foreign intervention', said Milman. 'Man is the same, to a great extent, in every part of the world and in every period. Society is part of his nature, and social forms being circumscribed in their variations, will take the same character. . . .'[1] He talks of the 'universal religion of man', of 'the universal tendency of man' to deify his legislators, of 'the universal religious sentiment' which makes the gods the parents of sovereigns and founders of dynasties.[2] 'Man, as history and religion teach, is essentially a religious being.'[3] But although Milman was in some respects a child of the 18th century, as all the Liberal Anglicans were, and must have been, there is in these remarks a tone of Vichian piety, a positive affirmation and wholehearted

---

[1] *Quarterly Review*, vol. 81, p. 323.   [2] *Ibid.* p. 324. [45]
[3] *Christianity*, vol. I, p. 8.

acceptance of man's religious nature, which is the measure of the difference between them and statements by Rationalist historians thinking in terms of the 'natural history of religion', which on the surface appear very similar. Robertson, for instance, wrote that 'without supposing any consanguinity between such distant nations, or imagining that their religious ceremonies were conveyed by tradition from the one to the other, we may ascribe this uniformity, which in many instances seems very amazing, to the natural opera-tion of superstition and enthusiasm upon the weakness of the human mind'.[1] The difference in tone is obvious.

History being one, then, there could be no real division between 'ecclesiastical' and 'secular' history. Keeping to the spirit if not to the letter of the *Scienza Nuova*, and following the lead of German biblical criticism, the Liberal Anglicans asserted that the history of the Jews was the history of any normal nation. For them man is everywhere and at all times the same, because he is fundamentally a religious being. This unity of religious experience in universal history, however, transcends the limits of any 'science of history' in the sense which, for convenience, it bears in this chapter, or as used by Rationalist historians. It is the basis of the Liberal Anglican belief in God's purpose in history, and is on a deeper plane of experience than anything which can be classified by a science of history.

In a science of history the past must be conceived as a single whole, like the world of Nature, composed of natural parts, each finding its place naturally in the whole. The past must be divisible naturally, for no science of historical development can be built out of an arbitrary division of the past. It is a presupposition of a science of history that natural divisions do in fact exist; it is for the science of history to determine these, and to work out the allied problem of the relation of these parts to one another and to the whole. The proper unit of historical study and the relations between the units in space and time are problems which are fundamental in any science of history.[2]

For the Liberal Anglicans, nations and the stages of development

---

[1] Quoted in F. J. Teggart, *Theory and Processes of History* (1941), p. 95.
[2] Cf., for example, Toynbee's *Study of History*, which is a science of history in this sense.

through which nations pass are the natural parts of the historical whole. Each national cycle is a complete example of development, and the stages of this development form 'analogous periods' comparable to similar stages in the development of other nations. Arnold showed that since childhood, transition and manhood are 'analogous periods' in the histories of Greece, Rome and the nations of modern Europe, comparisons drawn between the histories of Greece, Rome and England at any one of these stages are valid.[1] There are thus two kinds of historical parallels, those which are significant, because scientific, and those which are merely entertaining, of use only as literary devices. Arnold's *History of Rome* is full of entertaining parallels between the battles, great men, institutions and events of the history of Rome and those of Greece and modern Europe. But there are also parallels which illustrate and confirm a historical law; for example, that between the manly pastimes of the Spartans and the tournaments of medieval Europe.[2] These have nothing in common with, say, the gladiatorial combats of the later Roman Empire. They illustrate the fact that Sparta and Medieval Europe passed through a similar feudal stage of development. Again, Augsburg, in the critical period of its history, like Athens and Rome, had her noble family of popular principles: Sibot Stolzhirsch and his kinsmen acted the part of Cleisthenes and the Alcmaeonidae at Athens, of the Valerii and Manlius Capitolinus at Rome.[3] Nations at different stages of growth cannot be compared; examples drawn from the history of a nation during its childhood period and compared to the history of the same or of another nation in its manhood stage are not truly analogous. There is no historical significance, for instance, in a comparison between Charlemagne and Augustus, or Alexander, or Napoleon; one belongs to the childhood, the others to the manhood of nations. 'Thus', says Arnold,

to argue that the Romans were less bloody than the Greeks from a comparison between the factions of the Peloponnesian War and the struggle of the Commons against the Patricians is to compare the two nations under very different circumstances: it is instituting a parallel between the intensity of our passions in manhood and childhood. The

---

[1] *Thucydides*, vol. I, appendix I. [46]   [2] *Ibid.* p. 643.   [3] *Ibid.* p. 627.

bloody factions of Corcyra and Megara are analogous to the civil wars
of Marius and Sylla, of Caesar and Pompey, Brutus and Cassius and the
Triumvirs; the harmless contests between commons and patricians can
only be compared to those in Greece before the Persian invasion. . . .[1]
The state of Greece from Pericles to Alexander . . . affords a political
lesson perhaps more applicable to our own times, if taken all together,
than any other portion of history which can be named anterior to the
18th century.[2]

The 'modern' writers of Greece correspond to the 'modern' writers
of Rome, and both should particularly appeal to us, because we
are living in an analogous period.

Thucydides, Xenophon, the orators and philosophers of Athens are
not only abler than the English, French and German writers of the
Middle Ages, but their wisdom is more applicable to us—their position,
both intellectual and political, more nearly resembled our own.[3]

On translating the legends of Ancient Rome for his *History*,
Arnold wrote:

If I were to translate Herodotus it were absurd to do it in my own
common English, because he and I do not belong to analogous periods
of Greek and English literature. I should translate him in the English
of that period of our national cultivation which corresponds to the
period of Greek cultivation at which he wrote. The dramatic form
appears essential, which is also the style of the Bible, but not peculiar to
it, because it is characteristic of a particular state of cultivation which all
people pass through at a certain stage in their progress.[4]

Elsewhere he says:

In translating the prose writers of Greece and Rome, Herodotus
should be rendered in the style and language of the chronicles, Thucydides
in that of Bacon and Hooker, while Demosthenes, Cicero, Caesar and
Tacitus require a style completely modern—the perfection of the English
language.[5]

For Stanley, the period of the Judges in Old Testament history
is analogous to the Middle Ages.

No period of Jewish history so directly illustrates a corresponding
period of Christian history . . . . I know not where we shall find a
better guide to conduct us, with a judgement at once just and tender,
through the medieval portion of Christian ecclesiastical history than the

[1] *Thucydides*, pp. 633-4.   [2] *Ibid.* vol. III, preface, p. xx. [47]
[3] *Ibid.* vol. I, pp. 636-7.   [4] Letter of 20 Dec. 1837.
[5] *Miscellaneous Works*, pp. 354-5.

sacred record of the corresponding period of the history of the Judges. The knowledge of each period reacts upon our knowledge of the other. The difficulties of each mutually explain the other. We cannot be in a better position for defending medieval Christianity against the indiscriminate attacks of one-sided Puritanical writers, than by pointing to its counterpart in the sacred record. We cannot wish for a better proof of the general truth and fidelity of this part of the Biblical narrative, than by observing its exact accordance with the manners and feelings of Christendom under analogous circumstances. . . . These resemblances between the medieval history of the Jewish Church and the medieval history of the Christian Church are seen at every turn, and perhaps more felt than seen. Take any scene, almost at random, from this period, and but for the names and Eastern colouring, it might be from the 10th or 12th century.[1]

Stanley then proceeds to give some examples. The house of Micah and his Levite, he says, set forth the exact likeness of the feudal castle and feudal chieftain of our early civilization; the insecurity of communications is the same; the vows of monastic life, the vows of celibacy, the vows of pilgrimage have their prototypes in the vows in the early struggles of Israel. 'We are struck at Ascalon and in the plains of Philistia by finding the localities equally connected with the history of Richard Coeur de Lion and of Samson; but they are, in fact, united by moral and historical, far more than by any mere local coincidences.' In both ages there is the same long crusade against the unbelievers. The Moor in Spain, the Tartars in Russia, play the very same part as the Canaanites and Philistines in Palestine. Priests and Levites wander to and fro over Palestine, as mendicant friars and sellers of indulgences wandered over Europe. Hophni and Phineas became at Shiloh the prototypes of the bloated pluralists of the Medieval Church of Europe. 'In those days there was no king in Israel'; similarly, there was no settled government in Christendom in the Middle Ages. The schools of the prophets, the universities of Christendom owe their first impulse to this first period of Jewish and of Christian history. The Translation of the Ark was a festival which exactly corresponded to what in the Middle Ages would have been the Feast of the Translation of some great relic, as for instance the transporting of the Crown of Thorns by St Louis to

[1] *Jewish Church*, vol. I, pp. 308 et seq. [48]

the Royal Chapel at Paris.[1] The period of the Judges is in fact 'the medieval age of the Jewish Church'. Samuel is 'the last representative of the ancient medieval Church of Judaism'.[2] It is the 'old heroic age' of Israel.[3] Later, Stanley compares the Puritanism of the Jewish Church during the Exile to the Reformation of the 16th century.[4] Similarly, the history of the Russian Empire and Church is comparable to the history of the European Church. Both go through the stages of national development.

With many differences, produced by diverse causes, of climate, of theology, of race, the history of the Russian Empire and Church presents a parallel to the history of the whole European Church, from first to last, not merely fanciful and arbitrary, but resulting from its passage through similar phases, in which the likenesses are more strongly brought out by the broad differences just mentioned.

The conversion of the Slavs was to Constantinople what the conversion of the Germans was to Rome. Russia as well as Europe had its Middle Ages, though 'as might be expected from its later start in the race of civilization, extending for a longer period'. The Church of Russia had its Reformation, almost its Revolution, its internal parties and its countless sects.[5] If the Russian Church corresponds in its development to the 'European' Church, and if the phases of the latter are analogous to the phases of the Jewish Church, as recorded in the Old Testament, one would expect the Russian and the Jewish Church to be analogous. 'One special interest which the Russian ecclesiastical history possesses' according to Stanley, is 'its relation, both by way of likeness and illustration, to the history of the Jewish Church of old'.[6]

Milman's mythic and heroic periods were also analogous in the sense used by Arnold and Stanley. The Middle Ages are a mythic age, a second imaginative age; the Crusades are the heroic age of Christianity, corresponding to the period of the Judges in Hebrew history and to the heroic age of Greece. [49] Religion takes certain forms at particular phases of development. The monastic institution of the 'Brides of the Sun', for example, among the Incas of Peru, is 'but another illustration of the form which [religious sentiment]

[1] *Jewish Church*, vol. II, p. 82.   [2] *Ibid.* vol. I, pp. 408, 392.
[3] *Ibid.* vol. II, p. 18.   [4] *Ibid.* vol. III, p. 31.
[5] *Eastern Church*, pp. 340-1.   [6] *Ibid.* p. 343.

takes at certain phases of human society'. The Vestals of Rome and some of the earlier Asiatic religions, the Buddhist monasteries, the nunneries of the Roman Catholic world, find their anti-types in Peru.[1] Mexico, at the time of the Spanish Conquest, was 'advanced to a high state of what we may venture to call, without pledging ourselves to its origin, Asiatic civilization'.[2] The Toltecs are the Pelasgians of this civilization of Anahuac . . . to them are ascribed the buildings of the greatest solidity and magnificence, the monuments of 'Transatlantic Cyclopean architecture'. Mexico was to this civilization of Tezcuco as the sterner and more warlike Rome to the more polite and cultivated Greece.[3]

The fact of these natural periods in the social progress of all states, said Stanley, 'it has been one of the chief boasts of modern historical science to establish and elucidate'.[4]

We must judge whether a nation is in an early or an advanced stage, by these epochs; by them we learn what periods of civilization are alone truly analogous; by them we discover a modern history in the ages of Greece and Rome, and an ancient history in the nations of modern Europe; an affinity between the heroic ages of Paganism and the feudal ages of Christendom; between the era of Thucydides and the era of the Reformation; between the times of Alexander and Augustus and the times of Louis XIV.[5]

From a study of these analogous periods in the histories of different nations, then, general laws of a nation's progress can be drawn. It can be seen that all nations go through stages and crises according to a natural law of development; that each stage can be distinguished by its special characteristics, by the nature of the events of its social history, the scope and tone of its intellectual activity, the character of its art, especially its poetry, and the form of its religion; that the trend of its intellectual development is towards rationalism; and the inevitable tendency of its social development is to become more liberal;[6] that in this process the popular party (the Commons) of the transition period becomes the anti-popular party (the nobility of wealth) of the manhood

---

[1] *Quarterly Review*, vol. 81, p. 324.   [2] *Ibid.* vol. 73, p. 188.   [3] *Ibid.* pp. 196, 204.
[4] *Prize Essay*, p. 8. [50]   [5] *Ibid.* p. 9.
[6] Cf. Arnold, *Thucydides*, vol. I, p. 636. Thirlwall, for example, spoke of 'the natural tendency of the state toward a complete democracy' (*Greece*, vol. II, p. 99).

period; and that this movement is not in any way connected with the form of government or the names of parties.

The importance of these laws for the Liberal Anglicans, especially for Arnold, was that widespread knowledge of them should lead to social and political thought and action which was scientific and based on historical principles and not merely the result of self-interest or panic.

The examples of development which make these laws possible rest on the assumption that history is divisible naturally, and is a whole consisting of natural parts, and that any other than the natural divisions are arbitrary and meaningless. 'I hope these volumes', Arnold wrote, referring to his edition of Thucydides, 'may contribute to the conviction that history is to be studied as a whole, and according to its philosophical divisions, not such as are merely geographical and chronological.'[1] The dichotomy between 'Ancient' and 'Modern' history, was false in Arnold's eyes, an artificial division obscuring the real nature of history. He called for 'a more sensible division of history than that which is commonly adopted of ancient and modern'. There is in fact, he said, an ancient and a modern period in the history of every people, ancient corresponding to childhood, modern to manhood.

The largest portion of that history which is commonly called ancient is practically modern, as it describes society in a state analogous to that in which it now is, while on the other hand much of what is called modern history is practically ancient, as it relates to a state of things which has passed away. . . .[2] I must beg to repeat what I have said before, that the period to which the work of Thucydides refers, properly belongs to modern and not to ancient history, and it is this . . . which makes it so peculiarly deserving our study.[3]

The theory of the social progress of states provided the philosophical divisions, the natural periods, of history. 'Knowledge of these periods', says Arnold, 'furnishes us with a clue to the study of history which the continuous succession of events in chronological order seems particularly to require.'[4] Without such a clue history is meaningless, and any divisions of history into periods, or other units of study, which are made without this knowledge are useless.

---

[1] *Thucydides*, vol. III, preface, p. xxii.   [2] *Ibid.* vol. I, appendix I, p. 636.
[3] *Ibid.* vol. III, preface, pp. xviii-xix.   [4] *Ibid.* vol. I, p. 615.

They are completely devoid of significance, because unnatural. For instance, to take the accession of new dynasties, or an event like the Restoration of 1660, to mark the boundaries of the periods of English history is to cut violently into historical growth—a fatal vivisection, creating divisions which are merely artificial, and which 'give no idea of the beginning, middle or end of the history of a people'. For Arnold the Restoration is 'rather a subdivision of one particular period than the beginning or termination of a period in itself'.[1]

In his inaugural lecture as Professor of 'Modern' History, Arnold used the current academic two-fold division into 'Ancient' and 'Modern', but fitted his own conception of history to it. In the same way, Stanley, as Professor of 'Ecclesiastical' History, only accepted formally the implied division between ecclesiastical and secular history (in the title of his lectures), and hastened to point out, in his inaugural lectures, that no such division really existed. 'We must endeavour', he said, '. . . never whilst studying the parts to forget the whole; nor even so to lose ourselves in the whole as to neglect the study of one or more of the parts.'[2] 'In the history of the Church as in that of the world . . . there is a distinct unity of parts.' [51] In determining the beginning of his period he was 'fixing not merely the accidental limits of convenience, but the true limits involved in the nature of the subject'.[3] 'Ecclesiastical' history, so far from being exempt from the laws of gradual progress and development to which the history of other nations is subject, is the most remarkable exemplification of those laws. In no people does the history move forward in so regular a course, through beginning, middle and end, as in the people of Israel.[4]

Failure to realize the true nature of history as a whole consisting of natural parts meant that a science of history, properly speaking, was impossible, and if one immersed oneself deeply in any particular period (and Arnold recommended this as the best method of studying history),[5] one must realize its relation to the whole, otherwise there would be a danger of losing sight of the main

[1] *Ibid.* [2] *Eastern Church*, p. lxiv. [3] *Ibid.* p. xxiv.
[4] *Ibid.* p. xxvi. Of this Milman wrote: 'our opinions are as nearly coincident as may be' (*Herny Hart Milman*, p. 93).
[5] Stanley, *Life*, p. 14.

stream of history in the local cross-currents and checks, and this might well lead to a doubt whether there was any real direction in history at all. For this reason, Arnold considered the study of contemporary history, by itself, to be almost valueless.

The best example of national development, so far as social history is concerned, Arnold found in the history of Rome, which passed through all the stages of growth from infancy to maturity. (Rome was a model and type-history for Niebuhr and Vico.) This explains why the history of Rome was for Arnold, 'in some sort the history of the world',[1] and why he thought that the Roman Commonwealth ought to be understood 'by none so well as by those who have grown up under the laws . . . who are . . . citizens of England'.[2] This was because England provided a second best example of social development, though not a complete example, not a finished model. English historians, Arnold wrote, ought to be the best in the world, 'because our social civilization is perfect'.[3] The implication of this remark is that English social civilization was passing through a supremely important historical phase, in the natural course of its development, and under the very eyes of English historians, who were unaware of what was happening because their conception of history was not grounded on a science of history. [52]

If Rome was the best and most complete example of social progress which history had to offer, Greece was the purest example of cultural development, because it was the first.[4]

It was not necessary for the Liberal Anglicans to emphasize their belief that the nation was a proper unit of historical study, because this was axiomatic in 19th-century England, the framework of historical thinking generally. It was the one-ness of the nation's life, the organic conception, which it was necessary to emphasize. When Arnold defined history as the 'biography of a nation',[5] the vital word for Arnold was 'biography', springing, as it did, from his conception of history as a science, and from the analogy

---

[1] Stanley, *Life*, p. 115.   [2] *Rome*, vol. I, preface, p. vii.   [3] *Travelling Journals*, p. 51.
[4] Hare, *Guesses at Truth* (3rd ed., 1st series), pp. 59–60: Greece alone affords a type of the natural development of the human mind through its various ages and stages.
[5] *Lectures*, p. 27.

between the lives of nations and of individuals which was the starting-point of that conception. What the science of history had to determine, therefore, was not the fact of the nation as a natural part of the historical whole, because this could be taken for granted, but the natural periods in the nation's development. It was these periods accordingly which Arnold stressed as the proper units of historical study. The nation, however, remained the ultimate unit, the 'social atom', of the Liberal Anglican science of history, all nations going to make up a world governed by law. The histories of Greece, Rome and England were alike the histories of 'nations' in Arnold's mind. Thirlwall's Greece represented a cycle of national development. 'Alexander's invasion', he said, 'belongs rather to universal history than to the history of Greece'; for Thirlwall the history of Greece had come full circle before that event.[1] For Milman the history of the Jews was that of a 'nation', and for Stanley the history of Israel was likewise a complete cycle of national history. The nation remained the final unit of study, so far as the science of history was concerned. Thus the Liberal Anglicans considered race, not as a historical unit larger than the nation, but as a characteristic of it. The union of race, language, institutions and religion formed for Arnold the complete 'national personality'.[2] For Stanley 'race is to nations what family character is to individuals'.[3] It is the nation which goes through the stages of civilization, and the 'race' does so only in so far as it is comprehended by the nation. Race, therefore, did not provide the Liberal Anglicans with a unit of study more comprehensive than the nation. Any such unit was for them potential rather than actual. 'Civilization' at that time meant not a form of society but a process. There were degrees of civilization, but not civilizations. Stanley hinted that the relations between nations become defined and self-conscious in late periods of their civilization[4] (some such belief was Arnold's also, because the special danger of a manhood period, he thought, was international war),[5] but

---

[1] *Greece*, vol. VI, p. 120. [53]   [2] *Lectures*, pp. 31-2.
[3] *Quarterly Review*, vol. 126, p. 482. Buckle is criticized for neglecting the element of race.
[4] *Prize Essay*, p. 16: 'It is not till a late period that men understand their relations with foreign countries.'   [5] *Thucydides*, vol. I, p. 637.

he did not conceive of an earlier society or 'civilization' breaking up into smaller units, and becoming articulated, when such a society was in decay.

For Arnold, the nation was self-contained; the friendly intercourse between nation and nation, he said, is for the most part negative, and the external life of a nation seen solely in its wars, with scarcely any qualification. 'A state acting out of itself is mostly either repelling violence or exercising it upon others.'[1] Yet he hints at something larger in holding that the state is not only an instrument for the moral improvement of its individual members, that is, in its internal aspect, but is, or should be, moral also in its external aspect, as being part of 'the great body of organized states throughout the world, and still farther of the universal family of mankind'.[2] But this supra-national community (if it is one) is potential, not actual or historical. When he quoted with approval Niebuhr's remark that 1517 must precede 1688,[3] he missed the clue it afforded to a possible wider unit of historical study, comprehending the nation. The nation remained for Arnold the instrument of moral growth, the means by which the individual and mankind are brought to perfection.

(d) The Limitations of a Science of History

History, then, dealing with the stages of national development as natural parts of a larger whole, and aiming to discover the laws of national progress, was more than a mere branch of literature, [54] or philosophy teaching by examples, or a 'science' in the sense of an organized body of systematic knowledge, or as applying critical principles in the study of the past. It was a 'science' in that it dealt with a world governed by law. But as soon as this has been said it is necessary to state the limitations which were apparent to the Liberal Anglicans themselves in such a 'science' of history. It was, theoretically, a goal, an ideal; practically, a rough working hypothesis. Logic and history do not keep step; aspirations outrun objectivity. Only where the immediately practical aspect of a science of history is not stressed can such a science be worked out,

[1] *Lectures*, p. 10.   [2] *Ibid.* p. 17.   [3] Letter of 28 Jan. 1841.

as in the case of Vico, with anything approaching completeness. Arnold did not suffer from the *Halbheit* which was Milman's weakness as a thinker, but the Romanticism of both was characteristic of the Movement in England; the Liberal Anglicans did not make it their primary aim to erect a theoretical system, or to think out systematically the implications of their activity as historians. Thus, for example, though their conception of history is essentially idealist, the reader is left to find this out (with some difficulty) for himself; he is nowhere confronted with a formal and systematic statement or manifesto. Similarly the Liberal Anglican science of history was not erected into a system. Men like Arnold and Niebuhr, spoiling for the fray and at the same time conscientious historians, aware of the complexity of history, do not make good scientists or philosophers, at least so far as logic and completeness are concerned. Arnold had to confess that 'in history the laws of the science are kept out of sight, perhaps are not known',[1] and to deplore the fact that the scientific character of history has not yet been sufficiently made out, that 'there hangs an uncertainty about its laws which to most persons is very perplexing'.[2] 'History. . . ', he said in his lectures, 'does not seem to be sufficient to the right understanding of itself: the laws which, as it seems, ought to be established from the facts, appear even with a full knowledge of the facts before us to be infinitely disputable.' Yet he continued:[3]

I confess that if I believed them to be as really disputable as they have been disputed, the pain of such a conviction would be most grievous to bear. I am firmly persuaded, on the contrary, that setting out with those views of man which we find in the Scriptures, and those plain moral notions which the Scriptures do not so much teach as suppose to exist in us, and sanction; the laws of history, in other words the laws of political science, using 'political' in the most exalted sense of the term . . . may be deduced, or if you will, may be confirmed, from it with perfect certainty. . . . And if in this or in any former lectures I have seemed to express or to imply a very firm conviction on points which I well know to be warmly disputed, it is because these laws being to my own mind absolutely certain, the lessons of any particular portion of history, supposing that the facts are known to us, appear to be certain also: and daily experience can scarcely remove my wonder at finding

[1] *Lectures*, p. 390.   [2] *Ibid.*   [3] *Ibid.* pp. 391, *et seq.*

they do not appear so to others. That they do not appear so however is undoubtedly a phenomenon to be accounted for. And hard as it is, almost I think impossible to doubt conclusions which seem both in the way by which we arrived at them originally, and in their consistency with one another, and in their offering a key to all manner of difficulties, and in their never having met with any objection which we could not readily answer, to command absolutely our mind's assent; still I allow, that if they are convinced no minds but ours . . . we should be driven to the extremity of scepticism; truth would appear indeed to be a thing utterly unreal or utterly unattainable. Now on the contrary, what appears to me to be the laws of history, contain in them no single paradox; there is no step in the process by which we arrive at them which is not absolutely confirmed by the sanction of the highest authorities.

Arnold, then, believes that 'history has its laws',[1] that 'theoretically considered it is not a mere aggregation of particular actions or characters . . . but is besides this the witness to general moral and political truths, capable when rightly used of bringing to our notice fresh truths, which we might not have gained by *a priori* reasoning alone'.[2] He talked of 'the truths of historical science which I certainly believe to be very real and very important', of 'history in the abstract', of 'certain formulae which will enable the pupil to read all history beneficially', of his 'theorem', elsewhere of his 'experiment', of 'the method of historical analysis by which we endeavour to discover the key, as it were, to the complicated movement of the world'.[3] Stanley, in the essay which has already been mentioned, makes an enquiry, first into the *laws* of national duration in *themselves* and secondly into the *facts* as exhibited by history. The subject, he says, divides itself naturally into these two heads. He is going to 'discover the skeleton' of the growth of nations, 'freed from the various forms in which it has clothed itself', 'the golden clue of God's Providence'.[4]

History, therefore, according to the Liberal Anglicans, has its laws, though they are not as certain in their operation as the laws of mechanics.[5] Thirlwall compared the progress of mankind or that of a great community to a glacier, but said that it could not

---

[1] *Lectures*, p. 394: 'if history has its laws, as I entirely believe. . . .'   [2] *Ibid.*
[3] *Ibid.* pp. 81, 393; *ibid.*, p. 28; 'Use of the Classics' in *Misc. Works*, pp. 358-9; *Thucydides*, vol. I, appendix I; *Lectures*, p. 358; *ibid.*, p. 357.
[4] *Prize Essay*, pp. 4-5.   [5] Cf. Whately, *Bacon's Essays*, pp. 189-90.

be measured with scientific accuracy.[1] Real history was too complex for this.[2] The Liberal Anglicans, true historians as they were, could not exclude 'the play of the contingent and the unforeseen', but with the nation as the ultimate historical unit of their science of history they were able to make large allowances for it. Their laws applied to the internal history of nations, and thus left a large field open to the action of exterior forces, such as conquest by a foreign power. Such action does not bring in question the validity of the laws and the possibility of a science of history. The smaller one's unit of study, the easier it is to form a science of history, provided one believes that chance, at the worst, can only disrupt what would otherwise have been inevitable. Arnold recognized that the laws of progress may be upset or checked in their operation by external causes. At Augsburg the revolution of 1548 by which the nobles regained their power was the result of external causes, foreign violence in the person of Charles V. Arnold is very much aware of these disturbing causes, which, he says, have in fact generally interfered with the natural course of things. It is worth while to observe, he said in 1842, how little any real history is an exact exemplification of abstract principles, how our generalizations—which must be made, for so alone can history furnish us with any truths—must yet be kept within certain limits or they become full of error.[3]

But even where the disturbing cause is certain in its interference [he said in relation to the 1548 revolution at Augsburg] as in mechanics the resistance of the air always prevents a body from obeying the natural laws of motion, still the general principles of the science are universally held to be essential to the attainment of a true knowledge of it. Much more does this hold good in political science, where disturbing causes need not of necessity come into action, and what is true in principle may sometimes, as at Augsburg up to 1548, be no less true in practice.[4]

(e) Transition to the Philosophy of History

The Liberal Anglican science of history, then, had recognized limitations. But it could not be accepted as final by historians for

[1] *Remains*, vol. III (1861), pp. 281-2.
[2] For Arnold on the complexity of historical movement see *Sermons*, vol. IV, introduction, pp. v-vi. [55] [3] *Lectures*, p. 180. [4] *Thucydides*, vol. I, p. 628. Cf. *Lectures*, pp. 393-4.

whom God's Providence was an absolute presupposition. Considered in isolation, as it has been seen so far, as a whole, it had no existence for the Liberal Anglicans. It comes into conflict at too many vital points with their deepest convictions. Its logical implications, a complete relativism, fatalism, history made by man alone and governed by law, cycles of history which are pagan, not Christian, clash with the Liberal Anglican belief in a Universal standard of morality, free-will, divine interposition and progress under God's Providence. The realization of these problems, and of the basic idealism of the Liberal Anglican idea of history—the appeal to the individual mind as the ultimate historical reality—leads from the science to the philosophy of history.

The analogy between states and individuals, from which the Liberal Anglican science of history started, implies that the death of nations is inevitable and natural, like the end of all natural organisms. In the words of Hare, the life of nations, as well as of individuals, has its fixed course and term. It springs forth, grows up, reaches its maturity, decays, perishes.[1]

Nations after they have reached a high pitch of power and glory, have fallen and perished: in this there is nothing singular. The law of death—*Thou shalt surely die*—was not merely uttered against every child of man individually, but against every combination and society in which men can unite themselves together.[2]

The idea of the natural and inevitable death of nations was used by Hare to enhance the value of a belief in Christianity ('Only through Christianity has a nation ever risen again;' 'the Church of God alone . . . is indestructible'),[3] but rested on the conception of the nation as a complete biological and moral person, and cannot be reconciled with the Liberal Anglican belief in the power of the individual will in matters of faith.[4] By 1841, Arnold (never a Platonist, always an Aristotelian) was beginning to break away from the idea of the moral personality of the nation, and to realize the dangers involved in the metaphysical theory of the

---

[1] *Guesses at Truth* (2nd ed., 2nd series), p. 21.
[2] *Mission of the Comforter*, vol. I, pp. 333, 335. Cf. Thirlwall, *Remains*, vol. III, pp. 6-8. [56]
[3] *Mission of the Comforter*, vol. I, p. 333. [57]
[4] Sanders, *Coleridge and the Broad Church Movement*, p. 142.

state. Stanley says that 'he began to attach a new importance to the truths relating to a man's own individual convictions', and tells how 'In his latest lessons it was observed how, in reading Plato's Republic, he broke out into a solemn protest against the evil effects of an exaggerated craving after unity.' Arnold himself said:

I am myself so much inclined to the idea of a strong social bond, that I ought not to be suspected of any tendency to anarchy; yet I am beginning to think that the idea may be overstrained, and that this attempt to merge the soul and will of the individual man in the general body is, when fully developed, contrary to the very essence of Christianity. After all it is the individual soul that must be saved.[1]

History, from the Liberal Anglican point of view, could not be a natural world, composed of national biological wholes, because such a view leaves progress, and the moral world, out of account, and is fatalistic. What, then, was the relation of progress, a Liberal Anglican presupposition, to the world revealed by the science of history? Was the extinction of nations inevitable?

This was the question, the ultimate question of Liberal Anglican practical history, which Stanley undertook to answer in the essay of 1840, 'Whether states, like individuals, after a certain period of maturity, inevitably tend to decay', by emphasizing the reality of the moral, as against the merely fanciful nature of the physical analogy between states and individuals. All cyclical theories of history, such as those of Plato and Tacitus in ancient, and Vico in modern, times, he says, have rested, 'either in substance or in form', on this analogy. The analogy, properly considered, is two-fold. In speaking of the mind, the moral power, the virtue, the wisdom, of the nation we are plainly using the terms in the same sense as that in which we apply them to the individual. But to speak of the body of the nation is not only to extend, but absolutely to change the meaning of the terms. 'In the first case, that is, in regard to that moral being which alone is essential to nations, or individuals, the analogy is complete.' The moral analogy is based on reality independent of human applications of it, the physical analogy is the creature of our own imagination. 'The truth and error which seem to be united in the belief of an inevitable national cycle follow the two-fold division suggested by this double analogy.' The primary truth of moral science, that no one human being ever lost his moral life except through his own agency, applies also to nations. The fall of Rome and Jerusalem was owing to internal dissolution, and inevitable only for that reason. There is no resemblance between the latter end of an individual and of a nation. The decay of a nation finds its parallel and its laws, not in the inevitable physical dissolution of the individual, but only in his moral and self-caused enervation. 'The same moral analogy which forms the basis of belief in a national providence, furnishes a complete answer to the error which would substitute for it belief in a national fatalism.' The truths of the science of history had been disfigured by connection with the idea of the inevitable decline, death and decay of nations, as of men.[1]

It is typical of Liberal Anglican thought that the idealist interpretation of history, [58] by which is meant (without at present going any deeper into the matter) the acknowledgement of the individual mind as the ultimate agent (under God's Providence) of history, which is implicit in their conception of the intellectual development of nations, should become to some extent explicit only when it was face to face with the practical problem of the crisis of civilization. In Stanley's essay it is to meet this challenge that historical phenomena are explained in terms of mind. Because the 'moral analogy' is real, because history is not merely another name for biography, but rather (here Stanley quotes Carlyle) the 'conflux and essence of all biographies',[2] it is the advance of civilization (and by this Stanley means not the development of abstract reason in the Rationalist sense of the March of Mind—the phrase would have meant this in the mouth of a Utilitarian—but the development of concrete minds) which imparts to a nation its special qualities and brings to pass the great revolutions in the framework of the state. Starting from this fundamental historical reality, mind, the thinking and willing individual, he surveys the whole field of the decline and fall of nations. He sums up the social characteristics of civilization in the three great tendencies

[1] *Prize Essay*, pp. 5-7. [2] *Ibid.* p. 7.

towards equalization, division of labour (or variety) and co-operation (or unity). It is the 'development of civilization' which explains these tendencies.[1] Thus unity in war is discipline; in language, generalization; in philosophy, method; in politics, sub-mission to law and association—an interpretation of political development in terms of ideas. Co-operation, says Stanley, is a tendency only possible in a people which has at last been able to conceive in theory the idea of a state or community as distinct from the personal sway of an individual, the self-control of a freeman as opposed to the control of the slave, and has been taught by the experience of ages the immense superiority of collective over solitary exertions.

The keen insight of an advanced society into the wants and circum-stances of others, and the deep consciousness which men then first acquire of their own powers and ends, give birth both to that ardent desire of justice, which so instantly divides men into political parties and to those violent convulsions which the transition from custom to reason must always occasion in the moral and spiritual world.[2] It is not, in fact, till a late period that men begin to divide themselves into parties. It is not till the same epoch that they understand their relations with foreign countries.[3]

Here party spirit and nationalism are explained in terms of the development of mind.

Stanley's answer to the fatalism inherent in the idea of a historical world governed by law, therefore, is to point to the individual mind as the ultimate reality of history. It is an answer which leads logically to an examination of the Liberal Anglican conception of Progress (which is essentially the work of individuals—resting on the moral and intellectual exertions of each of us), because it did not lead on their part to any further enquiry, on idealist lines, into the nature of history, nor can it be proved that it rested on a deeper understanding of Vico. It was rather the result of an extraordinary union of evangelicalism, in so far as it emphasizes the salvation of the individual, [60] and the historical outlook. The sins of the nation were beyond cure, Arnold believed, repentance was too late to save it, [61] and it was to the individual that he turned in the crisis of civilization. It is a logical transition from the

---

[1] *Ibid.* p. 20.   [2] *Ibid.* p. 17. [59]   [3] *Ibid.* p. 15.

Liberal Anglican science of history to their philosophy of history, that is to say, from process to progress (the verbal distinction is not theirs), [62] from the history of nations viewed universally from the point of view of law, to the history of nations viewed universally from the point of view of purpose and moral effort. It leads to the idea of progress because it asserts that the things of the mind are the 'experience of ages', and are not lost for ever with the death of the nation but live on, recreated in the mind in future ages. Transition must be, to some extent, transmission. [63] This was in Milman's mind when he said that poetry rarely, if ever, renews its youth.[1] The cycles of national development are not self-contained, intellectually or morally. [65] In our day, each individual mind is heir to the wealth of nations which have run their course; a course which, as Stanley showed, all nations have completed as an historical fact, but not according to an inevitable law.

If we look both to the facts which precede and to the facts which accompany a nation's last stage, it would seem rather that the finger of Providence, so far as it can be discerned amid the perplexities of history, points perpetually in advance.[2]

The science of history cannot deal with true progress, because this is an accumulation, the result of transmission. Progress represents what is unique in each national cycle of history, and its characteristics therefore cannot be classified or compared. Progress, properly-speaking, is pure advance, and those characteristics of any national cycle of history which constitute such an advance must lie outside the scope of a science of history.

Just as the science of history cannot take true progress into account, so it has no concern with free-will or Providence. The Liberal Anglicans could not accept as final an interpretation of history which made it wholly the result of mechanical forces outside the control of men or the foreknowledge and (at special times) the intervention of God. [66] Thirlwall complained that free-will and God's Providence are both 'paralyzed and crushed' by the determinism inherent in a science of history.[3] Both Vico and Niebuhr strengthened the Liberal Anglican belief in Providence,

[1] Milman, *Latin Christianity*, vol. VI, p. 486. [64]
[2] Stanley, *Prize Essay*, p. 13.   [3] *Remains*, vol. III, pp. 281-2. [67]

[68] though modern interpreters would hold that to take Vico's lip-service to Providence at its face value was fundamentally to misunderstand his real meaning and purpose. [69] Practical history may be deterministic, like Marxian history, but practical history which is fundamentally Christian, cannot be.

The Liberal Anglican science of history, then, went so far, but no farther. It was necessary, but it did not explain everything. It covered the whole field of history but by no means accounted for it in its wholeness. It dealt with the progress of nations on certain levels, social and intellectual, and was useful on that account, but it did not touch the deeper levels of experience. From the point of view of a Christian, as well as from the Romantic point of view, these very limitations constituted its value, showing that even when the science of history had done its work, supposing even that it were possible to discover all the laws of historical movement, there would still be much to be accounted for. For even if man made his own history without any supernatural aid or guidance, the science of history could not deal with true progress. A science of history therefore which could not comprehend the whole of history could not be the expression of the universal plan of human history. It deals neither with true progress nor with God's purpose. From the Liberal Anglican point of view, therefore, it traces only a small and relatively unimportant part of the pattern which is human history. The whole pattern is the revelation of God's Providence.

The Liberal Anglican science of history may be compared to a pioneer who, in clearing the virgin forest, brings order into what was before a tangled chaos, and at the same time leaves the stark contours of its geological foundation visible to all, immovable, untouchable. This foundation is the pattern of true progress, God's purpose in so far as it is discernible. Coleridge had declared that the aim of his philosophy was 'to connect by a moral *copula* natural history with political history; or in other words to make history scientific, and science historical—to take from history its accidentality and from science its fatalism'.[1] This was the goal of the

---

[1] *Table Talk*, pp. 139-40 (12 Sept. 1831). The heading of this section is 'Mr Coleridge's System of Philosophy'.

Liberal Anglicans. In the science of history they attempted to make history scientific. They had now to take from science its fatalism. As inevitability, law, determinism recede, the science of history gives way in their minds to the philosophy of history. The crisis of civilization revealed by the science of history led the Liberal Anglicans to emphasize the individual and his salvation. As the future presses on us, Arnold said, it is for us to work while it is day, knowing that our efforts cannot be vain.[1] The science of history was to be an aid, not obscuring the true pattern of God's purpose by claiming for itself the whole field of history, and not thereby binding our own efforts by preaching our inescapable fate.[2]

---

[1] *Lectures*, p. 399.   [2] *Ibid.* pp. 395-6. [70]

CHAPTER III

THE LIBERAL ANGLICAN PHILOSOPHY OF HISTORY

THE Liberal Anglican science of history showed that progress, whatever it may be, is not the March of Mind in the purely Rationalist sense, because there is no true progress in that sense at all. On the Rationalist level of understanding, history is not progressive but cyclical; there are progresses, or rather processes, but no progress. The only 'March of Mind' which history reveals is the progress of the nation; only from this limited point of view is such progress visible, and its inevitable end is an intellectual barbarism worse than the barbarism of the nation's childhood. True progress cannot be revealed by the science of history, which is confined to the natural life-course of nations, [71] and the problem of its real nature remains. But the negative result of the science of history does in fact solve the problem, because if progress is not perfectibility in the predominantly material and intellectual sense of the Rationalist historians, it must be perfectibility in the moral sense, a sense in which religion and intellectual development are in perfect harmony. The fact of 'the moral and intellectual improvement of mankind' cannot be denied, and universal history, which shows unmistakably this general improvement, while remaining cyclical on certain levels, cannot be entirely cyclical. In other words, given the fact of progress, in some sense, and the rhythmical and not unilinear pattern of history, to discover the levels on which history is purely cyclical, purely natural and inevitable, is to demonstrate the nature of true progress, which stands apart from this natural process. Thus, by presenting in brief logical compass what in reality was an historical growth in the minds of the Liberal Anglicans, can their problem be solved for them. But, in fact, the Liberal Anglicans did not make systematically the verbal distinctions between 'science', 'philosophy' and 'history' which are so useful in the analysis and presentation of their thought, [72] and their idea of history as a whole grew not tidily, but in some confusion. Historically, their ideas on the science of history, as it has been called for the purpose of clearer exposition, did come to a fuller development first, but their philosophy of history did not spring simply and logically from this, but gradually took shape in their minds (though it never assumed the form of a final statement) in answer to practical problems more or less directly related to the fundamental problem of the nature of progress, and with a growing awareness and knowledge of the thought of the pioneers, Lessing, Herder, Kant, Hegel, who had faced the same problem. Thus, for example, the challenge of the literal interpretation of scripture was met by the theory of accommodation (in Milman's *History of the Jews*, 1829, and Arnold's *Essay on the Interpretation of Scripture*, 1831), and this theory, applied by Milman and Stanley to universal history, became the key-point of the Liberal Anglican philosophy of history. The challenge of the crisis of civilization, too, was ever present.

A useful landmark in the formation of this philosophy of history is provided by the 1848 edition of the *Guesses at Truth*, in which the pioneers of the philosophy of history are passed in review. [73] This essay is a miniature history of the Idea of Progress, and illustrates the extent to which the Liberal Anglican philosophy of history was indebted to the Germans. Belief in the perfectibility of mankind, says Hare, is a late growth in the world of thought and full of errors. Condorcet is unsatisfactory,[1] and elsewhere Hare makes it apparent that St Simon, too, does not meet with his approval. Hare would not accept 'these critical periods . . . in the sense . . . used by certain recent French theorizers, about the history of the world.'[2] 'It was in Germany that the idea of the progressiveness of mankind first revealed itself under a form more nearly approaching to the truth.'[3] Although Herder is dismissed as unsatisfactory (he 'had but vague conceptions with regard to the progress of mankind. He had discerned no principle of unity determining its course and end') [74] the answer which in fact the writer gives to

---

[1] *Guesses at Truth* (2nd ed., 2nd series), p. 51.
[2] Cf. 'Romanizing Fallacies', *Charges*, p. 69.
[3] *Guesses at Truth* (2nd ed., 2nd series), pp. 56 *et seq.*

his question: 'What is the true idea of the history of the world?' embodies Herder's central belief:

The philosophical idea of the history of the world will be, that it is to exhibit the gradual unfolding of all the faculties of man's intellectual and moral being—those which he has in common with the brutes may be brought to perfection at once in him as they are in them—under every shade of circumstance and in every variety of combination.

Hegel is criticized for regarding the historical process too much as a mere natural evolution, without due account of the fostering superintendence by which alone any real good is elicited. From what has been said, the writer concludes, we may perceive that the progress of mankind is not in a straight line, uniform and unbroken. . . . It is like the motion of the earth, which, besides its yearly course round the sun, has a daily revolution through successive periods of light and darkness.

Stanley hailed the book of Daniel as the first attempt at a philosophy of history[1]—the first forerunner of Herder and Lessing and Hegel. In the four Empires of the book of Daniel we see the first perception of the continuous succession of ages, the recognition of the truth that the story of the fortunes of humanity is not a mere disjointed tale, but is a regular development of epochs, one growing out of another, cause leading to effect, race following race in a majestic plan in which the Divine Economy is as deeply concerned as in the fate of the Chosen People. The expression of the universal plan of history is the purpose of the whole book, which contains the first sketch of the education of the world.

If, therefore, history is fundamentally rhythmical, and the fact of progress plain to Christian eyes, the pattern of universal history must be a series of forward steps, each cycle of national history representing, so far as true progress is concerned, an advance on its predecessor, and this must be God's plan in the unfolding of his purpose. True progress, then, is a gradual advance, through the childhood-manhood rhythm of nations, towards the final goal of God's purpose which it is not given us to see. Progress is a perfection of the things of the spirit, and 'progress' can only be cyclical on the lower plane, where, maturity passes over into a new

---

[1] *Jewish Church*, vol. III, p. 43; vol. I, p. 467.

barbarism. In so far as a period is in advance of its predecessor, it is so where the things of the spirit are concerned, for here alone is true progress. As Christianity represents the highest point of progress so far attained, it is only a Christian philosophy of history, that is, universal history from a Christian point of view, which will reveal true progress. The education of the human race, God's Providential government of the world, is not, therefore, inscrutable, but taken in conjunction with the science of history, and viewed on a grand enough scale, or in other words, when universal history is unravelled in terms of the theory of the social progress of states, it is plainly visible, if, in order to see it, one is standing where a Christian ought to stand. This is the relation between the 'science' and the 'philosophy of history' of the Liberal Anglicans. The science of history is its handmaid. It reveals the underlying rhythm or obbligato of true progress, describes the foundation in human history on which God's Providence works for the education of the human race.

Thus, as has been hinted already, 'progress' means two things for the Liberal Anglicans. From the point of view of the nation, it is the 'process of civilization', 'the natural internal progress of society', a succession of stages through which nations pass. True progress is that which makes each cycle of national history unique, and is revealed by the philosophy of history. Where each cycle is not unique, where it can be compared to other cycles, it is for the science of history to discover the laws of national development. In other words, there are movements, the swing of the pendulum, periodicity, on a national scale, but real progress only on the scale of universal history. The science of history deals with the parts, the philosophy of history comprehends the whole; national progress belongs to the natural world, true progress to the moral world. Man, as an animal, as part of the natural world, is completely organized and incapable of further growth, but, as a man, he is developing and growing in moral stature.

Universal history, then, is fundamentally rhythmical. Each period of civilization is also a period or epoch of universal history. For Arnold, the history of Greece, the history of Rome, and the history of modern Europe constitute three such periods of civilization, three steps forward on the path of man's intellectual and moral development. Each period has its childhood and manhood, its 'ancient' and 'modern' history, its barbarous state of culture and its 'philosophical or civilized' stage, as revealed in the history of nations. Thus, for Arnold, the history of modern Europe from the 16th century is 'the third full period of civilization'.[1] In Arnold's inaugural lecture, however, we are shown only two such periods, only two forward steps. This was probably because Arnold thought it necessary, as Professor of Modern History, to fit his ideas on history into the prevailing academic scheme of 'Ancient' and 'Modern'. His task as Professor of Modern History was to find a real distinction between Ancient and Modern history which would apply to the academic and chronological division, at the same time preserving his view of history.[2] He did this by combining his conception of moral growth (by stages, or periods of civilization), and his theory of the transmission of civilization in terms of race. Modern History, he said, begins with the German invasions, from them spring our modern nations, and our modern civilization. Our present period of civilization was brought into being by the contact of the German race with the gathered riches of the preceding period, the first period of civilization. The intellect of Greece, the laws of Rome, the moral and spiritual perfection of Christianity had culminated and been brought together in the later Empire. This 'mass' was transformed at the magic touch of the Germans, so that in 'Modern' history we have the ancient world still existing, with the added element of the German race with its peculiar qualities. 'This addition was of such power that it changed the character of the whole mass.' 'The peculiar stamp of the Middle Ages is undoubtedly German.'[3]

This is Arnold's theory of the transmission of civilization, a theory of the transition between two periods in terms of race. Roman law, Greek intellect, Christian ethics, he conceives as perfect in themselves. There is progress only if these fall into good racial ground. Morally, therefore, though 'our life is in a manner a continuation of Greece, Rome and Israel,' yet it 'exhibits a fuller development of the human race, a richer combination of its most

[1] *Miscellaneous Works*, p. 358.   [2] *Lectures*, p. 28.   [3] *Ibid.* p. 34.

remarkable elements', because the perfection achieved by Greece, Rome and Israel in their various fields of endeavour mingled with the virtues of the German nations, and the result was a step forward. Race therefore plays a large part in Arnold's idea of progress. It is the union of a fresh race with the achievements of the previous period of civilization which makes a step forward possible. Arnold's pessimism as to the future of civilization was due to the fact that, looking round on the world as it was, he could find no race fit to receive the torch. [75] Russia was the only possible hope, but the Slavs were for Arnold a part of our present civilization, bound up with its fortunes, so that they could not for that reason constitute the seed-plot of a new culture, and must be regarded as part of this one.

The real distinction between Ancient and Modern history is therefore twofold. In the first place, modern history from A.D. 476 is the biography of nations still living, 'beyond it is but the biography of the dead'. Arnold was a complete 'Germanist'. In the case of England he said, 'nationally speaking, the history of Caesar's invasion has no more to do with us than the natural history of the animals which then inhabited our forests.' Secondly, the 'universal' character of modern history, that is, the character that historians in a later period of civilization—presuming that there will be another period of civilization 'when existing nations have passed away like those which we now call ancient'—would recognize as its distinguishing mark, is that it is one step in advance of ancient history in the moral progress of mankind.[1] This is the explanation of various redeeming features of the childhood of modern history (in the Middle Ages) as compared with the childhood of Greece or Rome; for example, the Trugea Dei and the absence of slavery. The doctrines of Christianity made slavery impossible. Religion only separated the Grecian noble more widely from the inferior classes, teaching him to look down on them as beings of a different nature from himself, whereas the religion of modern history is, at any rate in theory, a force which binds, not one which divides, theoretically as well as practically, like the religion of early Greece. Indeed, all the softening and liberal

[1] *Lectures*, p. 33.

tendencies of Christianity serve to illustrate the fact of our moral progress compared with the ancient world. Arnold instances the 'order of gentlemen', 'the very delicacy of [its tenure] deprives it of all invidiousness'. Another advantage due to this fact of moral progress is our possession in a late age of a talisman against the inevitable excesses of sceptical thought characteristic of all late periods. This is a treasure of wisdom and of comfort which was denied to Plato; holding it in our hands, 'the utmost activity of the human mind may be viewed without apprehension, in the confidence that we possess a charm to deprive it of its evil'. 'Those who vainly lament that progress of earthly things, which whether good or evil is certainly inevitable' (this refers to the inevitable movement of the science of history) are comforted in remembering the inner strength of Christianity.[1]

Stanley's theory of race covers a wider panorama, being grounded on the discovery of the Indo-Germanic family of nations and languages. 560 B.C., when the predominance passed from the Semitic to the Indo-Germanic race, is Stanley's grand climacteric of universal history. [76] For Stanley, the end of the primeval epoch and beginning of the second period of universal history was accompanied by the eclipse of the Semitic races and the rise to historical significance of the 'Indo-Germanic or Aryan nations'. The year 560 was the date of the accession of Peisistratus and Croesus, 'from whose reign commences our distinct knowledge of Grecian life and literature'. From this time forward the Western world of Greece and Rome rises more and more steadily above the horizon, till it occupies the whole view. In that same great year arose also Cyrus, the Persian, hailed rightly (as we now know) by Isaiah as the deliverer, to inaugurate the fall of the old and rise of the new world; rightly, because we know that

the history of the civilized world was entering on an epoch when the Semitic races were to make way for the Indo-Germanic and Aryan nations which were thenceforth to sway the fortunes of mankind. With these nations Cyrus . . . was to be brought into close relation. . . . Of all the nations of Central Asia, Persia alone was of the same stock as the Greco-Roman and Germanic world. Cyrus, first of the great men whom Scripture records, spoke the tongue of the races of the West. . . .[2]

[1] *Thucydides*, vol. III, preface, pp. xxi-xxii.   [2] *Jewish Church*, vol. II, pp. 577 et seq.

Stanley reorganized Arnold's epochs of history around this conception of race. For him, 'Primeval', 'Classical' and 'Modern' history were the 'three great epochs, systems and races of mankind'.[1] Within and coinciding with these epochs, nations have each their own cycles, a beginning, middle and end. Primeval and Classical history each represent a full cycle, while the fate of the epoch of modern history is a problem of practical history. Each epoch has its own general characteristic (size was the main characteristic of primeval civilization), [78] as well as its predominant race. The epoch of primeval history extends from the dawn of civilization to the fall of Babylon; the second begins in 560 B.C., and the third, which is ours, with the Germanic invasions.

What is significant for the Liberal Anglican idea of history is the periodicity involved in this conception of the pattern of the past. This is essentially Vichian; and an answer to the March of Mind. Each new epoch is a new beginning, [79] in Milman's words, 'the dawn of a new civilization';[2] new in the light of progress because the gathered riches of the first epoch are the foundation of the second (thus Christianity has a 'second beginning' in our epoch); [80] a new beginning in the light of the science of history because the nations of the new epoch set out once more one their natural, unchanging course of development. [81]

There has been nothing in the Liberal Anglican idea of history, as presented so far, to oppose the possible deduction from it that man makes his own history entirely by his own efforts. This indeed is implicit in Milman's remark that the same social arrangements grow out of similar circumstances everywhere, and in Hare's, that a nation, in its childhood, mounts step by step 'without aid'.[3] This is Vico's contention, disguised only by his formal distinction between Jewish and Gentile history. It is fundamental to the Scienza Nuova that man does make his own history unaided, that he mounts up from savagery without any supernatural aid, solely in accordance with the universal principles of the development of society. It was, on the contrary, a Liberal Anglican absolute

---

[1] Essays chiefly on questions of Church and State, p. 467. [77]
[2] Christianity, vol. III, p. 486.   [3] Hare, Guesses at Truth (2nd ed., 2nd series), p. 159.

presupposition that man does not make all his history unaided by Providence (the central fact of history, the Christian revelation proved this—but this needed no argument). The problem of the origin of civilization was a life-long exercise for Whately, and Arnold was able to bring the ideas of Niebuhr and Vico to bear on it. Niebuhr argued in the *History of Rome*, against the 'conjectural' historians, that there were in fact no instances of a really savage people having spontaneously passed into civilization, and concluded that 'the society, as Aristotle wisely says, is before the individual, the whole before the part. Those speculators [the conjectural historians] do not perceive that the savage has degenerated or is originally but half-human.'[1] Whately and Arnold arrived at a different deduction. They agreed with Vico that all civilized peoples were originally savage, but the fact that there are no recorded instances of savage peoples having civilized themselves is for them an argument for the intervention of Providence. [82] They accept Vico's Providential guidance, which for him is purely formal, as reality. The origin of civilization therefore, far from being a proof that man makes his own history (which is the conclusion later commentators have drawn from Vico), is, on the contrary, a proof for Arnold and Whately that in the early stages, at least, it is God who is largely responsible for man's progress. The process which is studied by the science of history, that is, the process of civilization, is made possible in the first place by God. When Hare said that a nation in its childhood mounts 'without aid', this is because a nation in its childhood is in process of civilization (the childhood-manhood rhythm) and is consequently not under God's active Providence.

According to the Liberal Anglicans, God presided over the Creation and the early ages of the world. But man was only given supernaturally such knowledge as he could not otherwise have obtained. 'The first race of Mankind', Whately said, 'seem to have been placed merely in such a state as might enable and incite them to commence and continue a course of advancement.'[2]

---

[1] *History of Rome*, vol. I, p. 65. Cf. Arnold, *Quarterly Review*, vol. 32, p. 85. Arnold accuses Niebuhr of misunderstanding Aristotle.
[2] Whately, *Lectures on Political Economy*, p. 136.

The tendency towards progressive improvement which is natural to man does not come into play until man has been advanced by God to a state from which he can go forward to some extent on his own. In the early stages man must be taught by God; even certain material improvements (for example, the use of fire) are revealed supernaturally to him. The origin of language is, for Arnold, an example of this supernatural agency. We cannot, he says, conceive the inventing of language, because we cannot conceive the human mind acting without language. [83] This is just what Vico could conceive. Writing to Dr Greenhill, Arnold says:

> The student in history is as much busied with secondary causes as the student in medicine; the rule 'nec Deus intersit', true as it is, up to a certain point, that we may not annihilate man's agency and make him a puppet, is ever apt to be followed too far when we are become familiar with man and with nature, and understand the laws which direct both.[1]

It was an absolute presupposition of the Liberal Anglicans that all history is under God's Providence, so that in passing beyond the bounds of the law-governed world of the science of history, one is passing not into the realm of chance, but from a sphere ruled indirectly to one ruled directly, by God. God's Providence is twofold: active, as in the early ages of the world and in the Christian revelation, and permissive, when man is left to himself. The latter, God's 'ordinary Providence', said Arnold, is 'what we call the course of nature'.[2] The laws of history, the natural laws of social progress, are therefore under God's ordinary Providence, as are also natural causes, the constitutional differences which explain national character, and differences of geographical situation (for example, the presence of the sea: 'the mightiest instrument in the civilization of mankind')—causes in fact which are beyond human control, which 'affect the progress of society, that is, moral and intellectual progress'. Natural causes like these proceed 'directly from the inscrutable will of our Maker' and 'seem designed to humble the presumption of fancying ourselves the arbiters of our own destiny'.[3] Man's agency, which may be evil, may be nevertheless the agency of God's ordinary Providence. Dionysius,

[1] Letter of 31 Oct. 1836. [2] Sermons, vol. VI, p. 302.
[3] Thucydides, vol. I, appendix I, pp. 637-8.

for example, 'fulfilled that purpose of God's Providence which designed the Greek power in Sicily to stand as a breakwater against the advances of Carthage'.[1]

God's special Providence, apart from the Christian revelation and the origin of civilization, is responsible for special events, such as the retreat from Moscow, the outcome of the Punic War; natural causes, earthquake, plague, famine, to which historical laws cannot be applied, but which reveal God's manner of dealing with mankind in the course of his history; and miracles. Since all is under Providence, these unaccountable things which are beyond the scope of a science of history are under God's special Providence. The science of history cannot explain them. God's special Providence applies particularly to true progress, the moral and intellectual growth of mankind, just as his ordinary Providence covers the social progress of states. The latter is a natural process; the former impossible without God's direct intervention, in particular without the supreme revelation of Christianity. Because men could not have raised themselves unaided from their amoral brute condition, because in the early ages of the world they needed guidance, God's special Providence is seen at work most obviously and most vigorously in the childhood of historical development. This, for instance, is the age of miracles. God had to appeal to the bodily senses of such men because their intellectual faculties were un-developed. He had to appear in a striking form, appealing to the eyes and ears, through signs and portents. God could not appeal to man's reason, where there was no reason. His message was to certain individuals, chosen to be the medium of his direct revelations. These revelations were adapted to the faculties of a finite being of finite knowledge, but they placed him above and therefore in opposition to the more limited outlook of his age and society, so far as the things of the spirit are concerned. There is formed an enlightened minority which has to lead the nation in spite of the *vis inertiae* of the mass. In Milman's words:

This seems throughout to have been the course of providential government. Lawgivers, prophets, apostles were advanced in religious knowledge alone. In all other respects, society, civilization developed itself according to its usual laws.[2]

[1] *Rome*, vol. I, p. 464. [84]   [1] *Jews* (4th ed.), vol. I, preface, p. x.

The Old Testament story of Jacob and Esau provided Arnold with an illustration of the process, Esau being typical of a rude state of society 'where knowledge is very low and passion very strong', and representative of the popular morality of his age, Jacob being the type of the enlightened minority who try to live according to a higher principle, according to knowledge and not to passion and impulse or the opinion of one's fellows.[1]

According to Arnold, the revelation is twofold, consisting of 'the communication of knowledge' and 'directions for conduct', and it is adapted to the state of knowledge and of moral conduct reached by society in the natural course of things. 'Actions may even be commanded at one period which at another men would have learnt to be evil and which therefore never could be commanded to them.'[2] It is a revelation which becomes more and more indirect, increasingly an appeal to the reason rather than to the senses, as man progresses from primitive states of feeling to states of reason. As man grows in moral and intellectual stature, miracles recede, and man is left to his own powers and understanding and to his own moral strength.

The human species [says Arnold] has gone through a state of less fulness of moral knowledge, of less enlightened conscience, as compared with its subsequent attainments, just as every individual has done. Now this less perfect state, being a part of God's will, the training applied to it must have been suited to it; that is, it must have taken it as imperfect and dealt with it as such, not anticipating the instructions of a more perfect state, but improving it in its imperfection; not changing Spring into Summer, but making of Spring the best that could be made of it.[3]

For instance, God's command to Abraham to sacrifice his son was severely trying to Abraham's feelings, a moral test, but in no way startling to his conscience, because to Abraham there was nothing wicked in human sacrifice. It was in accord with the highest ethic of Abraham's age and society. Arnold compares Saul's instructions to slay the Amalakites with the *Iliad* VI, 55-62. 'In such a state of feeling lives were spared not from humanity, but from avarice or lust,' so that Saul's instructions, far from being an example of mere blood-thirsty revenge were really a test

---

[1] *Sermons*, vol. IV, pp. 94-5.   [2] *Ibid.* vol. II, p. 443.   [3] *Ibid.* p. 438.

of self-denial.[1] This is Arnold's doctrine of the interpretation of scripture, far-reaching in English theology in the 19th century, but also, as the principle of accommodation, the core of the Liberal Anglican philosophy of history. 'This principle', said Stanley, 'enables us to understand in a Christian and at the same time philosophic spirit, the whole history of mankind.'[2]

The principle of accommodation is the link, in the early stages, between God and man, later between progress and religion. 'Religion', said Milman, 'is one great system of accommodation to the wants, to the moral and spiritual advancement of mankind.'[3] 'Accommodation' is a bad word, Milman pointed out, because it implies art or design, while in reality it is the natural course of things.[4] In the natural course of things, civilization and religion keep step; if one outgrows the other there will inevitably be an adjustment, and the balance automatically righted sooner or later. An example of such an adjustment is provided by the Reformation. By the 16th century, civilization had outpaced religion, the mind of man had outgrown the trammels of the religion of the Middle Ages, and the Reformation, giving birth to a more rational form of religion, brought about the necessary and inevitable adjustment. The introduction of Christianity itself represents such an adjustment. [86] Many of the struggles and conflicts in the history of the Church, Hare pointed out, have been growing pains of this nature, attempts 'to force the man into the clothes of the boy . . . which at every motion, he rends'.[5]

Accommodation, the ability of a religion to adapt itself to progress, is thus the certain test of its strength and durability and future prospects. In particular it is the explanation of the success, and proof of the divine nature, of Christianity. In Stanley's words:

The everlasting mountains are everlasting, not because they are unchanged, but because they go on changing their form, their substance with the wear and tear of ages. 'The Everlasting Gospel' is everlasting, not because it remains stationary, but because, being the same, it can adapt itself to the constant change of society, of civilization, of humanity itself.[6]

[1] *Ibid.* pp. 446, 450, 453.   [2] *Essays chiefly on questions of Church and State*, p. 467.
[3] *Christianity*, vol. I, appendix III, p. 132.
[4] *Jews* (4th ed.), preface, p. x. [85]
[5] *Victory of Faith*, pp. 61-2. [87]   [6] *Sermons on Special Occasions*, p. 46.

The Liberal Anglican philosophy of history finds its most complete expression in Milman's three histories: of the Jews, of Christianity and of Latin Christianity (a projected history of Teutonic Christianity was never written). [88] The leitmotiv of this panoramic view of universal history is accommodation. In the history of the Jews it is, for Milman, proof of the authenticity of the Old Testament record.

Nothing is more curious or more calculated to confirm the veracity of the Old Testament history than the remarkable picture which it presents of the gradual development of human society; the ancestors of the Jews and the Jews themselves pass through every stage of comparative civilization. The Almighty Ruler of the world who had chosen them as conservators of the knowledge of his Unity and Providence and of his slowly brightening promises of redemption, perpetually interferes so as to keep alive the remembrance of those great truths, the object of their selection from mankind; and which nothing less, it should seem, could have preserved through so many ages. In other respects the chosen people appear to have been left to themselves to pass through the ordinary stages of the social state; and to that social state their habits, opinions and even their religious notions, were in some degree accommodated. God, who in his later revelation, appeals to the reason and the heart, addressed a more carnal and superstitious people chiefly through their imagination and their senses. The Jews were in fact more or less barbarians, alternately retrograding and improving, up to the 'fulness of time' when Christianity, the religion of civilized and enlightened men, was to reveal in all its perfection the nature of the beneficent Creator and the offer of immortality through the redemption of our blessed Saviour. . . . In our reverence for 'the Bible' we are apt to throw back the full light of Christianity on the older volume; but we should ever remember that the best and wisest of the Jews were not Christians—they had a shadow, but only a shadow of good things to come.[1]

It is a great error, Milman pointed out, to miss the fact of development in the Old Testament. 'The notion that the Mosaic narrative is uniformly exemplary, not history'[2] gives sceptics their chance to scoff at the morals of the patriarchs and the judges and kings of Israel. If the fact of progress is admitted, what appear to us as the obvious imperfections of Abraham or Saul are seen as the natural blemishes of their state of society.

---

[1] *Jews*, vol. III, preface, pp. iii *et seq.*　　　　　　[2] *Ibid.* vol. I, p. 36.

According to this view the objections of Volney and those who consider the Books of Moses as a late compilation . . . those of Bayle and Voltaire against the patriarchs and their descendants, fall to the ground at once. The seeming authorization of fierce and sanguinary acts which frequently occur in the Hebrew annals, resolves itself into no more than this—that the Deity did not yet think it time to correct the savage, I will add, un-Christian spirit, inseparable from that period of the social state. . . .[1] [For instance] Even in Abraham we do not find that nice and lofty sense of veracity which distinguishes a state of society where the point of honour has acquired great influence. It is singular that this accurate delineation of 'primitive manners', and the discrimination of individual character in each successive patriarch, with all the imperfections and vices, as well of the social state as of the particular disposition, although so conclusive an evidence to the honesty of the narrative, has caused the greatest perplexity to many pious minds and a great triumph to the adversaries of revealed religion. . . .[2] Had the avowed design of the intercourse of God with the patriarchs been their own unimpeachable perfection; had that of the Jewish polity been the establishment of a divine Utopia, advanced to premature civilization, and overleaping at once those centuries of slow improvement through which the rest of mankind were to pass, then it might have been difficult to give an account of the manifest failure. . . . Superior in one respect alone [as the depositories of certain great religious truths, the unity, omnipotence and providence of God] the ancestors of the Jews and the Jews themselves were not beyond their age or country in acquirements, in knowledge or even in morals; as far as morals are modified by usage and opinion . . . they acquired the virtues and the vices of each state of society through which they passed. . . .[3] A rude and uncivilized horde were not expected to attain that pure and exalted spirituality of religion which has never been known except among a reasoning and enlightened people.[4]

Thus Moses was 'a lawgiver who advanced political society to as high a degree of perfection as the state of civilization which his people had attained or were capable of attaining, could possibly admit'. Again, 'vows of celibacy were totally unknown among the Hebrews, and belong to a different stage of society', and the war of extermination against the Amalakites was justified by the war-law of nations of that age.[5]

The outcry caused by the publication of the *History of the Jews* is well known.

[1] *Ibid.* vol. III, preface, pp. iv–v.   [2] *Ibid.* vol. I, p. 35.
[3] *Ibid.* pp. 35 *et seq.*   [4] *Ibid.* vol. I, p. 111.   [5] *Ibid.* pp. 161, 202, 221.

The whole system of accommodation [said Milman] is looked upon with great jealousy. It is supposed to compromise the truth of the Deity, or at least of the revelation, a deception, it is said, or at least an illusion, is practised upon the belief of men.

But Milman could not assent to this view.

From the necessity of the case there must be some departure from the pure and essential spirituality of the Deity in order to communicate with the human race—some kind of condescension from the infinite . . . to become cognisable or to enter into any kind of relation with material and dimly mental man. All this is in fact accommodation. . . .

Milman's aim was to trace the gradual process of the development of society as exemplified by the Jews. His object, he explained, was 'strictly historical'.[1]

In the *History of Christianity*, Milman passes from the development of a 'nation' to the wider panorama of progress. As he passes from one national cycle to the next, he widens his view from strictly national to epochal history. 'The history of the Jews was that of a nation, the history of Christianity is that of a Religion.'[2] The theme, however, is the same.

Our history . . . will endeavour to trace all the modifications of Christianity, by which it accommodated itself to the spirit of successive ages; and by this apparently most skilful, but in fact necessary, condescension to the predominant state of moral culture, of which itself formed a constituent element, maintained its uninterrupted dominion . . .[3] [The author's object is] to portray the genius of the Christianity of each successive age, in connection with that of the age itself . . . to mark the origin and progress of all the subordinate diversities of belief . . . their progress from their adaptation to the prevailing state of opinion or sentiment: rather than directly to confute error or to establish truth; in short, to exhibit the reciprocal influence of civilisation on Christianity, of Christianity on Civilisation.[4]

Milman claimed originality for this design for the history of Christianity, at least in England, 'where the history of Christianity has usually assumed the form of a History of the Church, more or less controversial, and confined itself to annals of the internal feuds . . . in the Christian community or the variations in

---

[1] 'The object of this work is strictly historical, not theological' (*Jews*, vol. I, p. 35).
[2] *Christianity*, vol. I, p. v.   [3] *Ibid.* p. 47.
[4] *Ibid.*

doctrine or discipline, rather than to its political and social influence'. 'Our attention, on the other hand, will be chiefly directed to its effects on the social and even political condition of man.' There have been no Lives of Christ in England with a historic design, he said, none in which the author has endeavoured to throw himself completely back into the age of Jesus.[1]

Christianity, as taught by Jesus, was a rational religion, a 'universal morality', [89] yet aided by appearances which were intelligible to the more backward minds of that age, and of the Middle Ages. The miracles, angelic appearances and so on are not in general the vital and essential truths of Christianity but the vehicle by which these truths were communicated; a kind of language by which opinions were conveyed and sentiments infused, and the general belief in Christianity implanted, confirmed and strengthened. As we cannot but suppose that the state of the world, as well during, as subsequent to the introduction of Christianity, the comparative rebarbarisation of the human race, the long centuries in which mankind was governed by imagination, rather than by severe reason, were within the design or at least the fore-knowledge of all-seeing Providence; so from the fact that this mode of communication with mankind was for so long a period so effective, we may not unreasonably infer its original adoption by Divine Wisdom. This language of poetic incident, and, if I may so speak of imagery, interwoven as it is with the popular belief, infused into the hymns, the services, the ceremonial of the Church, embodied in material representation by painting or sculpture was the vernacular tongue of Christianity, universally intelligible and responded to by the human heart, throughout these many centuries. Revelation thus spoke the language, not merely of its own, but of succeeding times; because its design was the perpetuation as well as the first propagation of the Christian religion.[2]

The History of Latin Christianity is the story of the adaptation of Christianity to the rebarbarization or second childhood of the human race. [90] The science of history showed that this rebarbarisation was in the natural course of things, the philosophy of history deals with that element which is outside the natural course of things and therefore has to accommodate itself to it, that is, with Christianity. The relation, then, between Christianity and the course of history is one of condescension; it is this which accounts

---

[1] *Ibid.* pp. 48, 53.   [2] *Ibid.*, appendix III, pp. 129-32.

for its survival in the Middle Ages, and for its revival at the time of the Reformation. Civilization and Christianity both passed through the ordeal of the dark ages,[1] and Christianity, 'was constrained to accommodate itself to the spirit of the times . . . became splendid and imaginative, warlike and at length chivalrous'.[2] 'Where reason itself was about to be in abeyance, rational religion would have had but little chance.'[3] Iconoclasm is an example of the failure of 'a premature Rationalism, enforced upon an unreasoning age', the failure of religion to accommodate itself to the state of civilization.[4] Christianity in the Middle Ages had a new part to fulfil in the history of man.

However it might depart from its primitive simplicity and indeed recede from its genuine spirit, it is impossible not to observe how wonderfully (those who contemplate human affairs with religious minds may assert how providentially) it adapted itself to its altered position.[5]

In a society warlike and surrounded by enemies, Christianity had to become warlike in self-defence.

Christianity had subdued the world by peace, she could only defend it by war. However foreign then and adverse to her genuine spirit . . . however the very virtues of such a period might harmonize but doubtfully with the Gospels, it was an ordeal through which it must pass, the Church must become militant. . . .[6] Military Christianity was indispensable to the preservation of Christianity in its contest with [Islam.][7]

In an imaginative, mythical age, Christianity had to become mythical and imaginative. Mankind was passing through 'a new childhood, a second imaginative youth'; this was consequently the 'mythic period of Christianity'. The following are Milman's objects of study, 'as Europe sank back into barbarism':

the imaginative state of the human mind, the formation of a new poetic faith, a mythology and a complete system of symbolic worship; the interworking of Christianity with barbarism, till they slowly grew into a kind of semi-barbarous heroic period, that of Christian chivalry; the gradual expansion of the system with the expansion of the human mind; and the slow perhaps not yet complete, certainly not general, development of a rational and intellectual religion.[8]

---

[1] Christianity, vol. III, p. 39.   [2] Ibid. p. 128.   [3] Ibid. p. 318. [91]
[4] Latin Christianity, vol. II, p. 147.   [5] Christianity, vol. III, pp. 526-7.
[6] Latin Christianity, vol. II, p. 50; see Christianity, vol. II, p. 355.
[7] Christianity, vol. III, p. 529.   [8] Ibid. vol. I, p. 49.

Milman's attitude to the Middle Ages was a calm, scientific approach to a period which had for long been a battle-ground of practical history on which rival philosophies and faiths skirmished, a period which had aroused enthusiasm in some cases to the pitch of conversion to Catholicism [92]. His attitude was not one of patronage, of praise or of blame. It was an explanation based on a conception of the Middle Ages as an inevitable *ricorso*, a phenomenon laid bare by the science of history. The Middle Ages, according to this view of them, were natural, inevitable; a new mythic or imaginative period of the world which suppressed the growth of any strong intellectual energy, 'the necessary development of this state of the human mind'.

If the understanding of man in the dark ages was too much dazzled to see clearly even material objects, if just awakening from a deep trance it beheld everything floating before it in a mist of wonder, how much more was the mind disqualified to judge of its own emotions, of the origin, suggestion, and powers of those thoughts and emotions, which still perplex and baffle our deepest metaphysics.[1]

It was a mythic period, when poetry and history are inseparable, 'when legend and history were one, when it would have been equal impiety to assert the mythic character of the former as that of the authentic Gospel. . .'[2] 'Even theology maintained its dominion by in some degree accommodating itself to the human mind. It became to a certain degree *mythic* in its character and polytheistic in its form.'[3]

This kind of attitude to the Middle Ages was altogether too scientific for Carlyle. 'The "imaginative faculties?" "Rude poetic ages?" The "primeval poetic element?" Oh, for God's sake, good reader, talk no more of all that! It was not a Dilettantism this of Abbot Samson. It was a Reality. . . .'[4] 'Philosophic' vindications of medieval Christianity were perhaps more in the tradition of Rationalist historical thinking than in that of the Romantics, and there was much 18th-century furniture in Milman's mind.

Latin Christianity, then, is the Christianity of the Middle Ages, the religion of a mythic and heroic period, adapted to the intellectual and moral condition of such a period. Its vigour lay in this

[1] *Ibid.* vol. III, p. 534. [2] *Latin Christianity*, vol. VI, p. 524.
[3] *Christianity*, vol. III, p. 531. [4] *Past and Present* (Everyman ed.), p. 112.

adaptation. Its present weakness lies in its survival unchanged into a state of society which is to the Middle Ages as manhood to childhood. If the historical test of adaptation be applied to the present religions of the world, and to the prevailing forms of Christianity, true strength, that is to say, progress, would seem to be with Protestantism or 'Teutonic Christianity'. A history of Teutonic Christianity would have completed Milman's philosophy of history, his great panorama of true progress and universal history. Stanley, reviewing the *History of Latin Christianity*, wrote:

And now when we find that there is yet a third element of Christian life, younger than the other two—less defined, indeed, in its outlines, less vast in its proportions, but like those older systems, springing out of the heart of a mighty race, under the pressure of a great historical crisis—can we fail to hope that the Christianity which first appeared on the stage of the world's history, in the bosom of the German nations, at the Reformation, is not less surely a step in God's Providence—an instrument in the ultimate formation of Christendom—than the forms of ecclesiastical and religious life which rose out of the Greek race under the sway of Constantine, and out of the ruins of Rome under the auspices of Gregory? We will not anticipate the future volumes of the History of Latin Christianity by dwelling on the distinctive features of this, its noblest and we will not hesitate to add, its most genuine offspring.[1]

Milman's final word is faith in the adaptation of Christianity, a faith founded on his philosophy of history.

I pretend not to foretell the future of Christianity; but whosoever believes in its perpetuity (and to disbelieve it were treason against its Divine Author, apostasy from his faith) must suppose that by some providential law, it must adapt itself, as it has adapted itself with such wonderful versatility, but with a faithful conservation of its inner, vital spirit, to all vicissitudes and phases of man's social, moral, intellectual being.[2]

True progress in the final Liberal Anglican view is therefore synonymous with the development of true religion, that is to say, with Christianity. The very idea of progress itself was due to Christianity.[3] It is a pilgrim's progress (Stanley's inaugural lectures on Ecclesiastical history begin and end with quotations from

---

[1] *Quarterly Review*, vol. 95 (June 1854), p. 70.
[2] *Latin Christianity*, vol. IV, p. 627. [93]
[3] Hare, *Sermons preacht in Herstmonceux Church,*, vol. II, pp. 114-15.

Bunyan), the movement of the Church to perfection.[1] 'One religion, and that *one* because it is the truth,' said Milman, 'and that religion in its original purity, as taught in the New Testament, will co-exist and be co-extensive with the progress of knowledge.'[2] Outside this development, the Education of the Human Race, there is no true progress. Without Christianity, progress is fearfully uncertain, said Arnold.

All history begins in something which is evil; all our course whether as individuals or nations is a Progress, an advance . . . but history . . . apart from Christianity would make us regard this progress as fearfully uncertain. We are like men bewildered in those endless forests of reeds which line some of the great American rivers. It is death to remain, but yet if we move it may be that, while seeming to advance we shall but be going round and round and shall find ourselves hard by the place from which we set out at the beginning.[3]

A historical example on a grand scale of this *ricorso* without progress is provided by Islam. The East, left to itself, said Arnold, could only reproduce Judaism.[4] According to Hare, outside Christianity the cyclical order of history reigns triumphant and the past is strewn with the wrecks of civilizations. The Church of God alone . . . is indestructible. 'It is the idea of God that lifts us out of the eddying flux and reflux [*corso* and *ricorso*] of time, and fixes our being on that which is firm and lasting.'[5] It is Christianity alone which not so much breaks into the inevitable cycles of history as lifts the whole process on to the higher planes of true progress [95] by its effect on the minds of individuals. For example, Hare says:

It is a wonderful proof of the power of Christianity to expand and elevate the mind . . . that several of the Fathers living as they did among the falling and fallen leaves of the old world, and long before the first vernal germinating of the mind of the new world, should have been such great thinkers as they were.[6]

Geographically, progress is a Westward movement. Each new period of civilization has had a fresh birthplace in a continuous Westward advance. The East has remained stationary, its history has been merely cyclical in the sense of the science of history.

[1] Stanley, *Eastern Church*, p. lxxii.　[2] Milman, *Quarterly Review*, vol. 68, p. 411.
[3] *Sermons*, vol. IV, p. 2.　[4] Arnold, *Travelling Journals*, p. 91. [94]
[5] *Mission of the Comforter*, vol. I, p. 191.　[6] *Vindication of Luther* (2nd ed.), p. 79.

History in 'a higher sense', for Thirlwall, is the history of Greece, as opposed to that of Egypt.[1] The nations of the East, compared with those of the West, are mere vegetables, their progress is natural, not moral. For Milman, Mohammedan civilization is 'the highest it should seem attainable by the Asiatic type of mankind',[2] and speaking of Mexico at the time of the Spanish conquest, he said that it was advanced 'to a high state of what we may venture to call, without pledging ourselves to its origin, Asiatic civilization'.[3] Hare said, 'The brief effloresence of literature and science among the Mahometans, which itself was attributable in great measure to the portion of Christian truth mixed up with the errors of the Koran, or at all events to the lively conviction of the Divine Unity, passed away long ago.'[4] 'The Eastern Church was, like the East, stationary and immutable; the Western, like the West, progressive and flexible,' said Stanley. [97] The contrast between East and West is the greatest contrast which this earth affords, the contrast between Heathenism and Christianity, between the civilization of the ancient world of bygone ages and the civilization of modern Europe, between the Bible and the Koran.[5] According to Arnold, the mind of the East is incomprehensible to a Western historian. [98]

The course of the Christian religion has always moved onwards and from that onward movement derived its main strength. Christianity . . . has lived, it has flourished, it has expanded . . . not in proportion as it has remained within the influences of its first home but in proportion as it has receded further and further from them. 'Westward the Star of Empire has held its course', and westward has the sun of Christendom moved also.[6]

It is significant that Stanley, who travelled in Palestine as a young man, should cross the Atlantic in his old age, full of hope for the future of Christianity. [99]

Finally, progress is a unifying principle, which for Milman was introduced into the world by Christianity. [100] Progress is what

---

[1] *Greece*, vol. VIII, p. 205. [2] *Latin Christianity*, vol. II, pp. 50, 51.
[3] *Quarterly Review*, vol. 73 (Dec. 1843), p. 188. Cf. p. 196.
[4] *Mission of the Comforter*, vol. I, p. 198. [96]
[5] *Sermons on Special Occasions*, p. 114. The Koran has no progress, and therefore no sequence and no coherence (*Eastern Church*, p. 321).
[6] A. P. Stanley, *Quarterly Review*, vol. 95, p. 70.

Hare calls the perfecting of unity, not a unity like the medieval, which has been lost in actual political and religious division and a philosophy of selfishness . . . this was an outward material unity suited to the age. We need a spiritual unity with Christ as its head.[1] Unity, the desire for which is inherent in man and may be termed an elementary principle of his nature,[2] is to be distinguished from uniformity, which is characteristic of late ages, and a symptom of decline. Diversity is essential to unity. In illustration of this, Hare compares medieval Nuremberg with Georgian London. He quotes also the contest against the dramatic 'unities', as they were misnamed. Lessing and other critics since have shewn that this very seeking after uniformity was most inimical to unity. There is, he continues, a more real likeness, so far as unity is concerned, between Shakespeare's tragedies and those of the Greeks, though Shakespeare's is a higher form of unity since Christianity has enabled man to gain a much clearer sight of the unity which pervades all things. Thus 'the unity of Christian painting is deeper and higher than that of Greek sculpture'. Uniformity was a principle of Jacobinism.[3]

The Liberal Anglicans looked to this spiritual unity as the culmination of the education of the human race, the goal of universal history. It is a conception of the unity of history in a Christian, teleological sense. The unity of history, so far as the Liberal Anglican science of history was concerned, was the unity of process, the unity of the nation's life-course, the unity of the epochs of civilization through which the nation runs, the unity of the past as a whole consisting of natural parts. The nation's progress could be compared to the life of an individual, but the analogy could not be extended to mankind. Universal history, from the Christian point of view, presents no such unity as that which is the presupposition of the science of history. The history of mankind is not one in this sense—God being transcendent—and therefore there is no analogy between it and the individual, because for the Christian man is essentially not a unity. That the desire for unity is, as Hare showed, inherent in man, presupposes an existing

[1] 'Romanizing Fallacies', *Charges*, pp. 85-7.
[2] Hare, *Mission of the Comforter*, vol. I, pp. 263-4.   [3] See *ibid.*, pp. 226, 227, 229.

dualism in him of the moral and natural worlds. This is why Thirlwall, reviewing the essay on the education of the world in *Essays and Reviews*, objected to the analogy between the development of the race and that of the individual.[1] From the Christian point of view, mankind is only one ideally, not actually, potentially, not historically; there are, for the Christian, two worlds, and the unity of history must be a teleological unity. This final unity is the goal of history, not something with which to judge the past, but something to strive for now and in the future.

The history of man is no more the history of a changing identity, a developing organism, than it is the development of an abstract reason. Progress has, therefore, none of the inevitability of an organic growth, but is entirely dependent on our own individual efforts and our moral life. Such a view leads to a deeper understanding of history, because it is grounded on concrete reality, the individual mind. That the Liberal Anglicans touched this rock-bottom in the understanding of history has already been seen. They were brought to it by the undoubted fact of progress in relation to the historical fact of the hitherto universal death of nations. From thinking of the 'mind' of the nation they were forced to think of the mind of the individual, and to see that the concrete individual mind represents progress, and progress depends upon the individual mind.

It is of the nature of the philosophy of history, as such, that it sets itself a goal—that it is a relation of past, present and future. Even where it results in a complete determinism, it is nevertheless essentially practical; if not a ground for action, a ground for hope; if not a ground for hope, then at least a justification of despair, in either case, a relation of past and future. The concept of purpose in history is a projection of the past into the future. Sooner or later, philosophies of history are put into action. For the Liberal Anglicans, history was practical because their conception of history was fundamentally religious.

---

[1] *Remains*, vol. II, p. 27.

CHAPTER IV

PRACTICAL HISTORY

THAT it is possible to present the idea of history of the Liberal Anglicans both as a 'science of history' and as a 'philosophy of history' shows that for them history was nothing if not practical, a conscious relation of past and present. It was by no means an end in itself, a study of the past for its own sake, an intellectual exercise or emotional experience barren of results in the outer world, and unrelated to the duties and aspirations of everyday life, or to larger problems, social, political and religious. The science of history was related to the social and political problems of the day; the philosophy of history to a way of life and thought. History, if it were not a guide, [101] was nothing. It was, moreover, in its very nature, a force in the world. 'All readers of history', as Arnold said, 'are sure to catch some moral impression.'[1]

The unity of history, in whatever sense it was taken, meant that past and present formed a whole, the parts of which could not be intelligibly studied in isolation. History, for the Liberal Anglicans, was practical because it was a relation of past and present to form a whole which included the historian. As Thirlwall pointed out, the historian is himself in history, his very thoughts about the past are themselves a part of history. The historian cannot sever himself from the historical context or stand aloof from the processes of history as the scientist stands apart from the processes of science. Unlike the scientist, the historian is part of his subject. [102] This being so, the existence of the historian, as historian, is not justified by the mere contemplation of historical reality, or the search for historical truth. Unless meditation on history leads to action, it can have no meaning or value. The historian has a responsibility to society because he understands the inevitable movements of history, and knows that true progress is dependent on man's

[1] *Sermons*, vol. III, p. 206.

efforts for good. His is the special responsibility of a guide enlightened by an understanding of God's purpose, so far as it is visible, that is, in history, who can discern the goal ahead and whose faith is reinforced by this vision.

Thus the practical history of the Liberal Anglicans is not a mere recourse to history for eristic purposes, for examples, cases, precedents. History for them is practical, not in the 18th-century sense of philosophy teaching by examples, but because it is a whole, binding past and present, and because their idea of history is fundamentally religious. [103]

If the historian, therefore, wishes to understand the past, that is, to live actively in the past,[104] he must live actively in the present. For one thing, the science of history showed that a large part of what is miscalled 'ancient' history is in reality modern. 'Those who study the past times in books only', said Arnold, 'have no real understanding of those times, because they do not know or understand their own.' Again, 'He is a wiser man, and a surer guide, who knowing nothing of the Past, has yet had a large experience of the Present, and has observed it carefully, rather than the other, who is blind to the very world in which he lives, and therefore is perfectly incapable, with all his reading, of understanding a world in which he does not live.'[1] 'The Past is reflected by the Present', he said, 'so far as we see and understand the present, so far can we see and understand the Past, but no further.' This is why 'antiquarians and men calling themselves historians have written so uninstructively of the ancient world . . . for they did not understand the world around them.'[2] Arnold criticized Barante for writing the History of the Dukes of Burgundy like a Chronicler. 'We must remember . . .', he said, 'not so to transport ourselves into the 14th century as to forget that we belong really to the 19th; that here and not there, lie our duties; that the harvest gathered in the fields of the past is to be brought home for the use of the Present.'[3] It was Mitford's great merit that he felt his own times keenly.[4] Arnold thought that English historians ought to be

---

[1] *Sermons*, vol. VI, p. 244. Cf. *Miscellaneous Works* ('Use of the Classics'), p. 350: a classical teacher should be fully acquainted with modern history.
[2] *Lectures*, p. 109. [105]   [3] *Ibid.* pp. 402-3.   [4] *Ibid.* p. 109.

especially good, because England provided an excellent example of the natural course of social progress, and also because 'we have lived in a period rich in historical lessons beyond all former example; we have witnessed one of the great seasons of movement in the life of mankind'.[1] When John Morley stressed the need for practical history he appealed to a remark of Arnold's: that he would like to see a history of England traced *backwards*.[2]

This chapter, therefore, will be a study of the interaction of Liberal Anglican historical thinking and the most important aspects of Liberal Anglican practical thinking. As such it will have to deal with some of the practical, as opposed to the purely intellectual, influences in the formation of the Liberal Anglican idea of history.

(a) Social and Political: The Condition of England

Among the Liberal Anglicans, Arnold was the most actively interested in the condition of England, and he is the best representative of their political thinking. The distinctive feature of his political liberalism is its claim to be scientific, based, that is, on a science of history and laws of social development. [106] This claim is implicit in everything Arnold wrote on the political problems of his time. A study of history in the light of Niebuhr and Vico showed that the social development of the nation was determined by the struggle between classes for political power, and that the struggle between parties, history as politics on the most superficial level, provided no indication of the course of this development. Underneath political history as written in England in Arnold's time, underlying the clash of parties governed by the play of chance and personality, was the inevitable movement of the nation governed by law. This law was the key to social history, and without it political history was entirely meaningless. Arnold wrote to Bunsen:

It strikes me that a noble work might be written on the Philosophy of Parties and Revolutions, showing what are the essential points of division, and what are but accidents. For the want of this, history as a

---

[1] *Rome*, vol. I, preface, p. vi.
[2] *Critical Miscellanies*, vol. III, p. 9 ('On popular culture'); Stanley, *Life*, p. 183.

collection of facts is of no use at all to many persons; they mistake essential resemblances and dwell upon accidental differences.[1]

History properly studied, therefore, provided 'the true principle of all political division', which was not the ascendancy of the many or the few, not, that is to say, the type of government in power, but the relation of the government, of whatever type it may be, to the state of society in times of social calm, or to the potential state of society in times of social upheaval. There are no eternal principles of good or bad government.[2] We often regard a government as popular, said Arnold, when in actual fact it may be more fitly described as anti-popular. A 'popular party', for instance, the Whigs, which is really the party of wealth, is anti-popular in a manhood period, in which the natural state of society in the social development of the nation is the ascendancy of numbers. Whether a government is truly popular or anti-popular is not a question of the number of those taking a share in it, or of benevolent disposition or its opposite, but depends on the attitude it adopts to the inevitable development of society. A popular party is not always synonymous with a movement party.[3] Thus Conservatism may sometimes be ultra-democracy. Arnold instances Cleon's speech in Thucydides III.[4]

The great movement of the world is often wholly unconnected with the relations of the popular or anti-popular parties in any particular state, it may be favoured or resisted by either of them . . . .The mere change of time and circumstances may alter the character of the same party without any change on its own part: its triumph may be at one time an evil and at another time a good. This is owing to a truth which should never be forgotten, that government is wholly relative. There is and can be no such thing as the best government absolutely, suited to all periods and to all countries.

The 'fatal error' in all political questions is 'to mistake the clock'.[5] There is always an antagonism latent or active in society, the inner dynamic of the nation's life, which on the political and social planes makes it one, like an organism, ever growing or decaying according to the law of its being. Social development is the result

---

[1] Letter of 10 Feb. 1835.   [2] *Lectures*, pp. 239, 243, 249.   [3] *Ibid.* p. 247.
[4] Letter to Bunsen, 10 Feb. 1835.   [5] *Lectures*, p. 249.

of the clash of two principles which spring from an opposition inherent in human nature itself. There are therefore only two possible political divisions: the 'Conservatives' and the 'Advancers'. Arnold was an Advancer, and abhorred Conservatism because he believed that it sprang from a one-sided view of history and was inherent in the natural man, the very essence of habit, a part of the old Adam which it was man's duty to overcome.[1] All men who are reasonably well-off are Conservatives,[2] he said, and only the *argumentum ad ventrem* is able to rouse the mass of mankind out of their innate Conservatism. On the other hand, the Advance was of the realm of spirit and will, and in its most perfect form was Christianity.[3]

For the very reason that change is inevitable and in the natural course of things, it must not be forced. There is danger inherent in the process of social development. This process is within men's power to the extent that they can speed it up or hold it back, but in either case there is the risk of civil war and ultimate disaster. Indeed, history shows that the clash between classes in the final stage of a nation's progress is always fatal. At least, Arnold knows of no instances in which it has not been so.

In terms of contemporary politics, therefore, political wisdom lies in steering a middle course between 'Jacobins' and Conservatives. The science of history shows plainly enough what is to be expected at this stage of historical development, and what is to be especially avoided. The ascendancy of numbers is inevitable, but it is in our power, on the one hand, by futile resistance to what is inevitable to bring about the explosion of revolution, in which liberty and constitutional government perish, [107] on the other, to rush the process forward headlong into a Jacobinical anarchy which is equally destructive. [108] What is required of our rulers is action based on knowledge of the principles of historical development. We had arrived at one of those periods in the progress of society when the constitution naturally undergoes a change.

England, according to Arnold, had since 1688 been in the man-

---

[1] Stanley, *Life*, p. 109.
[2] Cf. Letter of 28 Nov. 1836: 'Men are all Tories by nature when they are tolerably well off.'
[3] Letter to Bunsen, 10 Feb 1835.

hood stage of a nation's development, analogous to the manhood stages of Greece and Rome, the period of the ascendancy of wealth. The Reform Bill crisis therefore was for him only superficially a struggle for political power between wealth and nobility. The real struggle which was developing in the bosom of the nation was the more deadly one between wealth and numbers, a struggle which bursts forth only when the opposing classes have reached the opposite extremes of beggary and luxury. [109] The great and hardest problem of political wisdom, therefore, was to prevent any part of society from becoming so degraded by poverty that their political enfranchisement becomes dangerous or even mischievous.[1] The widening rift between the rich and the poor, the *two orders*,[2] heralded the deadliest social conflict of all; one from which no nation had hitherto emerged successfully. Although Arnold supported the Ministerial Reform Bill and sympathized with the July Revolution, this fear, springing from his conception of history, and no mere momentary panic, led him to write [110] an article in the *Quarterly Review* on the subversion of ancient governments, in which he argues from the Grecian and Roman cycles of history (he appeals to Greece and Rome because their historical cycles are complete) against premature concessions to democracy. Too much liberty, he says, although it is the vital principle of every true political system is like too much oxygen.[3] Premature concessions in the history of Greece and Rome would have anticipated the dissolution of the bonds of society. The catastrophe of the drama as exemplified in ancient history, he says, is familiar to every schoolboy. What infatuation then prevents our applying this knowledge to the events passing before our eyes? Why should we hesitate, with these facts before us, to admit the inevitable conclusion that unless the better spirits be roused into instant and strenuous exertions, the domination of the base will be established, only to be succeeded by the last and lowest *genius*— that of the solitary tyrant? The writer believes that 'our age is passing from the long-sustained domination of the agricultural and manufacturing genii'.[4] The struggle in 1831 is a 'fearful *double*

[1] *Rome*, vol II, pp. 268-9 n.   [2] Letter of 24 Dec. 1830.
[3] *Quarterly Review*, vol. 45, p. 471.   [4] *Ibid.* pp. 450-1.

struggle . . . between the popular body and disunited aristocracy'.[1] It belongs however to every generation to render inevitable change gentle and inoffensive, or sanguinary and disastrous.

While the emphasis in 1831 was on the control of inevitable change and the danger of premature concessions to democracy, by 1835 Arnold had come to realize 'the enormous strength of the aristocracy', and to see 'clearly what hard blows they will not only stand but require, and that the fear of depressing them too much is chimerical'.[2] The idea of inevitable change, [111] and the belief that men can control it, [112] but not avert it, is the basis of Arnold's political thinking. He wanted to check all change that threatened to be violent or too hurried, to speed up the inevitable when it seemed to be arbitrarily (and therefore dangerously) [113] checked. Both in 1831 and 1835 his aim was change upon principle, not upon clamour.

The same outlook, springing from the same conception of an inevitable social development, is seen in Thirlwalls' *Tenth Charge* (1869). Referring to the Reform Bill of 1867, he said, 'We must all sympathize' with those people who fear 'the preponderance recently acquired by the democratical element in the Constitution', but the first thing which the righteous man has to do, is to satisfy himself

whether this change is a mere momentary fluctuation which may be expected to subside, or is a mighty stream of tendency, which no human power can arrest or control. If it is unmistakably marked with the character of a natural social development, then however much we may see in it to deplore or to dread, still, as believers in a superintending Providence, we cannot look upon it as merely evil; and instead of mourning over it, or . . . wasting our strength in a vain attempt to stem the tide which is carrying all before it upon earth . . . we shall hold it our duty to deal with it in a loving and hopeful spirit. . . .[3]

Arnold described his views as liberal but not popular, but more or less popular and more or less aristocratical according to circumstances, and they resulted in his political isolation. 'No party would own me', he said.[4] He appears in political thought midway between the Radicals and Conservatives. Actually his was a unique

---

[1] *Quarterly Review*, p. 452. [2] Letter to A. P. Stanley, 4 Mar. 1835.
[3] *Remains*, vol. II, p. 216. [114] [4] Letter of Nov. 1830; *Life*, p. 156.

position in the Reform Bill crisis. The science of history gave him a deeper insight into the crisis.[1] The preaching of class war was an abomination to him,[2] but he was not deceived by any temporary opportunist political alliance between the middle and working classes. He believed in a law of increasing misery based, like that of Marx, on a science of history, and in a widening rift between rich and poor. But he believed that it was possible to bridge this gulf and eventually to close it. The rich must be enlightened[3] in order that they may begin the process through education and social reform. The clergy were in a position of special responsibility as the only existing mediators between the two classes. Arnold approached the condition of England through the science of history. The tide of democracy was irresistible, he taught, and since the masses would come to political power in the natural course of things, it would be better for civilization if the social and cultural gap between the two nations were closed before this came to pass. Thus Arnold faced squarely the vaguely dreaded 'coming of democracy',[4] his vision clarified by the science of history. His faith was not in political remedies. He did not expect much from the Reform Bill;[5] though it was a necessary measure, political reform was unimportant in comparison with moral and intellectual reform, which was the aim of Arnold's short-lived paper, the *Register* (1831).[6] 'My great object in the Register was to enlighten the poor generally in the best sense of the term';[7] his aim was the *Christianizing* of men's notions and feelings on political matters.[8] Arnold's vision of unity, the ideal unity of Church and State in Christian England, is clearly related to his view of the state of the nation, and its growing disunity as revealed by the science of history. [116]

From this diagnosis of the state of the nation based on the science

---

[1] L. Trilling, *Matthew Arnold*, p. 50. [115]

[2] Carlyle's class-war doctrine is a 'Devil's doctrine' (Letter of 24 Dec. 1830).

[3] Letter to Carlyle, Jan. 1840.

[4] J. R. M. Butler, *The Great Reform Bill*. The word Democracy occupied in 1831 the position which Communism holds today. It was understood to mean something vaguely terrible which might 'come'.

[5] Letter to Susannah Arnold, April 1831.

[6] Letter to J. Ward (co-editor of *The Englishman's Register*), 27 April 1831.

[7] Letter to Whately, 11 June 1831.   [8] Letter to Ward, 27 April 1831.

of history and reinforced by it are derived the Liberal Anglican remedies: a broad conception of the Church to embrace the whole Christian nation, Church reform in order to save this great unifying force, education both for the rich and for the poor, and especially for the clergy as intermediaries between the rich and the poor, and political liberalism, which meant support for the 'movement', or rather, the 'improvement' party of whatever political complexion. The Broad Church as a practical force has its roots in the science of history. The characteristic Liberal Anglican approach to contempoary problems, calm, objective, judicial, broad, lifted above the clash of parties and sects, springs from the very nature of scientific history as they understood it, history, that is, viewed as a whole, impartially, objectively. Such a conception imparted a sense of proportion, as well as confidence to the Liberal Anglicans, and was apparently rare in England even in 1860.[1] In the violent social and religious conflict of the mid-nineteenth century, this impartiality was in itself both a remedy (as Stanley said, 'a general diffusion of comprehensive and tolerant views of past history'[2] was required) and a practical force. For the Liberal Anglicans, history was no party blunderbuss, but a healing instrument of scientific precision.

(b) The Crisis of Civilization

The condition of England was critical not only on the social and political planes, but on the deeper planes of religion and thought, and as such was part of the general crisis of civilization. This follows logically from the Liberal Anglican belief in the unity of the nation's life, because if the nation had reached the critical phase of manhood in its social history, the same must be true of all aspects of its life and thought. The Liberal Anglican Jeremiad against the spiritual tendencies of the age was reinforced by a conception of history according to which the inevitable products of the later stages of the nation's development were scepticism and barren intellectualism, a cosmopolitanism which destroys the poetry springing from the vigour of national life and feeling, a morbid

[1] Mark Pattison, *Memoirs*, p. 314.   [2] Stanley, *Jewish Church*, vol. I, p. 309.

self-consciousness, as in the later ages of Greece and Rome, which also destroys poetry by criticism and philosophy by 'false display', the disease of an enlargement of the understanding and the divorce between body and mind which subverts the balance of powers in the human constitution,[1] an indifference to error hardly less fatal than the barbarian indifference to all truth, luxury and the philosophy of luxury, the craving for 'excitement', [118] specialization, and the danger of 'the reduction of all things to uniformity and mediocrity' ('in its full development in the Western World').[2] Our pride in our enlightened age was in itself a most dangerous symptom. History showed that 'enlightenment' was the prelude to extinction. [120] Even novel-reading, 'a phenomenon which depends on causes completely beyond anyone's control', was a sign of decadence. Its parentage, said Thirlwall in 1861, did not raise any strong prepossession in its favour. 'We can trace it no further back than to an epoch in Greek literature, in the decline of the Roman Empire, when poetry was utterly effete and all the powers of the national mind were miserably enfeebled.'[3] In Stanley's words, ours was 'an over-heated civilization'. [121] 'To enquire into the nature of this decay', he said, 'at all times interesting, is peculiarly so to us, who standing on the grave of nations and on the verge of a crisis fraught, according to universal expectation, with no ordinary interest, have the deepest concern in knowing to what fate, at this advanced stage of society, and in this remarkable era, we ourselves are doomed.'[4] There was more speculation about cataclysm in the 19th century than is often allowed for. It was one of the strains which underlay the deep seriousness of the age. Readers of *Beauchamp's Career* will remember how Dr Shrapnel (who is modelled on Carlyle) discussed cataclysm with Meredith's hero. Such discussion was common in certain circles.

Liberal Anglican hatred of the philosophy of mammon, which reflected the spiritual condition of society, [122] leading to an enquiry into the nature of the progress which that philosophy

---

[1] Hare, *Guesses at Truth* (2nd ed., 2nd series), p. 285. [117]
[2] See above, chapter II (b), pp. 37-8. [119]
[3] *Remains*, vol III (1861), pp. 273-4.
[4] *Prize Essay*, p. 4.

assumed, resulted in the formation of a conception of history which revealed the place of the modern world, with all its ideas and beliefs, in the whole historical process. The science of history confirmed as symptoms of decadence all the evils denounced by the Liberal Anglicans, and showed that far from being the dawn of an era of indefinite material progress—heir to the unbroken lineage of the past—the modern world represented, at least on the level of material progress, an advanced stage in a pattern of inevitable cycles of growth and decay. History pointed not to an expanding future for the nations of Europe but to a second barbarism. Material progress was no criterion of growth, it may outlive true progress. As Coleridge had taught, there was all the difference of true and false progress in the distinction between 'cultivation' and 'civilization'. [123] Civilization was a word which, said Milman, needed closer definition. According to Milman, it was the height of moral perfection in a nation (in other words, Coleridge's 'cultivation'). According to Stanley, civilization was merely neutral; 'not necessarily good . . . not necessarily evil.'[1]

This view of the future of western civilization (the phrase is Stanley's) satisfied the ironic temperament of Thirlwall, [124] and a certain inborn, Puritanical, Old Testament strain, which is noticeable especially in Hare and Arnold, and which they shared with the Oxford Reformers [125] and with Carlyle. Arnold, for example, like Carlyle, [126] believed that nations, like individuals, suffered from the sins of their youth (a belief which Stanley refused to accept)[2] and he traced certain social evils of his time, such as 'landlordism' and the game laws, back to the feudal excesses of chivalry. For Arnold, 'the deep calm of the first seventy years of the 18th century' was 'the abused trial time of modern Europe', in which he was especially interested, as this period contained 'within itself the seeds of our future destiny'.[3]

It is also related, in Arnold's case at least, to the eschatological excitement of the 1830s, though 'the day of the Lord', for Arnold, was not the millennium of the Irvingites—a phenomenon on which Thirlwall poured scorn—but that which the science of

---

Milman, *Quarterly Review*, vol. 56 (1836), p. 350; Stanley, *Prize Essay*, p. 23.
[2] *Jewish Church*, vol III, p. 79.   [3] Stanley's *Life*, p. 440. [127]

history showed to be in the normal course of things the end of a
cycle of history.[128] In its more violent forms this was a temporary
phenomenon of the gloomy winter of 1830-1,[1] but the deeper
and broader current of religious feeling beneath it, of which the
Oxford Movement was but another expression, was the real inspiration of the Liberal Anglican idea of history. The idea of
history gave power and direction to the religious sentiment. It is
a cycle of thought which begins and ends in religion: from the
religious feeling sprang the distrust of 'civilization' which resulted
in the intellectual *tour de force* by which, with the aid of Niebuhr
and Vico, 'Civilization' was converted into a natural, cyclical
process of history; this confirmed the fatalistic outlook of Arnold
and Hare, and this fatalism, leading from the idea of the science of
history to the philosophy of history, from the natural to the
moral world, from law to purpose, emphasized the vital need for
true religion as alone consonant with true progress. Religion
alone exalts us above the cycles of history; when a nation loses its
hold on religion it collapses back into the natural cycles of
growth and decay, and, like a plant, dies inevitably. Religion is
life in a higher, moral, sense, above the natural life of nations.[2]
Only through religion can nations, like individuals, start life
afresh.[129]

Just as every age has its own characteristics, so also it has its
special dangers and opportunities.[130] In the natural progress of
society the early dangers are from distress, the later from prosperity.[3] The opportunities of an advanced age are spiritual opportunities. Miracles are ceased and prophets are no more, God's
special providence is withdrawn, and the individual is left to work
out his own salvation. This is Arnold's answer to the ultimate
question of practical history.

One great question still remains: if history has its laws, as I entirely
believe, if theoretically considered it is not a mere aggregation of
particular actions or characters . . . but is besides this the witness to
general moral and political truths and capable of bringing to our notice
fresh truths which we might not have gained by *a priori* reasoning

---

[1] J. R. M. Butler, *The Great Reform Bill*, p. 273.
[2] *Guesses at Truth* (2nd ed., 2nd series), p. 21; *Mission of the Comforter*, vol. I, p. 335.
[3] *Guesses at Truth*, 1st ed., vol. II, pp. 108-9.

only; still, it may be asked, is this theoretical knowledge available?[1]
Or is it powerless to alter facts? Are we swept to destruction
with our eyes open?

Arnold believed that the world as he saw it had not the resources to provide for a third period of civilization. But this view
was the result of his theory of the transmission of civilization in
terms of race. 'If our existing nations are the last reserve of the
world, its fate may be said to be in their hands. God's work on
earth will be left undone if they do not do it.'[2] The science of
history by itself could only point to our inevitable doom, and
this, Arnold pointed out, was the belief of some who held that the
destiny of present and future was fixed irrevocably to the past,
and that the greatest efforts of individuals could do nothing
against it. If this is so, he says, then our deliverance must proceed
wholly from a higher power. Arnold, however, did not end on
this eschatological note, but stressed the need for exertion. Surely
it is enough to know, he concludes in his final lecture, that our sin
may render unavailing the greatest goodness of our posterity;
our efforts for good may be permitted to remove, or at any rate
to mitigate, the curse of our fathers' sin. The answer to *nox ruit* is
'work while it is day'. On this note of pious exhortation Arnold's
enquiry into the future of civilization closes.[3]

Stanley's investigation of the same question[4] led to the conclusion that if there is to be any further progress in the history of the
world (and the Liberal Anglicans believed that where there is no
progress there must be decline), it will be through Christianity
and Christianity alone. He considered certain possible checks to decline, such as great men, philosophy, and healthy shocks,[131] but
said that owing to the frequent failure of these checks, a 'mightier
spell' was necessary. This did not mean that the city of the world
was to be destroyed (Stanley was altogether free from Messianic
expectation), because 'Chrisitanity is to be wrought out fully not
by the destruction of the kingdoms of the world but by their
adaptation with all their power, literature and institutions to its
own divine ends'.[5] The decline of nations was not inevitable, but

---

[1] Arnold, *Lectures*, pp. 394-5.   [2] *Ibid.* p. 39.
[3] Arnold, *Lectures*, pp. 399-400.   [4] *Prize Essay.*   [5] *Ibid.* p. 44.

was nevertheless hitherto universal. 'History exhibits not only the general fact of the decline of nations, but also their decline in the particular period of mature civilization.'[1] So far as our own civilization was concerned, Stanley believed that 'the day delays to go down, as though the catastrophe were for a time pre-naturally withheld'. Even if catastrophe ('the dissolution of all existing nations') is inevitable, there are enduring principles which will survive to form the ground of reconstruction, giving birth to 'new states in new and distant lands', as once they reconstructed the states of Europe out of the ruins of Greece and Rome.[2]

In 1857, in his inaugural lecture as Professor of Ecclesiastical History, Stanley, referring to Arnold's lecture of 1842, maintained that although the resources of nation and race were 'exhausted for the outer world in which our history moves', yet 'the Christian Church has a long lease of new life and new hope before it. . . .' If history was to end in the near future, he said, it would end with the Church unperfected, 'like an ungenial Spring cut short in full view of summer', with its acknowledged resources confessedly undeveloped, its finest hopes of usefulness untried.[3]

Meanwhile, in the dusk of civilization, while 'the day delays to go down', the proper knowledge of the nature of this crisis of our own age, based on a study of similar late ages in history, provides information as to our particular dangers, for example, inter-national war ('We may also learn by the experience of other societies in an analogous state to ours, that having happily out-lived the critical season of the transition from youth to manhood, what we should now most dread are accidents or constitutional disease produced by external violence: war is the great enemy of society in its present stage.' 'If this calamity be avoided the pro-gress of improvement is sure'[4]), party conflict, and all the spiritual evils of a late age which have already been considered. As progress depends entirely on Christianity, that is, Christianity informing all modes of experience, the division between religion and science, though it was to be expected in a late age, was es-pecially dangerous.

---

[1] Prize Essay, p. 25.   [2] Ibid. pp. 46-8.   [3] Eastern Church, pp. lxxviii et seq.
[4] Arnold, Thucydides, vol. I, p. 637. Written during the Belgian crisis of 1831. [132]

Stanley, contemplating in 1877 the 'vast, perhaps dispropor-
tionate advance of scientific knowledge', said,

If such a separation were indeed universally impending between the
the religion of the coming age and the progress of knowledge, between
the permanent interests of the Christian churches and the interests of the
European states, there would be cause for alarm more serious than any
of the commonplace topics suggested by the panics of religious journals
or the assaults of enraged critics;

and of Milman he said that it was one of his last anxious aspirations
that some means might be found to avert the wide and widening
breach which he seemed to see between the thought and religion
of England.[1]

The core of the Liberal Anglican doctrine, therefore, is the
saving power of Christianity in the present crisis of civilization; a
right understanding of the nature of progress; and a distrust of all
merely material and intellectual improvements which are divorced
from religion. The true idea of progress made it clear that
Christianity was the one saving force in a dissolving civilization.
The annihilation of religion in men's hearts and minds would
result in a return to barbarism, and the whole process of civilization beginning once more, with no forward step having been
taken. The wrong sort of belief in progress, 'its ordinary accepta-
tion', engenders a false sense of security, 'fosters presumption'.
Its believers 'enlist as drummers to beat the march of mind'.[2]
When such progress reaches its term, as it must do, the result is
despair and lack of faith which only serve to hasten the doom. A
true idea of progress, on the other hand, is the basis of hope even
in the darkest hour of the decay of civilization.

The problem of the true nature of progress was thus eminently
practical. For the Liberal Anglicans, belief in progress was a force
to be harnessed to truth and to religion. For Newman this
coming to terms with progress (for so it appeared) was of the
essence of liberalism, his arch-enemy; for he, too, saw the march
of mind as in reality the crisis of civilization.[3] In fact, this sense

[1] *Addresses and Sermons*, pp. 58-60, 93. [133]
[2] Hare, *Guesses at Truth* (2nd ed., 2nd series), pp. 63-4.
[3] C. Dawson, *Spirit of the Oxford Movement*, pp 51-3; C. F. Harrold, *John Henry Newman*, p. 234.

of crisis was common to the Liberal Anglicans and to the Oxford reformers, the starting-point of two opposite movements. Both appealed from it to religion as the one saving force (as Carlyle did also), but in opposite ways. Coleridge had defined the Church (in its universal aspect) as the sustaining, correcting, befriending opposite of the world.[1] The response of the Oxford Movement to the crisis of civilization was to lay stress on opposition and correction as the special work and glory of the Church; the Liberal Anglicans emphasized the sustaining and befriending aspects of religion. The one was moved by the spirit of dogma, the other by the spirit of history.

(c) Religion

(i) Romanism and Rationalism

That religion is not a special compartment of thought and action was the *leitmotiv* of all Liberal Anglican teaching, the fundamental principle of the Broad Church. Unity, the end of true progress, was not confined to their philosophy of history, but was the goal of their practical policy: comprehension, the religious unity, that is, a spiritual unity (the healing of schism), not an outward uniformity, of all Christian England. This ideal, seen most clearly in Arnold's theory of the essential unity of Church and State, a unity of ideals, was the Liberal Anglican response to the challenge of the crisis of civilization, which for the Liberal Anglicans was first and foremost a national crisis. In the face of this crisis, party conflict in Church and State, the disease of the age, and moreover unnatural, [134] was dangerous folly. Instead of uniting to face the danger, men were quarrelling over matters which in comparison with it were trifling and which, in historical perspective, were utterly unimportant.[2] However, although the very name of party was anathema to them, any policy, however comprehensive and large-minded, in an age of religious strife, was bound to carve out for its devotees a special position in the minds of men, and in spite of their express desire, they were

---

[1] *Constitution of Church and State*, p. 133.
[2] See e.g., Thirlwall (1851); *Remains*, vol. I, pp. 152-3.

eventually given their place and their label, the 'Broad Church'; a label which has undoubtedly served to obscure the real dimensions of their thinking. However, if their message, which was to all men, but especially to the nation (translated into 20th century terms it would be a call to 'Western Civilization'), was to be effective, they had to strike out a way among the conflicting creeds and religious passions of 19th century England, and this, given the doctrine of accommodation as central in their conception of history, was bound to be a middle way between irreligious rationalism on the one hand, and the prevailing 'Romeward tendencies' on the other.

From the practical point of view of religion, the Liberal Anglican idea of history was forged, as it were, between these two fires, just as from the practical social and political viewpoint, it was the condition of England which was the motive force. The distinction is superficial; for the real vision, the diseases were all part of the crisis of civilization, and the true remedies all inspired by one faith.

All observers are agreed on the essentially unhistorical nature of the ethos of the Oxford Movement. The idea of evolution was lacking in it,[1] its view of the past was the idealized romantic view extended to cover the early Church as well as the Middle Ages,[2] and it had no real understanding of the present.[3] The Liberal Anglicans were the first to emphasize this weakness. They attacked the Romantic medievalism which was a strong element in the Oxford Movement, and which tended to lead men to Rome. Hare showed that this medievalism, in itself a healthy reaction against the shallow rationalist break with the living past, became a perversion when it converted men to Catholicism. The comparison between past and present which was the cause of this Romeward tendency was fallacious. [135] In particular he criticized Kenelm Digby's 'apotheosis of the Middle Ages' as a misrepresentation of history. [136] Milman said of Chateaubriand that his Christianity was 'essentially the old poetic faith of the Middle

[1] C. C. J. Webb, *Religious Thought in the Oxford Movement*, pp. 18-19.
[2] Y. Brilioth, *The Anglican Revival*, pp. 120, 206, 208; Storr, *Development of English Theology*, pp. 255-6.
[3] Storr, *Development of English Theology*, p. 257.

Ages', that it had a sacred reverence for tradition altogether irreconcilable with the investigation of historic truth. [137] As early as 1826, the germ of Milman's philosophy of history is apparent in a sermon on the 'philosophy of preaching'. A religion which appeals solely to the imagination, Milman pointed out, is suited only to an imaginative age like the Middle Ages. [138] From the point of view of the Liberal Anglican idea of history, the strength of Catholicism in the Middle Ages, and of the early Church, its accommodation to a childhood age, was its weakness now. [139] A religion which appeals to the imagination and to authority is essentially as weak in the modern world as rational religion was weak in the Middle Ages. A view of the Middle Ages, therefore, which led men to Roman Catholicism, as it led Digby, was an example of history wrongly applied. Such a perversion of practical history must spring from a false view, an unscientific view, of the Middle Ages, from a misunderstanding of that philosophy of history which revealed the true role of the medieval Church.[1] No historian could deny the worth and value of medieval Catholicism, but the science of history made it clear that its whole value consisted in its adaptation to a state of civilization which by the 19th century had passed away everywhere, except where the old clothes of childhood still hung about the grown man. [140] The confessional, for example, was an example of authority which suited the childhood of nations, but was an anachronism in a manhood stage.[2] In the Church of England the condemnation of Colenso was another example of the exercise of an authority which was an historical anachronism. [142] It was a 'Romanizing Fallacy' to suppose that an institution which may have been good and useful at one period in the progress of society must also be good and useful at every other period, 'as though the calix which encloses and guards the bud, ought also to enclose the full-blown flower'. Institutions, subject like everything earthly to the law of change, are valuable relatively; only spiritual truths are absolute and permanent.[3] The unity of the Middle Ages was an outward,

---

[1] Hare, 'Romanizing Fallacies', *Charges*. pp. 80-4.
[2] Milman, *Savonarola and other Essays*, pp. 386-7, 388-9. [141]
[3] Hare, 'Romanizing Fallacies', *Charges*, pp. 80-4

material unity, suited to the age. To seek to return to it was an unhistorical Romanizing fallacy. Our need, said Hare, is a spiritual unity such as Rome, whether pagan or Christian, has never been able to comprehend.[1]

The appeal to history by the leaders of the Oxford Movement appeared to the Liberal Anglicans to be quite arbitrary. The Liberal Anglicans believed that effective action in the world sprang from a scientific approach to the whole of history, and that only when one has made such a study is it possible to go into action with all the confidence born of the knowledge that history is on one's side, at least with the sure knowledge of what tendencies to encourage and support and what to avoid and oppose. To exalt one century at the expense of another, therefore, to try to conform to the character of one particular age because one believes that age to have been right in its faith and in its aims, was utterly unhistorical.[2] Hare accused the Tractarians of 'pampering their fancies with delusive visions of former ages, and with fantastical wishes for their revival'.[3] To set up one particular age as a pattern of perfection and the goal of endeavour without reference to the whole of history was an appeal, not to history, but to one's arbitrary fancy. Argument from history meant argument from a scientific study of the whole of history. Properly speaking, it was not a question of argument, it was a question of realizing and understanding the inevitable and natural. Newman's theory of the development of doctrine was not based on such a study of history. To go to history in order to pick out the arguments that one approves, to construct a chain of doctrines across the centuries that are right and on the side of truth, was eristical, not historical. Newman's was not a true development, but a chemical mixture. [144] Contrasted in Hare's mind with the eclecticism of Newman was the genetical-historical method of the Germans, 'ever seeking to behold all things in their connection, as parts or members of a great organic whole . . . while the Eclectic is content if he can string together a number of generalizations'.[4]

Milman's criticism of Newman's theory of development was

[1] *Ibid.* p. 87 [143].   [2] Arnold, *Sermons*, vol. IV, introduction, pp. viii-ix.
[3] 'The Wants of the Church' (Charge, 1843), *Charges*, p. 25.
[4] *Guesses at Truth* (2nd ed., 2nd series), p. 238. [145]

that, according to it, Christianity was advancing to its perfect development while mankind was degenerating into the darkest barbarism and ignorance; and when this development of Newman's had reached its perfection, mankind was blessed with an unexampled intellectual, social and moral advancement.

Will religion only retrograde, while all things thus rush onward? . . . We too . . . have our theory of development. For us Mr Newman goes too far and not far enough. We believe that the development of Christianity, of the yet undeveloped or dormant part of Christianity, since the Reformation, has been immense; the development, we mean, of its morality, of its social influence, of its humanity. [1]

Newman's theory of development was based on the hypothesis of papal infallibility, and the claim that all historians must adopt some hypothesis if they would treat of Christianity. Hare criticized this argument, pointing out the difference between hypothesis and theory, words used indiscriminately by Newman. A hypothesis was a thing alien from history which a historian ought carefully to eschew except in cases where the scantiness of his materials compels him to supply their deficiencies by conjecture. It was the weakness of Milner that his ecclesiastical history was governed by one hypothesis. On the other hand, all intelligent contemplation of facts in their connection with one another is a theory. When a hypothesis has received the confirmation and verification of experience, it ceases to be a mere hypothesis and becomes a theory or a member of a theory. The confounding of theories with hypotheses belongs to the essence both of scepticism and of Romanism. [2]

Newman's weapon, said Hare, was the Jacobinical, unhistorical weapon of logic, which is a mere Cyclops, one-eyed, looking straight before it. [3] Thirlwall said that Newman's 'great intellectual deficiency' was 'the utter want of historical tact and judgement'. [4] Later commentators have endorsed this view. [5]

[1] *Savonarola and other Essays*, pp. 366-8; 'development . . . a word much misused' p. 384).
[2] Hare, *The Means of Unity*, note A, pp. 47-8, 52-3.
[3] *Contest with Rome*, note C, pp. 106 et seq. [146]
[4] *Letters: Literary and Theological*, pp. 260, 268.
[5] Brilioth, *The Anglican Revival*, pp. 117-18; Storr, *Development of English Theology*, p. 257; C. F. Harrold, *Newman*, pp. 223-5; Lecky, *Historical Essays*, p. 227; Pfleiderer, *Development of Theology*, p. 365; Tulloch, *Movements of Religious Thought*, p. 112.

Both in its theory and in its practice, therefore, the Oxford Movement was utterly unhistorical. But for this very reason it could hardly be a serious danger, it was a racing back against the tide of history,[1] superficially alarming, exasperating in its historical perversity, but lacking in real menace. The best way to combat it was to understand it as an historical phenomenon, as one of the ordinary oscillations in history.[2] It was, in fact, itself a symptom of the crisis of civilization. As Hare said, 'In ages when intellectual and moral energy is almost effete like that of Hadrian, people will . . . attempt to revive exploded superstitions. . . .' However 'that which has been once exploded cannot again become part of the organic structure of society. You might as well sow a husk'.[3] In 1859 Goldwin Smith, whose view of history as set out in his inaugural lectures bears a strongly-marked Liberal Anglican imprint, was confidently predicting the imminent downfall of the Papacy.[4]

Another symptom of the crisis of civilization was Rationalism. This was the greater danger, because the science of history showed it to be the natural development of a late age. Whereas the Oxford Movement was an attempt to assume the garb of childhood, to put on worn-out clothes, Rationalism, where it developed into an attack on religion itself, was only the logical or historical extension, as it were, of the normal process of history. It was the strength of religion to adapt itself to this process. The strength of Protestantism lay in being a rational religion in a rational age. This was the gauge of its validity. But a complete accommodation in an age of radical Rationalism would be the annihilation of religion and the extinction of civilization, and it can be argued that 'rational religion' is the thin end of the wedge, the beginning of such a denouement. The practical question implicit in the Liberal Anglican idea of history therefore is: when must rational religion begin to resist Rationalism? The Liberal Anglican answer was: when it begins to threaten the belief in God and His Providence and the essential truths of Christianity. An attack on these,

[1] Arnold, *Sermons*, vol. IV, introduction.
[2] Hare, 'Romanizing Fallacies', *Charges*, pp. 76-7; *ibid.* p. 79.
[3] *Ibid.* pp. 145-6.
[4] *Lectures on the Study of History*, p. 166.

at least neglect of them, was to be expected in a late age, in the normal course of things, but it was only by clinging to them that disaster could be avoided.[1] The Liberal Anglicans welcomed the spirit of German Neology (they were the pioneers of Biblical criticism in England) because they saw in this constructive criticism a weapon against the purely destructive scepticism of 18th-century Rationalism—it was to Rationalist criticism what Niebuhr was to Beaufort—but not when it went so far as to mythicize the events of Christ's life. The Germans, Milman pointed out, were capable of carrying Vico's principles to absurd lengths.[2] Thirlwall opposed *Essays and Reviews* because if the principles laid down in it were to be carried to their logical conclusion, Christianity would cease to be a religion, and as something merely floating on the stream of history, 'its final doom, as that of all that belongs to a mere state of transition, will have been irrevocably fixed by the nature of things'.[3]

The Liberal Anglicans, however, saw no necessary opposition between religion and the progress of knowledge, because religion and true knowledge advanced together.[4] Although the problems of science were problems of science, not of religion, and to be determined on scientific not on religious grounds, Hare said, irreligious science was an abomination.[5] It is from religion that science, if it is to be healthy, must draw its principles and its life-blood. As has been seen, the Liberal Anglicans regarded a split between science and religion as disastrous to civilization.

(ii) History and Theology

The theology of the Liberal Anglicans, like all their thought, is dominated by the idea of development. According to Arnold, the theologian's task was two-fold: the interpretation and the application of Scripture.[6] Given the Liberal Anglican idea of progress and the principle of accommodation, this meant that theology divorced from history was valueless, it could neither

[1] In proportion as a nation loses its hold on the divine idea it sinks back into barbarism (Hare, *Mission of the Comforter*, vol. I, p. 192).

[2] *Christianity*, vol. I, p. 122. The work of Paulus (*Leben Jesu*) Milman called 'ultra-rationalist' (*ibid.* p. 115).   [3] *Remains*, vol. II, pp. 51-2.

[4] Stanley, 'The Hopes of Theology', *Addresses and Sermons*, p. 93.

[5] *Charges*, p. 99.   [6] *Sermons*, vol. III, introduction, pp. viii *et seq.*

properly understand God's word nor properly apply it. As Milman said, unless due regard is paid to the predominant character of each age of civilization, the true philosophy, derived from considering human nature in every state and period of moral probation, could not be deduced from the lessons of history.[1] God's word was adapted to the prevailing state of society, and this must be understood if its eternal truths are to be discovered. The scripture, too, which is especially vital to us is the scripture which represents a state of society analogous to our own.[2] To grasp these principles implies an understanding of history as a whole. Moreover if religion is to be practically effective, the clergy must possess a knowledge of our own times [148] and if this is not to be meaningless, a knowledge of the past as well. Arnold demanded of the clergy a very comprehensive knowledge of the past: 'the great events in the political history of the human race, the great vicissitudes of opinion, the great influences upon morals, the great social changes which have been affected by and which have affected both.'[3] 'Ecclesiastical history', Joseph Milner in the vicarage library, was not enough.

To understand the modern Church we must understand the ancient, and vice versa, Arnold pointed out, nor must we leave the two periods unconnected.[4] What, he asks, can the clergy know of modern problems, even of modern church problems, if they are ignorant of history? [150] In order to be able to understand these problems and to play a useful and effective part in the world, a knowledge of history is essential, and this means a knowledge of history as a whole. It was the historical approach, and the spirit of Liberal Anglican history, calm, objective, which made Thirlwall's *Charges* so potent a force in the religious controversies of the 19th century.

Arnold's theory of the interpretation of Scripture is an application of the science of history to theology; and reflects the relativism of his political thinking. His belief that there is no eternally good or bad so far as government is concerned applies

---

[1] *Quarterly Review*, vol. 48 (1832), p. 428.
[2] *Sermons*, vol. II ('On the right interpretation . . . of the Scriptures'), p. 431. [147]
[3] *Sermons*, vol. III, introduction, p. ix.   [4] *Ibid.* vol. VI, p. 246. [149]

to God's government in the early stages of the world. As has been seen, God demands of men in one stage of society what men regard as evil in a later stage. The relativism of Arnold's theory of the interpretation of Scripture leads naturally to the Liberal Anglican view that there is no such thing as a theology for all time, but that each stage has its own theology.[151] Religions, in fact, are the product of the time and place, and must be studied in their context; only thus will religion, which is true eternally, emerge.

This view constitutes a theological revolution in England,[1] and as a result of it many old problems of theology were seen by the Liberal Anglicans in a new light. For example, they placed miracles in the framework of a conception of history. In the Old and New Testaments these represent the direct interposition of Providence, adapted to the child-like mind, sometimes 'consisting in the adaptation of a natural phenomenon to the time and place where its effects were needed'; in the Middle Ages they are, according to Milman, the products of an imaginative age. The 'Age of Miracles' was a historical reality; it had passed away with the childhood of nations. Prophecy, too, Arnold was able to explain as not so much anticipated history, as the enunciation of those eternal principles by which history is determined.

But this historical conception of theology involved a tension between history and religion which the Liberal Anglicans did not resolve, concerned as they were with the practical, at the expense of the speculative reason. They saw that the Bible was the greatest practical religious force in England, [152] and their aim was the immediately practical one of using the historical method to defend it against the purely destructive criticism characteristic of a rational age. To sift eternal truth, the truth of the philosophy of history, from historical truth, the truth of the science of history, was their aim. They saw, secondly, that the historical approach to Christianity was the most persuasive argument in an age governed by the idea of development. [153] It represented in itself an accommodation to the climate of 19th-century thought. Practical religion in the 19th century meant historical religion,[2] religion reinforced by the historical method and outlook, and historical

---

[1] See Stanley's *Essay on the Theology of the 19th Century.*   [2] See *ibid.*

religion, for the Liberal Anglicans, was inherently practical. Religion was a practical view of the world in relation to God's will, and God's will was revealed in history.

(d) Education

Arnold was appointed Headmaster of Rugby towards the end of 1827, he went to Rugby in August 1828, the theory of 'The Social Progress of States' was published in June 1830, and the essay on 'The Interpretation of Scripture' in 1832. The condition of England, the interpretation of Scripture, and the problem of education were the practical influences, as Niebuhr and Vico were the intellectual influences, which helped to form Arnold's idea of history. Arnold's mind was essentially practical and his idea of history would not have taken shape in an intellectual vacuum. Nevertheless his approach to these problems was not an empirical one, he brought to them the principles which are the foundation of his conception of history. His attitude to public school education, therefore, was not that of a Puritan moralist, his approach was in the first place a doctrinaire, determinist approach.

My object [he said in March 1828] will be, if possible, to form Christian men, for Christian boys I can scarcely hope to make; I mean that from the natural imperfect state of boyhood they are not susceptible of Christian principles in their full development upon their practice, and I suspect that a low standard of morals in many respects must be tolerated among them, as it was on a larger scale in what I consider the boyhood of the human race.[1]

This is a principle derived from the Bible, but from the Bible viewed as history, not as uniformly inspired. Arnold applied to Rugby not 'Old Testament principles', as Lytton Strachey asserts in his caricature of Arnold, but the principle of historical development. Rugby School, in Arnold's eyes, was not a flat moral level, it was a small-scale example of historical growth. From this conception sprang Arnold's great innovation and special contribution to public school reform: the use of the Sixth Form in the moral government of the school. There was nothing new in the prefect-

[1] Letter of 2 March 1828.

orial system. Both whereas, hitherto, headmasters had regarded the boys, as a whole, as an unenlightened mass, a feudal society, as it were, of tyrants and slaves (potential tyrants), necessarily at war with their masters, Arnold regarded them as an epitome of the life-course of a nation. They did not represent one state of society, therefore, but two. The majority of the boys were in the child-hood stage, in which 'knowledge is very low and passion very strong'. Their great need, therefore, was moral and intellectual guidance (public schools in Arnold's day did not accept this principle), but this was to be enforced, if necessary, because there was no appeal to reason where boys were concerned. They were in a state of bondage; they obeyed from fear rather than from love. Arnold used the language of the Law, not that of the Gospel, where they were concerned. [154]

The Sixth Form, on the other hand, were men, in Arnold's eyes, and he treated them as men, as equals. This was something quite new in public school education. [155] From the point of view of the majority of the boys, therefore, the Sixth Form represented the natural aristocracy of a childhood period. [156] From Arnold's point of view it represented a different historical stage from the majority. His appeal to it was through the reason. It was no longer in a state of bondage.

But if Arnold went to Rugby with a theory, experience at Rugby must have confirmed and clarified principles which are the basis of his theory of the social progress of states and of the interpretation of Scripture. For example, his constant use of the analogy between the stages of boyhood and manhood in states and individuals, and the dangers of the transition period in both, were no doubt due to this experience. At Rugby it was Arnold's duty to study the minds of boys, and this was for him an insight into the mind of nations in their childhood. Vico studied children and peasants to gain this insight. In Arnold's case, however, the end, as always, was practical. Arnold applied the Vichian, the Romantic, conception of mind to education, at a time when the theory of education in England was dominated by the *tabula rasa* psychology of the Utilitarians. For the latter, mental develop-ment, like progress, was unilinear. The child's mind had only a potential value, it was to be filled up with rational knowledge as quickly as possible. For the Romantics, the imaginative nature of the child's mind had an actual value in itself. Education, therefore, should be adapted accordingly; to force rational knowledge on to the child was a violation of natural development. In this, as in so much else, the Liberal Anglicans took the side of Coleridge and Wordsworth, against the Edgeworths, the *Edinburgh Review*, the Utilitarians and Owen.[1] Education, Arnold said, is a dynamical, not a mechanical process.[2] Arnold's theory of education, like his theory of the social progress of states, springs from the analogy between the development of states and individuals, and is governed by the relativism of the science of history. Just as memory and imagination are naturally strong in childhood ages, so these are the faculties which should be cultivated in the child. [157]

Everything has its proper season, and if summer be cut out of the year, it is vain to suppose that the work of summer can be forestalled in Spring. Fullness of knowledge and sagacity of judgement are fruits not to be looked for in early youth; and he who endeavours to force them does but interfere with the natural growth of the plant and prematurely exhaust its vigour.[3]

The historical education of the boy, in particular, should correspond with the natural history of nations. Children should be confronted with childhood periods: ages of heroism and of poetry. Pictures should be used, which should contain as much as possible the poetry of history. After this foundation, histories of one or two particular countries should be furnished, written poetically much more than philosophically.[4] Thucydides and Tacitus should be reserved until the most advanced stage of the boy's education. When he has reached manhood, the manhood periods of history should be revealed to him. At this stage, 'the particular subject of the history is of little moment, so long as it be taken neither from the barbarian, nor from the romantic, but from the philosophical or civilized stage of human society'. Now also the time is come when the pupil may be introduced to that

---

[1] Coleridge, *Biographia Literaria* (Everyman ed.), pp. 5-6; Wordsworth, *Prelude*, book v, ll. 222-363. See J. W. Adamson, *English Education, 1789-1902*.
[2] Letter of 2 March 1836.   [3] Arnold, *Miscellaneous Works*, p. 358.
[4] *Ibid.* p. 357. [158]

high philosophy which unfolds 'the causes of things', in other words, the science of history. 'In short, the pupil may be furnished with certain formulae, which shall enable him to read all history beneficially, which shall teach him what to look for in it, how to judge of it and how to apply it.'[1] Arnold wrote in 1833 that he was more and more suspicious of the mere *fact* system. 'My own lessons with the vith Form are directed now to the best of my power to the furnishing rules or formulae for them to work with . . . in history . . . general forms for . . . estimating the importance of wars, revolutions, etc.'[2] His method was a comparative method. He wrote to Stanley at Oxford, 'ancient history and philosophy will be constantly recalling modern events and parties to your mind',[3] and his favourite question in school is said to have been: 'What does this remind you of?'[4]

The theory of analogous periods also governs the principles of translation. In the choice of his words and the style of his sentences the boy should be taught to follow the analogy required by the age and character of the writer whom he is translating.[5]

History, therefore, should play an important part in any scheme of education, both because such an education is natural, corresponding to the growth of the child's mind, and because in its later stages (as the science of history) it is essentially practical, as well as being a training of the intellect. Not only did Arnold introduce modern history into the curriculum at Rugby (Guizot's *Civilization*, Ranke's *Popes*, Elphinstone's *India*, for example, were studied there,) but what is far more important, he completely revolutionized the teaching of the classics, [161] the staple of public school and university education and still studied as models of good taste abstracted from their historical background. The same revolution was begun by Hare and Thirlwall at Cambridge, and Stanley later carried on the work at Oxford. At both universities the tradition of Bentley and Porson of verbal, textual 'scholarship' was still supreme. For Arnold, as for Hare and Thirlwall, the study of the classics meant the study of classical

[1] Arnold, *Miscellaneous Works*, pp. 358-9. [2] Letter of 23 Oct. 1833.
[3] Letter of 4 March 1835.
[4] See *Life*, p. 85; Prothero, *Life*, vol. I, p. 362. [159]
[5] *Miscellaneous Works*, pp. 354-5. [160]

history, and this was not only ancient history in all its fullness of thought and action and development, but history in its universal aspect. [162] The fact that there is an ancient and a modern period in so-called 'ancient' history, meant that a man educated in the classics, 'even though he knows no history in detail but· that which is called ancient, will be better fitted for public life' than one who has considerable information (in the common sense of the term) about modern history, even though that information 'be twenty times more minute'.[1] In his inaugural lecture at Oxford, Arnold said:

We have in our familiar acquaintance with the history of the ancient world (or at any rate with some of its greatest historians) an immense help towards the study of modern history. Advantages neglected are our shame, and if we here are ignorant of modern history we are, I think, especially inexcusable.[2]

A classical education, provided that it was conducted on historical lines, was as practical as any form of utilitarian education, while a historical education could not be universal, could not therefore be practical, unless it was also classical.

Expel Greek and Latin from your schools and you confine the views of the existing generation to themselves and their immediate predecessors: you will cut off so many centuries of the world's experience, and place us in the same state as if the human race had first come into existence in 1500.[3]

Classical history alone provides two complete cycles of history: it provides both childhood and manhood periods. Modern history suffers from being incomplete. To depose classical studies from the place which they have hitherto occupied in every system of liberal education, said Thirlwall, 'would be virtually to sever the past from the present and so lose all sure guidance for the future, and to throw society back into a state of barbarism, in which all thoughts are engrossed by the concerns of the passing day'.[4]

But universal history could not be severed from religion, and this classical, universal, practical education of the Liberal Anglicans was thus necessarily religious in character; it could not be purely secular. The study of history, according to the Liberal Anglican

---

[1] Arnold, *Miscellaneous Works*, p. 360.   [2] *Lectures*, p. 42.
[3] Arnold, *Miscellaneous Works*, p. 349.   [4] *Remains*, vol. III, p. 349.

idea of it, would reinforce the close connection which Arnold established between intellectual and moral education. 'The moment you enter upon any moral subjects,' he said, 'whether moral philosophy or history, you must either be Christian or anti-Christian.'[1] It was because this principle was not admitted at London University that Arnold resigned his fellowship there, thereby in effect raising the crucial issue of English education in the 19th century. [163] And it was for the same reason that Gibbon was not studied at Rugby.[2]

In education, as in political thought and religion, the Liberal Anglicans struck out a middle way between the extremes of High Church conservatism and non-religious radicalism, between 'classical' and 'useful' education. [164] Education in 19th-century England reflected the social and religious divisions of the nation which it was the aim of the Liberal Anglicans to close. Conservative education, the old 'classical' education of the public schools and universities, was designed for the old House of Commons.[3] As such, the study of the classics as models of rhetoric was practical. Radical education for the 'industrious' classes, reacting in a class-conscious manner against 'classical' education, was utilitarian and non-religious. Liberal Anglican education was both classical (and therefore not banausic) and practical, but practical in a much wider social sense than the old 'classical' education, looking forward to the democracy which was destined in the natural course of things for full political power, and which had revealed its political awareness during the Reform Bill crisis; not practical in the purely empirical sense of the Utilitarians, condemned by Coleridge.[4] It was practical also from the point of view of social stability (the police aspect of education bulked very large in statesmen's minds in 19th-century England) because it was essentially religious, Christian in the broadest sense, a healing power in the land; universal therefore in the religious, but not in the utilitarian, *tabula rasa*, cosmopolitan, sense of universality; in fact a national education, 'designed for the education of English youth

---

[1] Letter of 28 Nov. 1837.
[2] Stanley, *Life*, p. 84. Arnold 'dared not' use Gibbon.
[3] J. R. M. Butler, *The Great Reform Bill*, p. 233.
[4] *Constitution of Church and State*, pp. 64-5. [165]

in the middle of the 19th century' [166]; 'its business', wrote Thirlwall, 'is not with human nature in the abstract, it is not to bring
up citizens of the world, but it is the fashioning of English minds
and hearts to fit them for such work as belongs to Englishmen.'[1]
A system of education adapted to the genius of our people, Thirlwall said, must be sound, solid and practical, rooted in the past,
but not offering violence to the law of continuity and progress by
which God works and reveals Himself in the history of mankind.[2]
The relativism of this theory of education should be contrasted
with Macaulay's programme for the education of India [167]
based, as it is, on the conception of progress and the assumptions of
Utilitarian psychology on which James Mill's *History of India*
rests. Thirlwall, as Bishop of St David's, championed the Eistedd-
fod and encouraged the study of Celtic remains, despite the open
opposition of *The Times*, which considered such studies 'a foolish
interference with the natural progress of civilization'.[3] This
remark gives us the measure of the difference between the idea of
progress of Thirlwall and the Liberal Anglicans and that of James
Mill, Macaulay and *The Times*.

The Liberal Anglican idea of education was designed to overcome 'the religious difficulty' which was obstructing the advent
of that state-controlled national education which alone could
save the nation from social disaster.[4] Milman argued that to
teach rational religion to children was absurd, because their minds
were not ready to receive it. The Bible should not be a school-
book, its value is for mature minds only. 'True religion is the
highest attainable point of knowledge.' The teacher therefore
should communicate what Milman calls 'the religion of childhood', not religion but 'religiousness'.[5] The Romantic theory
of education here cuts the Gordian knot of the religious difficulty
in theory, but at Arnold's Rugby it did so in practice. There was
no 'religious difficulty' in the reformed public schools of the
19th century.[6]

[1] Thirlwall, *Remains*, vol. III, p. 379.   [2] *Ibid.* pp. 382 *et seq.*
[3] See J. C. Thirlwall, *Connop Thirlwall*, p. 151.
[4] See Milman's article, 'The Education of the People' in *Quarterly Review*, vol. 78
(Sept. 1846).   [5] *Ibid.* pp. 401-7. [168]
[6] Cf. Milman's article, *Quarterly Review*, vol. 78, p. 420; R. L. Archer, *Secondary
Education*, pp. 53-4.

The aim of Liberal Anglican education was thus to heal the social and religious divisions in the nation. It was designed for all classes. [169] Culture should not be the exclusive possession of the rich; if working-class education was 'banausic' this was the fault of the more leisured classes. The education of the middle and working classes was an important sphere of Liberal Anglican activity, [170] and it was in the true Liberal Anglican spirit that the London Working Men's College of Maurice differed from all previous working class organizations in regarding 'human studies as the primary part of our education'.

(e) The Nemesis of Practical History

According to the Liberal Anglican science of history, the modern period of civilization, whose childhood was the Middle Ages, was rapidly nearing its final phase. This prognosis, however, in the eyes of 19th-century middle class liberals, must have seemed daily to be more and more divorced from the plain facts of progress, so that in the realm of ideas it was the march of mind which was triumphant; 'Civilization' in the sense of the Rationalist historians. 'The day delayed to go down', and the symptoms of decay, Utilitarianism, the philosophy of material progress, triumphed. The Liberal Anglicans appeared to be wrong in direct proportion as they themselves were strengthened in their opinions. So far as the crisis of civilization and the idea of true progress were concerned, therefore, they found themselves intellectually in a minority. It was just in so far as their history was practical, a relation of past and present, that it appeared in the 19th century to be false. Moreover, the great religious movement of the 1820s and 30s, to which their idea of history was so closely related, instead of gathering irresistible momentum, fell away from under them with the increasing material progress of the century, broke up and crumbled into warring sects at their feet, so that they became the last thing that they could have wished, one of the pieces merely, a party with a label, 'the Broad Church'. In the critical years, too, though their warnings were plain enough, the intellectual basis of those warnings, the historical diagnosis, was beyond the mental horizon of the educated public in England. Intellectually, they would have been more widely appreciated in the second half of the century, but in the returning prosperity of those years their warnings were forgotten. It was not until the turn of the century, and later in England, as once again the crisis of civilization sharpened visibly, that civilization became a problem rather than an assumption. By this time, the problem and the historical resources which were brought to its solution had grown beyond all recognition.

Thus the Liberal Anglican idea of history ran into the sands of the middle class prosperity of the Victorian Age and, after Arnold's death in 1842, underwent no further significant development. The Liberal Anglican goal was not a system of thought. Action, not systematic exposition, followed, and influenced, the formulation of their views. Their conception of history is the foundation of their religion, their teaching and their formal Histories. This is why historians of History who have examined them in closed compartments, viewing Milman and Stanley as 'ecclesiastical historians', Thirlwall and Arnold as 'classical historians', have missed the Liberal Anglican idea of history as a whole.

It is also owing to its practical nature that the historical thinking of the Liberal Anglicans suffers from a logical tension between their religion and the historical *Weltanschauung*. The Liberal Anglicans did not attain the complete historical outlook: the Vichian emancipation of history from the direct interposition of Providence. Thus, in Arnold's doctrine of the interpretation of Scripture, God's commands are adapted to the prevailing state of morality. But if they are adapted in this manner, how, one may ask, is this morality improved? According to Arnold, the progress of mankind is 'provided for', perfection is 'prepared for, although not immediately made attainable' in that God gives 'general principles of duty', but the conclusions which follow from these general principles 'with regard to our particular relations in life were not at the same time developed and men did not at once develop them for themselves. Their notions therefore on many particular points of practice were really irreconcilable with the principles which they acknowledged; but the inconsistency did not strike them; and revelation did not as yet interfere to make it palpable.'[1] But how can revelation interfere without destroying the principle of accommodation? To be logical one must sacrifice either the principle of accommodation or the belief in God's intervention in man's history.

If God commanded Abraham to sacrifice Isaac in accordance with the ethic of the time, that human sacrifice was not evil, but on the contrary, if commanded by God, good, how can He say 'Thou shall not kill' without offending that ethic? If man took this moral step by himself, what prevents him from taking them all, and making the whole of his moral and intellectual progress unaided? Arnold indeed talks of the 'acquisition' of purer views 'by later generations'.[2]

The doctrine of accommodation, moreover, is a double-edged weapon, and can be used to justify any departure from Gospel Christianity. Eternal principles, Milman was careful to point out, are not merely the result of a certain stage of civilization, [171] but how can Gospel principles, the universal religion of Christianity, be said to survive at all in a period like the Middle Ages, when Christianity accommodated itself to the state of society and became warlike and imaginative? Applied to politics, the principle of accommodation resulted in a complete relativism. For Arnold and Milman there were circumstances which justified despotism. [172] The appeal to a science of history, to inevitable laws of historical development, is the most dangerous of all the justifications of political obligation. It can justify any political iniquity.

And if religion accommodates itself to advancing Rationalism, which is the Liberal Anglican argument for Protestantism, how far is this to go? Why should not religion accommodate itself to the second intellectual barbarism, as it did to the first imaginative one?

Another logical difficulty concerned the question of missions. Dr Fausset in his criticism of Milman's *History of the Jews* pointed to the incompatibility of historical relativism with missionary activity. Why convert to a rational religion a people unfit for it? [173] There is an argument here for leaving all missionary

---

[1] *Sermons*, vol. II, pp. 438-40. [2] *Ibid.*

activity to Roman Catholics, to an 'imaginative' religion. Whately said 'Christianity is designed and is calculated for all mankind, except savages and such as are but little removed above the savage state',[1] and yet was himself a supporter of missionary activity. Stanley overcame this difficulty by appealing to the Vichian 'common sense' (*sapienza volgare*) of nations.

No doubt to a mere childish and barbarian intellect the idea of complexity is difficult to grasp: but after all, in presenting to uncivilised or half-civilised nations the truths of a religion which, if it be anything, ought to correspond with the results of the highest civilisation, we must be content to trust ourselves in some degree to the common sense and common reason of mankind, which even in the most barbarous races, is not wholly extinguished. . . .[2]

The Liberal Anglican idea of history was, in fact, of the nature of a compromise, a *via media*, being the result of practical, no less than of purely intellectual, problems. The climate of religious opinion in England, illustrated by the hostile reception of Milman's *History of the Jews*, must therefore be taken into account in listing the inconsistencies in this conception of history. The Liberal Anglicans had to go carefully if the offence created by their work was not to be its undoing. They had, in fact, to accommodate their thinking.

The presupposition of a science of history is the universal acceptance of its laws. But the first thing which Arnold's successor at Oxford did was to condemn the search for laws in history, and in setting up 'Society', the 18th-century Rationalist concept, as his unit of study, made a science of history, in the Liberal Anglican sense, impossible. [175] Goldwin Smith, also, whose philosophy of history is that of the Liberal Anglicans, rejected the idea of a science of history, and described Vico's law, 'that of revolving cycles of men and events', as 'wild and fruitless as a dream'.[3]

Although the study of history never lost its practical character

---

[1] *Lectures on Political Economy*, p. 184.
[2] Sermon for the day of intercession for Missions, 1877 (*Sermons on Special Occasions*, p. 293. [174]
[3] *Lectures on the Study of History* (1859–61), p. 47. [176]

in England in the 19th century (Seeley, Acton, Freeman, for example, illustrate this), the study of the past 'for its own sake' became the work of professional historians, while the future of practical history lay, on the one hand, with the socialism of Marx, based on a historical pessimism similar in many respects to that of the Liberal Anglicans, and, on the other hand, with the science of history of the Positivists, based on the optimistic, Rationalist view of civilization which the Liberal Anglicans considered as itself a symptom of decline. The study of the past itself became deeply influenced by positivism and the methods of the natural sciences, and the reaction against positivistic history was a reaction against the idea of history as a science at all. In this reaction, the autonomy of history was vindicated; it was shown to be an independent discipline, a world of experience of its own.

From the critical standpoint of modern historical thinking, therefore, the Liberal Anglican idea of history, as presented so far, is not history [177] at all. What, therefore, is its place in the historical movement proper, as seen, that is, in the light of later developments, and in relation to the background of historical thought in England in the first half of the 19th century?

CHAPTER V

THE 'HISTORICAL MOVEMENT PROPER' AND THE LIBERAL ANGLICANS

THAT the Liberal Anglican idea of history was practical and liberal does not distinguish it in any real way in the world of historical thought in England in the first half of the 19th century. There was no significant departure, as yet, from the age-long tradition of history as a conscious relation of past and present governed by practical issues, [178] and liberalism, in one form or another, was the dominant characteristic of the historical thinking of the age. Men's reflection on the past was, however, still dominated by the Rationalist tradition of the 18th century, and in particular, by the sensation psychology, with its essentially unhistorical presupposition of the uniformity of human nature. 'Mankind,' as Hume had said, 'are so much the same in all times and places that history informs us of nothing new or strange in this particular,' and it is the Liberal Anglican opposition to this conception, and to the Rationalist tradition generally, which is important for the history of history. The positive side of this opposition lies in what may be called the Vichian or Romantic philosophy of mind, which from the point of view of the development of history proper forms the most valuable element in the Romantic Movement, though many so-called Romantics did not subscribe to it. Before describing the nature of this philosophy of mind as it is found in the historical thinking of the Liberal Anglicans, there is one distinguishing characteristic of their idea of history which springs from its essentially practical nature: its impartiality.

(a) The Nature of the Impartiality of Liberal Anglican History

Impartiality is not usually a property of history which is self-consciously practical, but the goal of Liberal Anglican endeavour was unity in Church and State, and party-spirit, as they saw it, was one of the most dangerous symptoms of the crisis of civilization. From the Liberal Anglican point of view, therefore, history which bore the label of a party or sect was not practical; to project one's own standpoint in the controversies of the present into the past, on the level of political history, was merely an invitation to the other side to do likewise. [179] It was, as Coleridge saw, the spirit of party, never more rampant than in the 19th century, which blinded men to the lessons of history.[1] The whole practical aim of the Liberal Anglicans in studying the past was to take soundings from beneath the clash of parties and sects, and in comparison with this aim—a science of history, formulating laws of historical movement, a philosophy of history whose goal was unity—Hallam, Macaulay and Grote, to name three of the most self-consciously 'impartial' contemporary historians, (though, for that matter, Mitford claimed impartiality[2]) are rightly classed with the historians who drew their inspiration from the spirit of party. Whereas the liberalism of this triumvirate was almost their religion, their all-in-all, the liberalism of the Broad Church was grounded on Christianity, on the fundamental religious needs and instincts of the individual. The inspiration of the Liberal Anglicans was the Coleridgean vision of spiritual unity. [180]

It might seem ludicrous to speak of impartiality in writing the history of remote times [Arnold said], did not those times really bear a nearer resemblance to our own than many imagine; or did not Mitford's example sufficiently prove that the spirit of modern party may affect our view of ancient history. But many persons do not clearly see what should be the true impartiality of an historian.[3]

Impartiality, for the Liberal Anglicans, did not mean the absence of a standpoint (the objectivity of the scientist was ultimately impossible in the study of history), [181] it meant having the best standpoint, one which, though itself beyond the domain of the processes of purely political history, was yet in history, and this Christianity alone could provide. They were not historians first and Christians afterwards. The spirit of true history was the spirit of Christian ethics; [182] the Coleridgean ideal: truth uttered in charity was their aim. [183] They saw that real historical understanding meant

---

[1] *Table Talk*, pp. 147, 149.   [2] *History of Greece*, vol. IV, pp. 118, 358.
[3] *Rome*, vol. I, preface, p. x.

sympathy, not judgment. This was a doctrine to which John Mill paid lip service, to the scarcely veiled disgust of the hagiographer of the Utilitarians, Alexander Bain, who wrote that this doctrine, preached by Goethe and echoed by Carlyle, 'was in everybody's mouth and had its fling'.[1] It was a Coleridgean doctrine also.[2] Arnold, alone among the Liberal Anglicans, found it difficult to sympathize with his opponents. His zeal was inclined to outrun his impartiality. Hare said of Milner that 'his inability to understand or sympathize with any other than one special modification of the Christian character' was injurious to his history.[3] Historians, Hare said, were apt to write mainly from the understanding, which has no eye for the rich varieties of real life, but only sees its own forms and fictions, and only one side of human nature—the worst. The historian should be also a poet; he should see human nature as a whole. To gain this insight requires charity as well as imagination. We are apt to try every one that ever lived by our own standard of right and wrong, a standard which is a proper one to try the only persons we never try it by—ourselves.[4]

The question of impartiality, therefore, in its narrower sense of holding the balance fairly, which Macaulay praised in Hallam, did not arise for the Liberal Anglicans, because in their view of history there were no scales to hold. If they were not advocates, like Mitford, neither were they judges, like Hallam.[5] In so far as they did sit in judgment and condemn, as Arnold condemned Caesar, and Thirlwall condemned Alexander the Great, they were acting not in accordance with this strictly historical ideal, but were asserting the claims of an absolute as against a purely historical morality. [185] The finest example of this ideal impartiality provided by the Liberal Anglicans is Milman's *History of Latin Christianity*. [186]. It was an impartiality inherent in their conception of a science of history, and in the broad-minded charity of their practical religion.

[1] *J. S. Mill*, p. 58.
[2] Sanders, *Coleridge and the Broad Church Movement*, p. 62.
[3] *The Means of Unity*, note A.
[4] See Hare's dialogue on poetry and history (*Guesses at Truth* [3rd ed., 1st series], pp. 367 *et seq.*, especially pp. 394, 397-9). [184]
[5] '[Hallam's] work is eminently judicial. Its whole spirit is that of the bench, not that of the bar' (Macaulay, *Essays* [Oxford, 1913], p. 3).

(b) The Romantic Philosophy of Mind

There was nothing original in England about Arnold's quest for a science of history. Such a quest was in the tradition of the historical thought of the 18th century. Utilitarian liberalism, in the hands of J. S. Mill, was to be scientific, resting on a science of history, and Macaulay found it useful to appeal to the inductive method of science, to the tradition of Bacon, to support the Whig interpretation, though this was something of a façade.[1] But the loyalty of the Liberal Anglicans to the tradition of Coleridge and the first generation of Romantics, and their conception of the nature of progress, sundered their idea of history from that of both Whigs and Utilitarians. While Macaulay and the Utilitarians were agreed as to the static nature of morality, progress—the work of individuals, with the state playing the role of policeman only—being essentially intellectual in character (though the phrase 'moral and intellectual progress of Mankind' was sometimes used, illogically, as Buckle was aware, seeing that the men who used it held fast to their belief in the uniformity of human nature), progress for the Liberal Anglicans meant moral progress and could not be conceived apart from the state, which was its prime agent and an essential force in the education of the world. The Utilitarian science of history as seen, for example, in Buckle's *History of Civilization*, was founded on the assumption of a progress exclusively intellectual in character, whose arch-enemy was the 'protective spirit' in whatever form. In Mill's *System of Logic* a science of history meant a science of progress (in the neutral sense of the word, meaning that the course of history never returns upon itself), in alliance with psychology, the universal 'principles of human nature'; the presupposition of the Liberal Anglican science of history, on the other hand, was the cyclical movement of history which Mill ascribes to Vico and rejects. [187] A science of progress, in Mill's sense, was, for the Liberal Angli-

---

[1] Leslie Stephen, *English Utilitarians*, 1900, vol. II, p. 86. *Edinburgh Review*, vol. XLIX, pp. 188-9. For Macaulay's chemical method, see his essay 'On History' in *Critical and Miscellaneous Essays*, Philadelphia, 1841, vol. I, p. 185.

cans, impossible. The 'principles of human nature', which make such a science possible for Mill because they are unchanging, in the Liberal Anglican view are governed by a progressive development which constitutes the education of the world, 'the advance of the moral character of the race', in Goldwin Smith's words. What is static for Mill is dynamic for the Liberal Anglicans, and what constitutes progress in Mill's mind, 'the principal phenomena of society', are, for the Liberal Anglicans, the ground of a possible science of history in so far as they are governed by a law of cyclical movement.

The Utilitarian idea of progress, in fact, was really the Rationalist 18th-century conception, a progress without development, and this was not only because they refused to view the state as a growing organism (the past, as they saw it, being nothing more than an aggregate of hard facts), but further, because development or evolution in history, properly considered, is the development of concrete mind as a whole, not simply the progressive accumulation of intellectual achievement, the march of abstract reason.

According to Leslie Stephen, it was the distrust of the idea of development by the Utilitarians as 'mystical', not springing from experience (that is to say their own experience, in the light of the association psychology, applied to the whole past) which accounts for the inadequacy of their science of history, and it was this evolutionary idea, by which is meant not only, as Cobban[1] has shown, the historic conception of the national community, but, allied to it, the Romantic philosophy of mind, that constituted the inmost nature of the revolt of Coleridge and the first Romantics against the 18th century. It was this two-fold conception that sundered the Liberal Anglican science of history from the Utilitarian science of history, as well as from Whig (and Tory) party history. It is a great gulf fixed between two worlds of thought in 19th-century England. This evolutionary idea is sought in vain in J. S. Mill, and Buckle, in the 'chemical method' of Macaulay and the Whig (and Tory) collection of lessons from historical experience. Of Macaulay, for example, it has been said: 'That society and the human intellect have laws of organic

[1] *Edmund Burke and the Revolt against the 18th Century.*

growth, the stages of which cannot be transposed, any more than the periods of youth and old age can be transposed in the life of an individual, was a conception which never dawned even faintly on Macaulay's mind.'[1]

According to Leslie Stephen, Darwinian theories marked the point at which a doctrine of evolution could be allied with an appeal to experience,[2] but the alliance is seen in Liberal Anglican thought, in a conception of history which stresses the autonomy of the moral and the natural worlds, of history and nature,[3] and which is not indebted to the concept of natural evolution. In the Liberal Anglican science of history an appeal to the 'hard facts' of experience was allied to the evolutionary idea. The 'hard facts' which explained the dynamic evolution of society, for Arnold, were the facts of the class-war, hard and real enough in the England of the first half of the 19th century, but which neither Whigs nor Utilitarians could be expected to welcome as a principle of historical interpretation.

Cobban says that it was not until the empiricism of the Utilitarians and the evolutionary idea of the intuitionists had become linked that the historical movement proper was possible.[4] In that case the pioneers in England of the historical movement proper were the Liberal Anglicans, because the link which Cobban [188] postulates is seen in their historical thought. They appealed to the hard facts of historical experience as well as to the organic conception of the state, and at the same time (and this, in the history of the development of the modern historical outlook, is fundamental) they rejected the Rationalist sensation psychology which demands a universal psychological man, which to the Romantics was a vicious abstraction. And it was because they belonged to the tradition of Burke and Coleridge, and, as Hare said of Niebuhr, 'maintained the historical side of the question in the great controversy as to the first principles of government, in opposition to those who would refer all such matters to the absolute decrees of the reason',[5] that they were open to the

[1] Cotter Morison, *Macaulay* (1882), p. 104.   [2] *English Utilitarians*, vol. III, p. 375.
[3] 'The enlargement of our knowledge—whether in the sphere of nature or of history....' (Thirlwall [1861], *Remains*, vol. III, p. 283).   [4] *Edmund Burke*, p. 262.
[5] *Vindication of Niebuhr* (1829), p. 21.

influence of those German thinkers who were the real exponents of the historical movement proper. They hailed Niebuhr, Savigny and the rest as allies in the struggle against the Rationalists and Radicals. Niebuhr, Hare said exultingly, 'is with Burke and against the Contrat Social'.[1]

The Liberal Anglican interpretation of history, therefore, was an idealist interpretation in two senses; in the first place, their philosophy of society was idealistic, in the Coleridgean tradition. [189] 'Every society', said Arnold, 'must have in it something of community; and so far as the members of it are members, so far as they are each incomplete parts, but taken together form a whole, so far, it appears to me, their joint life is the proper subject of history.'[2] For Stanley the mind of the nation was the concentration in its utmost strength of the moral and intellectual nature of the individual. What in an individual we see faintly, in a state we see distinctly developed, he said; what in solitary cases may be stunted or irregular, in the 'united mind of a whole people' attains its full proportions.[3] Secondly, the Liberal Anglicans interpreted the development of a society in terms of its growing mental life. The changes in the social condition of the nation, as Stanley said, though they may give a colour to its thoughts and feelings, were yet only changes in its outward form.[4] The nation, like the individual, must be interpreted in terms of mental development, of the changes in its inner life. Coleridge, attacking superficial explanations of the French Revolution, had said that that 'which alone deserves the name of a cause' was 'the predominant state of public opinion . . . the ascendancy of speculative principles or the scheme and mode of thinking in vogue'.[5] Hare attacked the 'exoteric' history which accounted mechanical inventions the great agents in the history of mankind, as another form of the Materialism which cannot comprehend or conceive anything except as the product of some external cause. [190] Arnold in his lectures exhorted the would-be student of modern history to begin by reading the contemporary writers (Comines for

[1] *Ibid.* Hare quoted a passage from Niebuhr's *History of Rome*, 'in which the author seems almost to have snatched a feather out of Burke's plumage' (p. 25).
[2] Arnold, *Lectures*, p. 5.   [3] Stanley, *Prize Essay*, pp. 6-7.   [4] *Ibid.* p. 12.
[5] *Statesman's Manual* f 16.

15th-century France, for example) in order to see not only the events of the period, but the minds of the actors and the 'prevailing tone of opinion and feeling'.

The reason of this rule is evident: that it is important to look at an age or country in its own point of view; which of course is best to be obtained from a native and contemporary writer. Such a history is in fact a double lesson: it gives us the actions and the mind of the actors at the same time, telling us not only what was done, but with what motives and in what spirit it was done. Again the language of a native contemporary historian is the language of those of whom he is writing; in reading him we are in some sort hearing them, and an impression of the style and peculiarities of any man's language is an important help towards realizing our notion of him altogether.[1]

Arnold also recommended the study of the second-rate literature of a period, 'in order to discover what was the prevailing tone and taste of men's minds; how they reasoned; what ideas had most possession of them; what they knew and what use they made of their knowledge'. Finally, we must imbue ourselves with the spirit of a period, he said, 'by enquiring into the state of art, whether in painting, sculpture or architecture [Arnold had no ear for music] or as exemplified in matters of common life'.[2]

There is, however, a further sense of the idealist interpretation of history, and that is where history is interpreted in terms, not of the national mind (which is an abstraction), but of the concrete reality of the individual mind. The Liberal Anglicans and Coleridge are both idealistic in this sense when the ideas, the idea of the constitution, of man's moral freedom, and so forth, are emphasized as historical realities existing in the minds of individuals; such ideas, Coleridge said, are 'the most real of all realities'.[3] Arnold, for instance, talked of the *idea* of his life, meaning the object of his personal endeavour, and this is an historical fact. [191] But when Coleridge goes beyond this, [192] upholding, as he appears to do, the reality of ideas independent of the individual, ideas laid up, as it were, in some heaven of historical evolution, the Liberal Anglicans did not follow him. Their interpretation of history is not idealist in this sense. In the face of the crisis of civilization, they even came to doubt the idealist

[1] *Lectures*, pp. 86-7.   [2] *Ibid.* pp. 99, 107.   [3] *Constitution of Church and State*, pp. 7-12.

philosophy of society, because in the breakdown of the community it was the salvation of the individual soul which was all-important. It has been seen how Arnold in 1841 thought that the idealist principle, when fully developed, was contrary to the very essence of Christianity, and how Stanley had shown that the corruption of nations is due solely to the corruption of its individual members. The latent evangelicalism of Liberal Anglican historical thought is incompatible with root-and-branch philosophical idealism, the metaphysical theory of the state. As a result of it, they insisted on the ultimate historical agency of the will of the individual. 'Human character, as modifying and modified by circumstances, man controlling and controlled by events, must be the historian's ultimate object,' Hare said.[1]

Coleridge, moreover, was temperamentally inclined to neglect facts at the expense of principles. According to Muirhead, he would have welcomed the Hegelian dialectic as an illustration on the grand scale of what he meant by a 'directing Idea'.[2] The Liberal Anglicans agreed that history should be read not for the mere facts alone, but for the general principles beneath the facts, and that the only cure for the ills of the day must be sought in 'the collation of the present with the past, in the habit of thoughtfully assimilating the events of our own age to those of the times before us',[3] but their approach was more truly empirical. Arnold, for instance, found Coleridge's *Church and State* 'historically very faulty'.[4] The Liberal Anglicans were, after all, historians in a sense in which Coleridge was not.

History for the Liberal Anglicans, then, was history viewed from within (it was idealistic in this sense; the proper sense where history is concerned) because it was for them the development of concrete mind, not the march of a universal abstract reason, or the unfolding of an idea or ideas. It is interesting to see that Grote, whom Leslie Stephen describes as one of the most orthodox of the Utilitarians, who 'seems to prove that the Utilitarian who was most faithful to his most vital principles was especially qualified

---

[1] *Guesses at Truth* (3rd ed., 1st series), p. 375.
[2] J. H. Muirhead, *Coleridge as Philosopher*, p. 99.
[3] Sanders, *Coleridge and the Broad Church Movement*, pp. 54-5.
[4] Letter of 26 Jan. 1840.

to be a historian',[1] was praised by Stanley for having realized this historical aim in his *History of Greece*, that is to say, for having portrayed the Greek mind in its successive stages of development. Grote's 'great achievement', said Stanley, 'not merely to Grecian history but to all historical study of whatever kind', was 'the keen discrimination with which he presents, not merely distinct characters, but distinct types of character in the lineage of the Grecian mind, whom before we had been accustomed to regard much as we usually regard the fixed stars—their distance from each other being lost in comparison with the distance from ourselves'.[2] In this 'great representative of Utilitarian history', 'more of a Millite than Mill',[3] Stanley acclaims the 'mystical' idea of evolution.

This conception of development, which is of the inmost nature of the historical movement proper, seen first in Vico's psychology of nations, and a presupposition of the whole German historical movement, informs the historical thinking of the Liberal Anglicans, but is not found in those who, like the Utilitarians, Macaulay and Scott, held the assumption underlying the sensation psychology of the uniformity of human nature. To the empirical tradition of Locke, Hartley and the Mills, to which Macaulay and Scott belonged, [194] the Liberal Anglicans (and Carlyle) [195] opposed a Romantic philosophy of mind which is ultimately Vichian in origin. The two worlds of historical thought in England in the first half of the 19th century are thus divided ultimately by psychological theory, and from the critical point of view of modern historical thinking, it is the Vichian element (the historical philosophy of mind) in the Liberal Anglican idea of history which is seen to approximate to a method more truly historical than that of the historians of the Rationalist tradition. Many of the marks of a real historical discipline spring from it, because, if mind has a different hue in different ages, if, in Carlyle's words, 'the inward condition of life . . . is the same in no two ages', the historian, if he is to truly understand the past, must endeavour to

---

[1] Leslie Stephen, *English Utilitarians,* vol. III, p. 337.
[2] Inaugural lecture (1857), *Eastern Church,* p. lii. [193]
[3] Leslie Stephen, *English Utilitarians.*

enter mental worlds which are totally different from his own. If he is to do this, he must find his criteria of experience in the time and place which he is studying, and not import a standard of his own. In order to understand a childhood period, for instance, it is necessary to shuffle off the intellectual coils of a rational age and become child-like, entering the childish mind and viewing its world from within. [196] It is a principle of the Vichian philosophy of mind, for example, that the Old Testament cannot be understood in the light of the New, but only in the light of its own mental life. As Hare said, speaking of the understanding of the Middle Ages, 'the difference is important between the entrance of an object into the mind, and the entrance of the mind into the object.'[1] Truth has a different appearance from age to age, he pointed out, and the only standard of judgment is contained in the living principles which manifest themselves thus diversely. [197] To demand of all ages and countries that they shall correspond in every tittle with our own and to condemn them when they do not, is a vulgar delusion.[2] It is the mark of the unphilosophical class of historians that 'not having a right insight into the necessary distinctions of ages and nations they . . . measure others by their own standard and so misunderstand and misjudge them'.[3] Milman, no doubt with James Mill's *History of India* and perhaps also Macaulay's minute on 'Education in India' in mind, said that the historian should be superior to that 'contemptuous wisdom . . . which refers everything to one standard; and disdainfully condemns, because they differ from preconceived and European notions, all institutions, usages and literature, of which it condescends not to either the origin or the genius'.[4] Of Elphinstone's *History of India*, Milman said it was 'the best, if not the most popular'.[5] Elphinstone had simply described the culture of India, whereas Mill's object had been not to understand it, but to fix it in the scale of civilization, that is to say to judge it by an exterior and arbitrary standard.

---

[1] *Guesses at Truth* (1st ed.), vol. II pp. 63-4.
[2] Hare, 'Romanizing Fallacies', *Charges*, p. 83. [198]
[3] *Guesses at Truth* (2nd ed., 2nd series), p. 71.
[4] *Quarterly Review*, vol. 68, p. 379.
[5] Arthur Milman, *Henry Hart Milman*, p. 200.

As a result of this Vichian philosophy of mind, which is fundamental in their historical thought, the Liberal Anglicans avoided certain errors of historical method embraced by the Positivists. They did not, for example, take natural science as a model for the methods of history, as the Positivists did, because they were aware of the fundamental differences between the historian and the scientist; they saw that the historian, unlike the scientist, does not stand outside his subject; that the historian, as such, can find no objective standpoint; that all purely historical thinking, like other forms of thought, is wholly relative; that the historian is himself in history, and is therefore liable to prejudices and subtle influences which he must constantly guard against.[1] This idea of the relativity of historical thought is a logical result of the Vichian philosophy of mind, according to which the history of an imaginative age is 'poetic history', because all forms of intellectual activity in such an age are 'poetic', while the history of late age is 'reflective history'. As Milman said, 'the early life of Becket has been mystified both by the imaginative tendencies of the age immediately following his own, and by the theorising tendencies of modern history'.[2] Joinville was a 'poetic' historian. 'Each age,' Milman said, 'will have its own characteristic way of looking on the Past; each will have its own philosophy of history; each be misled in the appreciation of characters, or in ascertaining the magnitude of events, by the haze of its own passions and prejudices.'[3] History advances with the movement of the world, and since, as has been seen, according to the Liberal Anglican philosophy of history, this movement is synonymous with the advance of Christianity, 'we must encourage the hope that although not altogether clear, our moral sight will become more keen and just; that our judgements on the past will not only be formed on the more complete evidence of more extensive information, but on sounder, wiser and more truly Christian principles'.[4] Even the idea of the relativity of historical thought is yoked to the needs of practical religion, but such an encouraging outlook as Milman's is only possible on the presupposition of

[1] Thirlwall, *Remains*, vol. III, p. 281-2.   [2] *Latin Christianity*, vol. III, p. 433 n. [199]
[3] *Quarterly Review*, vol. 50 (1834), p. 306.   [4] *Ibid.*

moral progress. Only great faith could turn historical relativism into a gospel of good cheer. Milman was the most optimistic of the Liberal Anglicans.

History, which for the Utilitarians and Positivists was a collection of atomistic facts, was for the Liberal Anglicans ultimately an indivisible whole which included the historian. But this unity of history was not a 'mystical' conception imposed by the historian on the facts, but was reached by way of the abstractions, the scaffolding, as it were, of the science of history, which, in its turn, rested on a study of the past for its own sake, in other words, on what Positivists call the 'hard facts' of history. But this ground of the Liberal Anglican idea of history was much broader than the historical experience of the Positivists and Utilitarians, because it included that imaginative experience which the latter tended to despise and reject. In an idealist interpretation of history, properly so called, the only historical facts are ideas. Hare examined the nature of historical facts and pointed out that they are composed of the different, often divergent, ideas of witnesses. 'Very few histories tell us what has really happened. They tell us what somebody or other once conceived to have happened, somebody liable to all the infirmities, physical, intellectual and moral, by which man's judgement is distorted.'[1] For Milman the miracles and angelic appearances of the New Testament were 'hard facts'; whether they were 'actual appearances or impressions produced in the mind of those who witnessed them, is of slight importance. In either case, they are real historical facts.'[2] Of the miracles surrounding the life of St Benedict, Milman said, 'History, to be true, must condescend to speak the language of legend; the belief of the times is part of the record of the times.'[3] 'Fiction at times becomes history. It is as important to know what men were believed to do, as what they actually did.'[4] The Liberal Anglicans believed that fiction was fact for the historian, and that miracles happened in so far as they were believed to have happened. The most valuable part of history, Arnold believed, was 'that which relates to a people's mental powers and habits of thinking'. Here

[1] *Guesses at Truth* (3rd ed., 1st series), p. 368. See also pp. 372-3, 374.
[2] *Christianity*, vol. I, p. 131. [3] *Latin Christianity*, vol. I, p. 415. [4] *Ibid.* vol. III, p. 545.

also, Grote departed from his orthodox Utilitarianism. The very fact that he did not believe in the historical basis of the Greek myths makes it all the more significant that he should devote the first two books of his history to them as examples of imaginative experience.

It is a corollary of the Vichian philosophy of mind that the field of historical experience is not bounded by the 'common sense' or any other criterion of the historian. As R. G. Collingwood has shown, the historian's criterion of experience is not a ready-made body of experience by which he judges the statements contained in his authorities, not a standard of common sense or probability, but his experience *qua* historian.[1] The Liberal Anglicans did not formulate a statement like this, but a similar attitude is pre-supposed in their historical thinking, in particular, in their revolt against the 18th century and its standard of rational experience.

It is clear, from what has been said, that the word 'Romantic' must bear a special meaning in the history of history, if it is to be of any use. To use the same word to describe the historical thinking of Scott and Macaulay and that of the Liberal Anglicans and Carlyle is obviously stretching it beyond the limits of usefulness. The real test is the Vichian or Romantic philosophy of mind, as opposed to the Rationalist uniformity of human nature; this, from the point of view of the history of history, successfully separates the sheep from the goats.

It was because the Liberal Anglicans were Romantics in this sense that the influence on their thought of Scott and 'local colour' history was negligible in comparison with the influence of the German historical movement. The Liberal Anglicans were concerned with this movement in the three main departments of classical philology, Biblical criticism and the philosophy of language; but in all three departments the Vichian philosophy of mind was a fundamental presupposition, it being the aim of the new critical technique to examine its objects in the light of the larger historical whole of which they formed a part, the mental life of a people at a given period. [200]

---

[1] *The Idea of History*, pp. 139-40.

'Local colour' history and antiquarianism help in the understanding of the mind of past ages only in so far as the externals, in
which they delight, are seen as the expression of that mind and
used to gain insight into it, but by the English local-colour
Romantics the outward trappings were not used for this purpose. [201] Scott's resurrection of the past is historically convincing
only so long as the world which he is describing is his own world
of experience, or one very near to it. Rationalist historian as he
was, he did not recognize the existence of whole mental worlds
fundamentally different from his own. The theory underlying the
historical reconstruction of the Waverley Novels was the 18th
century doctrine that men are everywhere fundamentally the same
in their mental habits. Tried by the test of the Vichian psychology of nations, Scott is a Rationalist and Sensationalist. [202]
Hare described his 'genius' as 'external' and 'superficial'[1]; these
are the stigmas of Rationalism, which, according to Hare, 'had
done little more than skim the froth of history'.[2] If the novels of
Scott served as an incentive in the resurrection of the past, and
this cannot be denied, he was no safe guide where the Middle
Ages or Antiquity were concerned. The Liberal Anglicans had to
extend the understanding which he showed in the 'Scotch novels'
to types of mind remote from their own; the problem did not
exist for Scott. To do this, they had to assert the historical canon
which is diametrically opposite to that of the Rationalists: that
the historian entering the mind of the past should begin by
expecting to find in it nothing similar to his own world of experience; [204] that the historian's mind must be ready to receive
and consider anything, things even which are outside his personal
experience and the experience of his age, because to reject such
things is to apply an arbitrary standard to the past, such as the
Rationalist standard of enlightenment. The assault on the criterion
of the uniformity of rational experience, which is the basis of the
scepticism of the enlightenment, in particular of Hume's *Essay on
Miracles*, [205] and the much-quoted example of the King of Siam
who refused to believe in the existence of ice, [206] used for the

---

[1] *Guesses at Truth* (3rd ed., 1st series), p. 81.
[2] *Mission of the Comforter* (3rd ed., note H), p. 270. [203]

same purpose by Carlyle, is related in Liberal Anglican thought, as in Carlyle, to a deeper understanding of history, to the Vichian philosophy of mind, according to which the uniformity of experience applies only to man as a 'digesting-machine', not as the possessor of a mind.

More vital to the historian than the 'local colour' of the Romanticists, therefore, from the Liberal Anglican point of view, was philology and the philosophy of language as studied in Germany, studied, that is, in the light of history, as allied to and inseparable from history, which was in effect a deeper understanding of the use of 'local colour' in the reconstruction of the past, 'local colour' being related to the particular, concrete mind of a people at a given stage in its development.

Hare believed with Vico and the German philologists (those of the historical school) that 'philology ought to be only another name for philosophy in its highest sense'. 'Its aim', he said, 'should be to seek after wisdom in the whole series of its historical manifestations. As it is the former usually mumbles the husk, the other paws the kernel.'[1] In 1866 Thirlwall wished it could be said that the 'abuse of classical literature', the study of things for the sake of words and not words for the sake of things, was altogether a thing of the past among ourselves.[2]

Words still formed the greater part of the historical evidence left by the past, and language was the most immediate and intelligibly self-revealing expression of mind with which the historian had to deal. [208] Donaldson, a philologer of the German, as opposed to the Bentley-Porson, school, whom Arnold described as 'almost the only Englishman who promises . . . to be a really good philologer',[3] wrote in 1839:

There is in fact no sure way of tracing the history . . . of the early inhabitants of the world except by means of their languages. . . . It may seem strange that any thing so vague and arbitrary as language should survive all other testimonies, and speak with more definiteness, even in its changed and modern state, than all other monuments however grand and durable. Yet so it is: we have the proof before us every hour.[4]

---

[1] *Guesses at Truth* (2nd ed., 2nd series), p. 326. [207] [2] *Remains*, vol. III, pp. 306-7.
[3] Letter to Bunsen, 25 Feb. 1840. [4] *New Cratylus*, p. 11.

Emphasis on the importance of the distinction between words and things was a legacy of the Noetics to the Liberal Anglican idea of history, handed on from Copleston[1] to Whately, and from Whately to Arnold; [209] from being a logical axiom (as found first in Copleston) and then a principle of the Noetic revolt against the prevailing textual and purely verbal classical 'scholarship', it became a maxim of history, blending ultimately with German historical philology. It was a corollary of the Liberal Anglican science of history that words, to be properly understood, must be studied in relation to their historical background, because their content alters with the development of the national mind. As Arnold, for example, pointed out, the names of parties, the terms 'popular' and 'anti-popular' used in political history, mean nothing outside their historical context, and have to be seen in relation to the social progress of states. German philology opened a wider prospect; nothing less than the vision of the essential oneness and universality of all aspects of historical study as the reconstruction of the mental life of the past.

The philology of the German school was Vichian and implied the reconstruction of the past in its wholeness; it was a reconstruction of the mind of the past; in Wilhelm von Humboldt's words, philology was 'the knowledge of human nature as exhibited in antiquity', for Boeckh, it was 'Erkenntniss des Erkannten', *cogniti cognitio*. [210] For the Liberal Anglicans it was the glory of German philology that it studied every aspect of the expression of an age, everything which was of significance in the interpretation of a particular mental life.

Of Heyne, Donaldson wrote, 'The difference between him and his predecessors consisted mainly in this, that he did not limit his investigations to the narrower field of the ancient authors, but combined it with all the newly applicable resources of the archaeology of art, of the principles of taste, and of literature in general,' and of Winckelmann, that he 'laid the foundations of the archaeology of art, a most important application of philology in the wider sense of the word.'[2]

The true scholar [Donaldson said] is . . . not merely a student of the

---

[1] Whately, *Remains of the late Edward Copleston*, p. 123.   [2] *New Cratylus*, p. 25.

Greek and Latin languages and an interpreter of the authors who have written in them. It is his business to lift the curtain which has fallen on the glories of the past: to bring Athens and Rome again upon the stage, to enable the modern reader to regard the old authors and the events of which they write with the eyes of a contemporary. . . . The Greek and Latin authors must be read together and in connection, and we must endeavour to peruse them with as little interruption as possible from modern and extrinsic associations.[1]

The sources of history, therefore, were not confined to the written word. For Vico, medieval heraldry, for example, was a language, and Milman echoed this principle of interpretation when he described the ceremonial of the medieval church, the painting and sculpture, as the 'vernacular tongue of Christianity, universally intelligible . . . .'[2] 'Original records', Stanley said, 'are not confined merely to contemporaneous histories, nor even to contemporaneous literature . . . .' 'Study, if possible, the scenes of the events, their aspect, their architecture, their geography, the tradition which has survived the history, the legend which has survived the tradition, the mountain, the stream, the shapeless stone which has survived even history and tradition and legend.'[3] Stanley had acted on this principle in his travels in Sinai and Palestine (1852-3). 'What insight into the familiar feelings and thoughts of the primitive ages of the Church can be compared to that afforded by the catacombs', he said, criticizing Gibbon and Mosheim for 'hardly noticing' them.[4]

The Liberal Anglicans were perhaps the first English historians (apart from antiquarians) to indulge in extensive and systematic travel, as historians (Stanley visited every country about which he lectured, including Russia), realizing, as O. Müller realized, that the country itself is one of the chief documents of the historian. [211] Arnold wrote: 'I can better fancy the actors when I have got a lively notion of the scene on which they are acting.'[5] and in his lectures stressed the importance of geography in the study of history. This attitude should be contrasted with that of James Mill, who stated expressly, in setting out the qualifications of the

1 *New Cratylus*, p. 36.   2 *Christianity*, vol. I, p. 131.
3 *Eastern Church*, p. lvii.   4 *Ibid.* p. lviii.
5 Letter of 12 Apr. 1840.

historian, that personal knowledge of a country, 'a residence in India or a knowledge of the languages of India', far from being necessary to the understanding of its history, was, in fact, 'to express myself moderately, not indispensable'.[1] Grote never visited Greece and, compared with the Liberal Anglican interest in historical geography, Macaulay's visits to the scenes of historical events were antiquarian in their aim; his interest is external, and if he can compare foreign scenes to the English countryside, he is delighted to do so.[2] In this context, Macaulay must be judged not by these excursions, but by his minute on 'Education in India', which would have received the approval of James Mill. The historical geography of the Liberal Anglicans, on the other hand, was allied to the Romantic philosophy of mind; its two sources were German philology and the rediscovery by the Lake Poets of the interaction of locality and mind. [212] 'As the poetry of the Asiatic nations may be termed the poetry of the sun, so the Edda is the poetry of ice,' said Hare. Geography was a clue to the varying types of mental life of different nations. Hare pointed out, for example, that nature was the mother of the imaginative mind of nations in their infancy, which for a long time scarcely regards itself as separate from nature. 'When it speaks, you rather hear the voice of Nature speaking through it, than any distinct voice of its own.'[3] Stanley (who knew Hare and had read the *Guesses at Truth*) in his Greek tour of 1840-1 'felt ... how poetical had been the mind of the Greek nation, how deeply it was impregnated with the general spirit of the scenery', and 'delighted to trace its mythology in the action and reaction which existed between the scenery and the imagination of Greece. He felt that natural objects determined the national belief',[4] and, in his *Sinai and Palestine* (1856), he wrote, 'the most important results of the insight into the geographical features of any country are those which elucidate in any degree the general character of the nation to which it has furnished a home'.[5]

---

[1] *History of British India*, preface, p. xiii.   [2] Trevelyan, *Life and Letters*, p. 498.
[3] *Guesses at Truth* (3rd ed., 1st series), pp. 54-5. Homer was 'the father of poetry springing in the freshness and simplicity of childhood out of the arms of mother earth' (p. 60).   [4] Prothero, *Life*, vol. I, pp. 271-2.
[5] *Sinai and Palestine in connection with their history*, p. xii.

For the Liberal Anglicans, the encyclopaedic knowledge of the past which was essential to historical reconstruction, philology as studied in Germany was, in the words of Wolf, not an aggregate but a whole. Its goal was the interpretation of a mental life in its complete individuality. It was the influence of the German historical movement, with its presupposition of the Vichian philosophy of mind, which made the Liberal Anglicans pioneers in England of the historical movement proper, and they were open to the full refreshing force of this influence because they had rejected the sensation psychology which, more than the general ignorance of German prevailing at this time, more even than the individualism of the Utilitarians, was the real barrier in England to a true historical method.

The experience to which the Liberal Anglicans appealed was thus much deeper and fuller than that of the Utilitarians or Positivists, because the science of history, which the Liberal Anglicans saw was possible on the levels of political and intellectual history, and which for the Utilitarians was all-in-all, was for the former only a part of the whole historical field, and that not the most vital part. They probed beneath these levels to the working of mind in all its manifestations, but the Romantic vision of the essential unity of historical reconstruction was not an end in itself. [213] For them, as for Vico and the Germans, philology and philosophy, properly considered, were one, and the end, as always, of this fuller experience was the practical application of the new history. Philological, historical and philosophical research was, in Arnold's words, to minister to divine truth.[1]

The revolution caused by the Vichian philosophy of mind in English historiography is illustrated by the contrast between Milman's interpretation of the Middle Ages and that of Hallam. Hallam, with his Rationalist lack of sympathy, made no attempt to understand the medieval mind. Milman, like Hallam, refused to patronize the Middle Ages in the unhistorical romantic way [214] (there is nothing so unhistorical as patronage of the past), but, unlike Hallam, his aim was to understand the medieval mind, interpreting it in accordance with the Vichian psychology as an

[1] Letter to Bunsen, 10 Feb. 1835.

imaginative period, and from the point of view of universal history, and in accordance with the Vichian philosophy of history, as a second imaginative period. (To understand any past age, Hare said, we should consider it in a two-fold light; first gain the fullest and most definite conception of its peculiar features and character; and then contemplate it with reference to the place it holds in the history of the world.)[1] Together with this emphasis on the continuity of history (the place of the Middle Ages in universal history), which is lacking in Hallam, goes Milman's clear notion of the unity of medieval civilization in itself, as an imaginative religious era, organized outwardly round the monarchial unity of the Papacy. [215] Hallam had organized his sketch of the Middle Ages round the nations of Europe, thus projecting his view of 19th-century Europe into the Middle Ages, missing the outward unity of the period by neglecting its essentially religious character and failing therefore to see its inner unity. Milman's *History of Latin Christianity* was hailed by Stanley as a complete epic and philosophy of medieval Christendom.[2] In his inaugural lectures he singled it out as an example of ecclesiastical history in the true sense of the word. [216] It is only in histories of historiography that Milman is an 'ecclesiastical' historian in any narrower sense.

Thus the imagination, distrusted by orthodox Utilitarians and Positivists, was seen by the Liberal Anglicans to be essential to the understanding of history. [217] Their position, in fact, was akin, in many striking resemblances, to that which was later systematized and made self-conscious by idealist philosophers reacting against Positivitism in the second half of the 19th century, because these thinkers (Dilthey and Croce and the rest) were only thinking out in full the implications of the historical practice of Vico and the German movement. The Liberal Anglicans may be said to represent in England the tradition of real historical thinking, as against the Positivists, who represented a revitalized 18th-century Rationalism inimical to it, and it is this element of true historical understanding—the Vichian or Romantic philosophy of mind—in the Liberal Anglican idea of history which must be considered

---

[1] *Guesses at Truth* (2nd ed., 2nd series), p. 72.   [2] *Life of Milman*, p. 224.

as truly historical and belonging to the historical movement proper. In this we see something which is neither science, nor philosophy, nor the philosophy of history, but history in its own right, a discipline which asserts its independence by handling science, philosophy and the philosophy of history according to methods which are its own.

(c) A Vindication of the Liberal Anglican Science of History

The same critical outlook which appreciates this element of true history in the Liberal Anglican approach to the past must condemn the whole apparatus of the 'science of history', remembering however that on the one hand, together with this vision of a possible science based on the facts of historical development, went the rejection by the Liberal Anglicans of *a priori* systems of history, such as that of Hegel, and on the other hand, that they took no short cuts to the science of history such as led to the Utilitarian cul-de-sac of Buckle's *History of Civilization*, or to the absurdities, based on the analogy between the life of the state and the life of the individual, the starting-point of Arnold's science of history, of Draper's *Intellectual Development of Europe*. The delight in the complexity of history, which was the mark of Romanticism, as well as their very desire for a scientific practical history [218] had this healthy effect on their historical thinking: they saw that the idea of the unity of the periods of history must not mean a neglect of the 'recessive' factors in favour of the 'dominant', which is the great failing of all attempts at a science of history from Buckle to Spengler. [219] It has already been seen how fully aware they were of the limitations and difficulties of the science of history. They did not attempt to iron out the strains and stresses of historical movement. 'He who would learn wisdom from the complex experience of history', said Arnold, 'must question closely all its phenomena, must notice that which is less obvious as well as that which is most palpable, must judge not peremptorily or sweepingly but with reserves and exceptions.' Historical oversimplification was the great weakness of the Oxford Movement.[1] Moreover, their divisions of the past are not self-contained; their

---

[1] *Sermons*, vol. IV, introduction, p. vi.

periods and epochs are bound together dynamically. Events in one period produce results in another, the characteristics of one period survive into the next, and ultimately all history possesses the unity of a great progressive evolution. [220]

Moreover, if history is not a science, the Liberal Anglicans never conceived a science of history which comprehended the whole past and was the final interpretation of its processes, because they could not accept the ultimate identification of the moral and natural worlds which such a science of history implied. When J. S. Mill hailed Arnold as a pioneer in England of the science of history (though, according to Mill, he showed only 'few and faint' signs of being one), [221] he did not point out that Arnold's thought went beyond the science of history, the extension of natural laws to the past of mankind (which for Mill was the ultimate stage of 'historical philosophy'), to a world of moral progress, a philosophy of history, in which these laws had no existence. The lack of such a philosophy of history was noticed by Stanley in Grote's *History of Greece*. [222] The Liberal Anglican dichotomy of the world of nature governed by natural law, and the moral world of progress in which men are free agents under God's Providence, is the basis of Goldwin Smith's attack on the science of history of Comte and the 'Necessarians'. 'Effort is the law, if law it is to be called, of history', he said,[1] and this is the kernel of Liberal Anglican thought. The science of history foundered on the rock of the individual will, and it became necessary at this point, as has been seen, to change ship.

The Liberal Anglicans realized that there were analogies between 'natural history' and history properly so-called (in both the processes of development were gradual), [223] but although they were in close contact with some of the founders of geology (Arnold, whose interest in geology was life-long, was the friend of Buckland, Thirlwall of Sedgwick—both Buckland and Sedgwick, however, were 'catastrophists'),[2] their conception of history developed independently of the concept of natural evolution. The autonomy of the moral world was fundamental in their idea

[1] Goldwin Smith, *Lectures* (1859–61), p. 95.
[2] J. W. Judd, *The Coming of Evolution*, pp. 28, 44.

of history, and the uniformitarianism of 19th-century evolution is analogous to Rationalist history, with its presupposition of the uniformity of experience, not to Vichian history, in which there is no such uniformity. [224] The Liberal Anglican attitude to Darwinian evolution was summed up by Stanley: 'It is not the descent, but the ascent of man which reveals his true nature.'[1] If the ultimate historical reality was the individual will, as the Liberal Anglicans believed, 'natural' history, history governed by laws like the world of nature, was a contradiction in terms where progress was concerned, and held good only on the levels of the science of history. Law could not govern the whole historical world as it governed the natural world, because progress was dependent on the moral effort of the individual.

The object of the Liberal Anglican science of history was the attempt to discover certain general laws of social and intellectual movement as a guide and a sure basis for action in the practical problems of the condition of England and the crisis of civilization. This attempt was of benefit to the study of history in England in that it postulated a widening of the historian's field of study and a greater emphasis on social and cultural, as opposed to purely political, history. As Arnold said, 'It should be borne in mind that history looks generally at the political state of a nation; its social state, which is infinitely more important, and in which lie the seeds of all the greatest revolutions, is too commonly neglected or unknown.'[2] For Milman, history 'will embrace everything which concerns man, religion, laws, manners, usages, the whole of human life'.[3] This broadening of the historian's field of study was essentially practical; the Liberal Anglican motive in this respect was the same as Macaulay's when, in his essay 'On History' (1828), he called for a broader study of history. [225] In neither case was it primarily a romantic motive, a delight in social history for its own sake; it was essentially the same practical motive as that of the 'philosophical' historians of the 18th century. Such a widening of the field of historical study, therefore, was by no means an innovation on the part of the Liberal Anglicans, nor on the part of

[1] *American Sermons*, p. 206 (1878).   [2] *Rome*, vol. II, p. 368.
[3] *Jews* (4th ed.), vol. I, preface, pp. iii–iv.

Macaulay, nor was there anything original in their assault on the dignity of history. It was of the nature of the 'philosophical history' of the Rationalists to deal with many aspects of civilization beneath the notice of the so-called dignity of history. [226] This was true, for example, of Priestley's *Lectures on History*, which Arnold read in his boyhood and mentioned in his lectures at Oxford, though the best example is provided by the 'grand sociological display' (as Bain called it) of the second book of James Mill's *History of India*. Coleridge attacked the dignity of history in his *Biographia Literaria*, [227] also from a practical point of view, and Whately, in 1818, declared that he defended the Waverley Novels on the grounds that private individuals and minor occurrences, taken collectively, were of higher importance than the great characters and events of history.[1] When, later, therefore, Whately insisted on the importance of the ordinary day-to-day transactions of men, as against wars and revolutions which only hindered 'progress', [228] he was carrying on the tradition of Eden, Macpherson, Hall and the statistical historians of the late 18th century.

The Liberal Anglican revolution, which Whately does not seem to have comprehended fully, consisted not in the widening of the sphere of historical interest, but in viewing the new factors as parts of a whole, of an organism which goes through different stages of growth, with different characteristics at each stage. It was the conception of the wholeness of all aspects of the nation's life which was new in English historiography.

Another result of the Liberal Anglican idea of history, due more exclusively to the Liberal Anglicans than the widening of the sphere of historical interest, was the historical approach to the Bible, which they were practically the first in England to regard as neither above nor beneath the notice of critical historians. This last fortress to stand out against the advance of the historical spirit in England was betrayed, as it were, from within, by churchmen militant against Rationalism, who regarded the Old Testament as constituting a cycle of universal history, amenable to law (from the point of view of the science of history), and a natural part of a

[1] *Life and Correspondence*, vol. I, p. 37.

greater whole. In a 'people of the Book' such as were the English, in an age of bibliolatry (so it seemed to Coleridge and the Liberal Anglicans), this represented a signal triumph for the spirit of history.

Finally, it was a corollary of the science of history that the study of the past should be as scientific in technique as possible. It is this aspect of Liberal Anglican history, their introduction of the critical methods of the Germans, their admiration of Niebuhr, their appreciation of Ranke, their dependence on O. Müller and many others, which has attracted the attention of later historians. Because this study of the Liberal Anglicans is not primarily concerned with the workshops of historians, with the technological aspect of their activity, it is sufficient to notice that, in the Liberal Anglican idea of history, scientific history and a science of history are found together, the latter undoubtedly acting as a spur to the former, because if the foundations, knowledge of the past, were not constructed with the most scientific and critical apparatus possible, there could be no confidence in any structure raised on the foundations. The basis of the whole structure of the Liberal Anglican idea of history was in fact the critical study of the past for its own sake, which is what is meant by history at the present day.

It has not been pointed out, either, in the story of Niebuhr's influence in England, that his historical 'intuition' would present no barrier to his acceptance by historians of the Coleridgean school, whereas Macaulay could not accept it;[1] and it was George Cornewall Lewis, a Utilitarian in spirit if not in name, who demolished this part of his method.

Intermingled with error, therefore, in the Liberal Anglican idea of history are many aspects of what has later come to be considered as correct historical method. The Liberal Anglican science of history, to a much greater extent than the Utilitarian and Positivist structures, and just in so far as it was hesitant because inseparably bound to a deeper experience, looks to the future, at least where history proper is concerned. In condemning the structure as a whole, there is much which can be taken artificially from

---

[1] G. O. Trevelyan, *Life and Letters*, p. 316.

its place in the Liberal Anglican science of history, and applauded as belonging to the tradition of history proper. This is true also of the Liberal Anglican philosophy of history.

(d) A Vindication of the Liberal Anglican Philosophy of History

The philosophy of history, the assertion of a purpose governing the whole past, is generally considered at the present day to be no business of the historian as such, it is *ignoratio elenchi*. Nevertheless, two life-giving historical doctrines spring from the Liberal Anglican belief in its validity: the indivisibility of history, and the ultimate historical reality of the individual mind.

For the Liberal Anglicans, sacred and profane history were one, not because all history is one on the level of the science of history (the truths of 'sacred' history are not found on this plane of experience), but because all men, as a fact of history, are fundamentally religious, all civilization has its origin in the religious instinct (as Vico taught), and progress is the education of the human race in Christian morality. The idea of the education of the human race as a moral development binds all history together into one whole, and the idea of the unity of the human race is a necessary presupposition of the philosophy of history. Freeman, in his conception of the unity of history, emphasized linguistic uniformity as the basis of his belief in its validity. It is the comparative method in philology, he said, which has taught us 'that the study of history is one study . . . that no parts of history are more truly modern—if by modern we mean full of living interest and teaching for our own times—than those which the delusive name of "ancient" would seem to brand as something which has wholly passed away, something which, for any practical loss in these later times, may safely be forgotten'.[1] This was an echo of Thomas Arnold, but the unity of history of the Liberal Anglicans was primarily a teleological unity, in fact, a Christian philosophy of history. Man was 'the same in all ages' for them because he was a religious being, and because the goal of all history was spiritual unity. There was a 'unity of history' (if the term is to

[1] Freeman, *The Unity of History* (1872), pp. 9-11.

be applied to Freeman's idea) in the 18th-century conception (fundamental in the Rationalist view of history) of man as everywhere and at all times possessing the same mental machinery (machinery of perception and association being 'mind'). [229] It is this view which corresponds to uniformitarianism in geology, [230] the one being, from the point of view of the intuitionists, no less mindless than the other. The Liberal Anglicans would have called it a 'uniformity of history', corresponding to the uniformity of the processes of the science of history. Freeman's conception also, from the Liberal Anglican point of view, is a uniformity rather than a unity, being actual, not potential. [231] The whole object of the Liberal Anglican philosophy of history was to show that progress depends entirely on the efforts of individual men; as such it was a reaction against the logical end of a science of history carried à outrance: Determinism. In the Liberal Anglican idea of history, the unity of the philosophy of history stands over against the uniformity of science; in followers of Coleridge, there can be no doubt which was the more vital conception. Thus the Liberal Anglican philosophy of history is grounded firmly, like their theology, on that ultimate historical reality: the individual will.

This view of man's relation to an infinite whole—the education of the human race; the infinity which is experience—this vision of unity, is an essential of romanticism.[1] It is fundamental in the thought of Carlyle, [232] whom most observers agree in describing as the epitome of romantic history in England, and Carlyle's was the contemporary conception of history in England which the Liberal Anglican idea most closely approaches. (All the Liberal Anglicans admired Carlyle; Arnold and Thirlwall were his personal friends.) Though the systematic uniformity of a science of history is wanting in Carlyle (because he thought that our knowledge of experience, such as it was, was not sufficient to form the ground of such a science[2])—and in this he had broken more completely than the Liberal Anglicans with the Rationalist tradition—the conception of the rhythmic nature of historical movement, which is a presupposition of the Liberal Anglican science of history, underlies all his thought. [233] For Carlyle, too,

[1] Cf. Muirhead, *Coleridge as Philosopher*, p. 28.　　　　　[2] See 'On History'.

history which was not a conscious relation of past and present was mere antiquarianism, and Arnold recognized in the *French Revolution* a work of practical history. [234] Both Carlyle and the Liberal Anglicans regarded *a priori* systems of history as blarney, [235] both Arnold and Carlyle had little faith in purely speculative reasoning. Carlyle, too, had rejected perfectibility and distrusted progress, and was militant against rationalism, utilitarianism, and mechanical psychology. History, for Carlyle as for the Liberal Anglicans, dealt with concrete mind (the essence of innumerable biographies), not abstract reason. [236] For both, man was fundamentally a religious being. The crisis of civilization dominated Carlyle's thought, also, [237] and his response was the Liberal Anglican appeal to the individual to work while it is day. For both, the historical spirit was the spirit of sympathy, not judgment.[1] Finally, if, as has been recently demonstrated, Carlyle's profoundest interest was in social biography, then it coincides with that of Arnold. Both men were absorbed, as historians, by the mechanism of change. [238]

(e) Conclusion

For J. S. Mill, it was the possibility of a science of history which constituted the great revolution in historiography in the 19th century. He did not point out that the science of history, as he conceived it, stood in the unbroken 18th-century Rationalist tradition, and that for history the fundamental revolution was the Romantic, Vichian philosophy of mind, because he would not have admitted the validity of this philosophy. Even Lecky, who was no Utilitarian, apparently did not see that between Vico on one side and Condorcet on the other there was the unbridgeable gulf of incompatible psychological theories, and he places both thinkers in the same tradition of philosophical history.[2] In the same undiscerning way he classes together the scepticism of Vico, Beaufort and Niebuhr.[3] This is because Lecky was indebted to both traditions, that of Milman and Coleridge, and that of Buckle

[1] Morley contrasts Carlyle's sympathy with Macaulay's habit of always judging (*Miscellanies*, vol. I, pp. 182-5).

[2] See *A Victorian Historian* (1947) (Lecky's private letters), p. 10.

[3] *European Morals* (1946), vol. II, p. 82.

and Condorcet. It is this spirit of compromise, this scarcely conscious reconciliation of opposites, this eclecticism which is the result of a failure to approach the history of history historically, that would make an investigation into the influence of the Liberal Anglican idea of history so difficult a task. Fortunately it is one which is beyond the scope of this study.

It only remains to exercise that final task of the historian: the application of a tourniquet. Such a tourniquet is applied by Cobban to the flow of thought of Burke and Coleridge, when he says: 'The leaders of the first generation of romanticism died one by one, beaten and broken men, perishing among the spears of triumphant Victorianism, in which the individualist and utilitarian eighteenth century came finally into its own',[1] because the ideas of those men, strongly reinforced by German historical speculation and method, passed into the Liberal Anglican idea of history. How far the ideas of the Liberal Anglicans themselves perished amidst the spears of triumphant positivism (one aspect of the 18th century coming into its own) is another problem. It is because most modern historical thought has passed beyond the positivist stage, that the Liberal Anglicans, with all their errors, are seen in this chapter as marching on the highroad of history proper, not wandering among the byways of pseudo-history. The future progress of historical thinking alone can decide whether they will continue to occupy the crown of the road. Meanwhile, an understanding of the Liberal Anglican idea of history is the key to the development, in England, of what Renan has called the true philosophy of the 19th century: the historical movement proper.

---

[1] A. Cobban, *Edmund Burke*, p. 273.

NOTES

[1] THOMAS ARNOLD (1795-1842): Headmaster of Rugby, 1828; Regius Professor of Modern History at Oxford, 1841.

RICHARD WHATELY (1787-1863): leading 'Noetic' at Oriel; succeeded Nassau Senior as Professor of Political Economy, 1829; Archbishop of Dublin, 1831.

JULIUS CHARLES HARE (1795-1855): disciple of Coleridge; translator (with Thirlwall) of Niebuhr's *History of Rome* (begun 1827); Lecturer in Classics at Trinity College, Cambridge, 1822-32.

CONNOP THIRLWALL (1797-1875): *History of Greece*, 1835-44; Bishop of St David's, 1840.

HENRY HART MILMAN (1791-1868): Professor of Poetry at Oxford, 1821-31; Dean of St Paul's, 1849.

ARTHUR PENRHYN STANLEY (1815-81): pupil and biographer of Thomas Arnold; Dean of Westminster, 1864.

[2] Klaus Dockhorn, *Der Deutsche Historismus in England* (Göttingen, 1949) deals with Thomas Arnold, Julius Hare and Thirlwall in connection with the influence of the German 'Historical Movement' in England. It is the only work that I have seen which realizes the importance of the Liberal Anglicans in the history of English historiography, and I take this opportunity of acknowledging my indebtedness to it. I have referred to it in my notes.

[3] 'The cloud still led the way; but their prudent leader likewise secured the assistance of Hotah . . . who . . . had been accustomed to traverse the desert' (*History of the Jews*, vol. I, p. 141).

[4] In 1839 Arnold saw Wordsworth receive an honorary degree at Oxford, and wrote: 'remembering how old Coleridge inoculated a little knot of us with the love of Wordsworth, when his name was in general a bye-word, it was striking to witness the applause' (Letter of 6 July 1839). The letters of Arnold quoted in these references are from the *Life* by Stanley.

[5] Cf. Hare: 'We must bear in thought that the progress of mankind, if there be any, has . . . as is plain from every portion of history, never been uniform and rectilinear; that according to the law of the whole creation, it has had its periods of alternation, its ebbs and flows, its nights and days, its winters and summers, and that these may

have been measured out by centuries; that the same life does not go on waxing in vigour indefinitely, but wanes and decays and perishes, though succeeded by other lives, in such a manner that the realm of life is continually enlarging; that the blossoms do not remain on the tree along with the fruit, but fall off to make way for the fruit, which however does not ripen until after an interval of comparative bareness' (*Mission of the Comforter* [3rd ed.], p. 273 n. 11).

[6] Belief in the perfectibility and progressiveness of mankind, according to Hare, was a late growth in the world of thought and full of errors, yet a belief in accordance with the precepts of Christianity (*Guesses at Truth* [2nd ed., 2nd series], p. 75).

[7] Cf. also p. 246: 'All large states have their savages; the richest and most civilised the worst' (*Guesses at Truth*).

[8] There is a good warning in *The Idea of Nature* (p. 128) where Collingwood describes 'that frivolous and superficial type of history which speaks of "influences" and "borrowings" and so forth, and when it says that A is influenced by B or that A borrows from B never asks itself what there was in A that laid it open to B's influence, or what there was in A which made it capable of borrowing from B'.

[9] Cf. Milman in 1831: 'The *Scienza Nuova* of G. B. Vico has at length been translated into both German and French, and coinciding in a remarkable manner with the tone of thinking prevalent among the continental writers of the present day, many of whose speculations it had anticipated, is acquiring a tardy fame and winning its way to something like a European reputation' (*Quarterly Review*, vol. 44, pp. 128 *et seq.*). Milman's edition of the *Scienza Nuova* was the 2nd. (1730).

For Vico's reputation and influence in England see Fisch and Bergin, *The Autobiography of G. Vico*, pp. 83 *et seq.*; Robert Flint, *Vico*, p. 231. Croce's appendix II (*The Philosophy of Giambattista Vico*, London, 1913) deals with Vico's European influence.

[10] His mind, Hare said in his preface to Arnold's *History of Rome*, vol. III, was rather that of the statesman than the philosopher. 'Arnold, who had a deeper feeling than any man, perhaps, of his own standing, for the evils in the social condition of England and who, directly and indirectly, had done more than almost any other single man, though but a small part of what he desired and meditated, for remedying them' (Hare, 'The Wants of the Church' [Charge 1843], *Charges*, note A, p. 52).

'If ever . . . there was a mind intensely English in the practical, ethical

bent underlying all his studies and all his work, it was Arnolds'
(Tulloch, *Movements of Religious Thought* [1885], p. 62). Cf. Stanley's
Life, p. 106.

[11] 'The same mental condition, to which he owed his power of
sympathy and his irresolution, hampered him as a thinker and gave
an unscientific turn to his mind' (Prothero, *Life and Correspondence of
Stanley*, vol. I, p. 241).

[12] Without a comprehensive survey of history (that is, one which
'extends to whatever illustrates the character of the human species in a
particular period, to their reasonings and sentiments, their arts and
industry') the statesman, says Hallam, 'would form very erroneous
estimates of events, and find himself constantly misled in any analogical
application of them to present circumstances. Nor is it an uncommon
source of error to neglect the general signs of the times and to deduce
a prognostic from some partial coincidence with past events, where a
more enlarged comparison of the facts that ought to enter into the
combination would destroy the whole parallel' (Hallam, *The Middle
Ages*, vol. III, pp. 268-9). Cf. vol. I, p. 67 n. The unjust encroachments
of courts, the intemperate passions of the multitude, etc. are 'among
the eternal lessons of history' and 'will never cease to have their
parallels and analogies'. This corresponds to Arnold's historical outlook before 1824.

[13] Arnold condemns the scorn shown by the Germans towards the
18th century. Cf. p. 88: 'the full light of the 18th century (we beg
Niebuhr's pardon for the expression) *Quarterly Review*, vol. 32'.

[14] Niebuhr's method, says Acton, was the visible sign of the new
doctrine of fixed lines, invariable laws and overruled action of men.
'The right sphere of these operations is the primitive obscurity. They
could not flourish in the daylight.' How the Liberal Anglicans overcame the determinism inherent in a science of history is related in ch. III.

[15] That Arnold thought so is stressed in the *Quarterly Review* article
already quoted, where he criticizes German historians for being unpractical in the moral sense. They are too apt, he says, to be carried
away by the intellect and to forget their moral responsibilities (vol.
32, p. 87).

[16] Vico is quoted in Arnold's *Thucydides* I, appendix I, and in a
letter to T. F. Ellis, 26 June 1830. 'I am delighted that you have given
Vico his due.' (An anonymous article on Vico appeared in the *Foreign
Review* in 1830.) Lionel Trilling calls Vico and Niebuhr 'Arnold's two
masters' (*Matthew Arnold*, p. 52).

[17] Though it is true that the article was 'slightly altered by Coleridge here and there, so that I am not quite responsible for all of it' (see letter of 22 August 1825). The leitmotiv of 'The Social Progress of States' (1830) is seen in the 1825 article—Vico is mentioned in the former but not in the latter. The writer of the latter shows how the first steps towards liberty have been the result of a contest not between the rich and the mass of the community, but between the rich and the noble. Hence that which is a popular party in one stage of society becomes at a more advanced stage an oligarchical one. In Cicero's time the contending parties were the same as in modern times: the rich and the multitude. Further quotations from the 1825 article are given in ch. II (*a*) (ii) 'The Social Progress of States'.

See also Arnold, *Thucydides* I, preface, p. xii. Niebuhr 'has rendered an essential service to Grecian history no less than to Roman by being practically the first writer who developed the original relations of the families of nobles and of the commons to each other, and the first composition and gradual advance of the latter to an equality with their former masters'. In a note Arnold adds 'I say "practically" because Vico's work was so little known as to have produced no perceptible effect on the state of historical knowledge.' This answers Vaughan (*Studies in the History of Political Philosophy* (1925), vol. I, p. 236 n.), who can find no reference to Vico in Arnold.

[18] Arnold, says Gooch (*History and Historians*, p. 319), was far better fitted to portray the life of a State than to reconstruct the faint outlines of an early civilization. His strength grows as he advances. . . .

[19] Cf. Antoine Guilland, *Modern Germany and her Historians* (London, 1915): 'Niebuhr was truly haunted by this taste for the actual' (p. 66). 'He was the first among modern writers to attempt to understand and determine the individual life of each nation' (p. 64).

[20] Niebuhr, says Arnold, seems almost to believe in a gradual degeneracy of the human race from some high pitch of bodily and mental excellence which he supposes it to have attained in the earliest stages of its existence. . . . He will not believe . . . that the aborigines of Italy were a mere horde of savages, and treats with contempt the opinion that mankind has gradually advanced from a condition of rudeness to civilization and knowledge (*Quarterly Review*, vol. 32, p. 85).

[21] 'I saw Niebuhr at Bonn . . . and am satisfied from my own ears, if I had had any doubts before, of the grossness of the slander which called him an unbeliever' (Letter of 24 Aug. 1830).

[22] This Vichian view of the Homeric monarchies is not found in

the article of 1825 where Arnold says 'the earliest governments were either monarchies or aristocracies' (*Quarterly Review*, vol. 32, p. 78).

[23] Cf. Thirlwall's *History of Greece*, vol. 1, p. 286: 'What has been said shows that the Cretan constitution was strictly aristocratical, like those which prevailed throughout Greece in the Heroic Age.' Cf. vol. 1, p. 394.

[24] The influence of Vico is seen in the remark that this priest-king society is the first transition from domestic or patriarchal to something like civil society.

[25] The Second Infancy represented by the Middle Ages is a Vichian idea. Was it an interpolation of Coleridge's? S. T. Coleridge was acquainted with the *Scienza Nuova* at this time.

[26] Contrast Arnold's opinion of 1824 regarding feudal aristocracies. Cf. *Rome*, vol. 1, p. 228. The inequality of the first stage of society is 'neither unnatural nor unjust'.

[27] Lectures v, vi, and vii of Arnold's *Introductory Lectures on Modern History* are an elaboration and examination in greater detail, with regard to English History from the Reformation, of the theory of the social progress of states, showing how the popular party tends to become anti-popular, e.g. in the Wilkes case, and at the time of the French Revolution; a change 'very important to dwell upon because it is the result of a natural law'. His object in these lectures, he said, was to exemplify from that history which is most familiar to us all the method of historical analysis by which we endeavour to discover the key, as it were, to the complicated movement of the world, and to understand the real principles of opposite parties amidst much in their opinions and conduct that is purely accidental (*Lectures*, p. 357).

[28] The dichotomy was made by the Liberal Anglicans. Cf. Stanley, 'The Social as opposed to the more strictly moral and intellectual, characteristics of civilization' (*Prize Essay*, 1840, p. 19).

[29] The poetry of reflection, that is, of an advanced age, 'awakens feelings absolutely unintelligible to men in a less advanced condition', according to Arnold, 'though all men have the same feelings' (*Miscellaneous Works*, pp. 254-5). Cf. Goethe, 'The imagination has its own laws, to which the understanding cannot and should not penetrate' (*Conversations with Eckerman*, Everyman ed., p. 212). 'Man becomes . . . in the different stages of his life, a different being' (p. 383). Hare, 'The imagination and the feelings have each their truths, as well as the reason' (*Guesses at Truth* [3rd ed., 1st series], p. 260).

[30] See Croce's *Aesthetic*, ch. v. Vico makes of poetry a period in the

history of humanity. Poetry precedes intellect, but follows sense. It is an imaginative phase of consciousness, but one possessed of positive value. The imaginative phase is altogether independent and autonomous with respect to the intellectual, which is not only incapable of endowing it with any fresh perfection but can only destroy it. Poets are the senses, philosophers the intellect of mankind. Imagination is stronger in proportion as reason is weaker. Cf. Croce, *Philosophy of Vico*, ch. IV.

[31] Cf. R. Flint, *Vico*, p. 133: 'His *Scienza Nuova* has not inaccurately been described as a psychology of nations. He saw that just as biography should trace the development of the mind of the individual, so history ... should trace the development of mind in humanity.' Croce, *Philosophy of Vico*, p. 46: 'The *Scienza Nuova* might be called ... a philosophy of Mind with special attention to the Philosophy of Imagination.'

[32] 'Romanticism can be defined only in terms of pure psychology' (Legouis and Cazamian, *History of English Literature*, p. 995). 'The "wonder" of the Romanticists is the enthralling discovery, the progressive lighting-up of an inner horizon, which extends beyond the limits of clear consciousness; it is the perception of objects in the magic garb with which our fresher vision invested them of yore, and which our tired eyes had forgotten' (p. 999).

[33] 'The most valuable part of history, that which relates to a people's mental powers and habits of thinking' (*History of Rome*, vol. II, p. 63).

[34] Cf. *Sermons*, vol. IV, p. 7. Our work at Rugby would be unendurable, says Arnold, if our eyes did not look forward (i.e. past the transition period of boyhood to manhood).

[35] This idea was 'in the air' at the time. Cf., for example, Peacock's *Four Ages of Poetry* published anonymously in 1820, and Macaulay's essay on Milton, 1825.

[36] This principle is used to attack Grote (see *Quarterly Review*, vol. 78, p. 124). Milman takes Thirlwall's side against Grote in believing in the historical content of the *Iliad*. There is, for Milman, an essential difference between mythic and heroic legend. The first is purely creative, the second has a basis of fact.

[37] 'It is remarkable that, as India has followed the same course of philosophic development as Greece, so its poetical life has the same analogy. It should seem that it is the regular process of civilization' (*Quarterly Review*, vol. 68, p. 392). The religious poetry comes first; the part of the Vedas which consists of hymns to the gods corresponds to the ancient Orphic poetry which we must assume to have existed at

one time in Greece. The *Ramayana* and *Mahà Bhàrat* are the 'two *Iliads*' representing the heroic, warlike age of the people. Like the *Iliad* they are far from deficient in real historical information.

[38] Cf. *Quarterly Review*, vol. 45, p. 39: 'The [Hindu] drama evidently appears to belong to a much later, and more refined, and less poetic age.' Cf. *ibid.* vol. 68, p. 395, and *Horatius Flaccus*, p. 84, for an explanation of literary development in terms of political maturity.

[39] 'Whether states, like individuals, after a certain period of maturity, inevitably tend to decay' (Stanley, *Prize Essay*).

[40] Cf. Thirlwall's *Greece*, vol. VIII, p. 98: 'Society in its highest stage of refinement had relapsed into the wildness and disorder of its infancy.' (Cf. *ibid.* vol. II, p. 196.) Cf. Hare: 'When we view [man] in his natural state, at whatever stage of it, from the infant rudeness of blind ignorance down to the expiring torpor of an effete refinement. . . . ' (*Mission of the Comforter*, vol. I, p. 366).

[41] 'Ecclesiastes' is the work of such a period (*History of the Jews*, 4th ed., vol. I, p. 325 n.).

[42] 'The systematical connexion of moral truths is a purely intellectual process . . . and commonly carried to its highest perfection, like the theory of art, in periods when practice has begun to decline and perhaps has sunk into the grossest corruption' (Thirlwall, *Remains*, vol. III, p. 336). Cf. *Guesses at Truth* (3rd ed., 1st series): 'When a nation reaches its noon . . . it occupies itself . . . in examining and analysing. . . .' (p. 311).

[43] Hare pointed out the difference between the unconscious feeling for Nature of early periods with the self-conscious 'taste for the picturesque' of late periods. 'The mind of a people when it first awakes is full of its morning dreams . . . for a long time it scarcely regards itself as separate from Nature. It lies in her arms and feeds at her breast and looks up into her face and smiles at her smiles. . . .' etc. (*Guesses at Truth* [3rd ed., 1st series], p. 54). There is almost a quality of Spengler in these remarks.

[44] Can one make this distinction between the Romantic and the Rationalist historian: that the one sees himself as submitting to a natural rhythm, the other imposes a pattern of order on the Past?

[45] Cf. *Latin Christianity*, vol. III, p. 222. Pilgrimage may be considered as belonging to the universal religion of man. All the religions of antiquity possess a family resemblance. Milman refers the reader to the study of comparative mythology, e.g. to Creuzer (see *Christianity*, vol. I, p. 10).

[46] Cf. his letter of 10 April 1842: 'It is a pity that Elphinstone had not a more profound knowledge of the ancient western world, which continually illustrates and is illustrated by the state of things in India.'

[47] The period of Roman civilization, Arnold said, from the times of the Gracchi to those of the Antonines was 'far more completely modern' than the period of the Reformation, which was still an age of strong feeling and intense belief, and 'accordingly this is one of the periods of history we should do well to study most carefully' (*Thucydides*, vol. III, p. xx).

[48] The analogy, says Stanley, is useful as a defence of medieval Christianity against 'the indiscriminate attacks of one-sided Puritanical writers'. One need only point to its counterpart in the Sacred record. Similarly, it is a defence of the Old Testament narrative against destructive criticism.

[49] 'The mythic period which lasted throughout the middle ages' (*Savonarola*, p. 490); 'the mythic age of Christianity' (*Christianity*, vol. III, p. 531).

The Crusades are 'the heroic age in the ordinary, not the Christian sense . . . which would seek its heroes rather among the martyrs. . . .' The Crusades ought to have been the heroic age of Christianity in poetry but their Homer arose too late (*Latin Christianity*, vol. III, pp. 237-8). See *ibid.*, vol. v. Of Edward I's statement of his claim to the crown of Scotland, Milman says: 'It is a singular illustration of the state of human knowledge when poetry and history are one, when the mythic and historic have the same authority even as to grave legal claims. . . .' (p. 218); 'Allegorical picture was the language of the times. The Church had . . . employed it to teach . . . Christian truth. . . . It had certainly been used for political purposes' (p. 516).

Cf. *ibid.* vol. I: 'The monastery of St Andrew was a perpetual scene of preternatural wonder. Fugitive monks were seized upon by devils . . . others were favoured with visits of angels. . . . Such was the poetry of those days' (p. 432); cf. *ibid.* vol. VI, p. 526: 'No cold later epic on St Louis will rival the poetry of Joinville.'

'The period of the Judges is the heroic age of Hebrew history' (Jews, vol. I, p. 187).

'The *Iliad* and *Odyssey* were a Golden Legend, which made the traditionary fables catholic throughout Greece, just as they made the Trojan War, from a loose and vague tradition, a great universal reality to the imaginative faith—the only dominant faith of that period of all-ruling song' (*Quarterly Review*, vol. 78, p. 134). 'The religion itself was the *poetry* of Christianity. The sacred books were to the Christians what the national epic and the sacred lyric had been to other races of antiquity' (*Christianity*, vol. III, p. 466).

[50] In this connection Stanley refers the reader to Arnold, Whately and Niebuhr (and does not mention Vico, which might suggest that the 'analogous periods' were worked out from a study of Niebuhr).

[51] . . . 'an onward progress from scene to scene, from act to act, towards an end yet distant and invisible; a unity and a progress such as give consistency and point to what would else be a mere collection of isolated and disjointed facts' (Stanley, *Lectures on Eastern Church*, p. xxxvi).

[52] This remark is misunderstood by Thompson and Holm (*History of Historical Writing*; see vol. II, pp. 280 n. 2, 281): Dr Arnold's 'complacent remark in 1830 about England's "perfect social civilization" '. Dr Arnold was the last person to have been complacent on such a topic.

[53] Cf. J. C. Thirlwall's *Life*, p. 106: 'Thirlwall's History of Greece remained, even after Grote had written, the only History filled with a continuous sense of the unity of Grecian destiny in decline as well as rise.'

[54] Arnold had the greatest distaste for Livy as a mere literary historian (Stanley's *Life*, pp. 114, 250). Contrast Macaulay, who admired him greatly (G. O. Trevelyan, *Life and Letters*, p. 316).

[55] One or more nations may be in advance of or behind the general tendency of their age and from either cause may be moving in the opposite direction. The tendency itself is liable to interruptions and short counter-movements. The opposite tendency exists in an undercurrent perhaps, here and there it struggles to the surface. The great movements of history 'never have the world wholly to themselves'.

[56] Nations, said Hare, like individuals, can only enter into the Kingdom of God through much tribulation. The destruction of the Roman Empire, for instance, prepared the way for the Christianizing of the Northern nations (*The Duty of the Church in Times of Trial*, p. 48). 'The moral year, like the natural, is not one continued spring and summer, but has its seasons of decay' (*Guesses at Truth* [2nd ed., 2nd series], p. 66).

[57] Cf. *ibid.* p. 353: Outside Christendom, says Hare, 'the smouldering ashes of extinct civilizations' cover the desert, 600,000,000 souls strong.

[58] As expressed, for example, by Taine in his chapter on Carlyle (*History of English Literature* [New York, 1871], vol. II, p. 447): 'His

[Carlyle's] special feature, the special feature of every historian who has the sentiment of actuality, to understand that parchments, walls, dress, bodies themselves are only cloaks and documents; that the true fact is the inner feeling of men who have lived, that the only important fact is the state and structure of their soul, that the first and unique business is to reach that inner feeling, that all diverges from it. We must tell ourselves this fact over and over again: history is but the history of the heart, we have to search out of the feelings of past generations and nothing else.'

[59] According to Vico, the idea of justice grows with the development of rational mind, which represents the drawing near of Mankind to the rational mind of God. See, e.g., H. P. Adams, *Life and Writings of Giambattista Vico*, pp. 135, 155–8.

[60] 'The great Evangelical truth—Evangelical in its literal sense and true to the depths of human nature—that nations and individuals alike can leave their past behind them, and start afresh in the race of duty' (Stanley, *Jewish Church*, vol. III, p. 79).

[61] Letter of 10 May 1839: 'The real evil which lies at the bottom of the Chartist agitation is, I believe, too deep for any human remedy. . . . So far from finding it hard to believe that repentance can be ever too late, my only wonder is that it should ever be otherwise than too late, so instantaneous and so lasting are the consequences of any evil once committed.'

[62] 'Progress' as used in Arnold's theory of the 'Social Progress of States' had no teleological implications and was equivalent to process, or course. In Mill's *System of Logic* (1843) 'progress' is used neutrally. According to Bury, in 1857 Spencer used progress also in a neutral sense, but recognizing that a word was required which had no teleological implications he adopted *evolution* six months later (*Idea of Progress*, pp. 371 n. 3, 341).

[63] It was a constant theme of Liberal Anglican preaching that we are not better than our fathers, but more richly endowed; see, for instance, Thirlwall, *Remains*, vol. III, p. 381.

[64] Cf. Hare, *Guesses at Truth* (3rd ed., 1st series), pp. 59–60. With regard to modern poetry, when we are looking at any question connected with its history, we ought to bear in mind that we did not begin from the beginning. . . . Owing to this, and perhaps still more to the influence . . . of Christianity, we from the first find a far greater body of reflective thought in modern poetry than in ancient. Dante is not, what Homer was, the father of poetry springing in the freshness and

simplicity of childhood out of the arms of mother earth: he is rather, like Noah, the father of a second poetical world, to whom he pours forth his prophetic song, fraught with the wisdom and experience of the old world.

In the realm of social history the nobility of modern times represents an advance on the nobility of Greece. We must take into account the softening and liberal tendencies of Christianity (Arnold, *Thucydides*, vol. I, pp. 669-70).

[65] See Arnold, *Lectures*, p. 33: morally our life is in a manner a continuation of Rome, Greece and Israel. Cf. p. 36. See also Milman, *Christianity*, vol. I, p. 46. In spite of the *ricorso* represented by the Middle Ages 'the indelible difference' effected by Christianity remained.

[66] Cf. Arnold (?) 1831: 'We are not mere puppets, whirled around by a machinery over which we can exercise no control; it belongs to every generation to accelerate or retard its own progress' (*Quarterly Review*, vol. 45, p. 469).

[67] Thirlwall calls it the 'philosophy of history'. This equals our (and Goldwin Smith's) 'science of history' or Max Nordau's 'causal' as opposed to 'teleological' 'philosophy of history'.

[68] Cf. the article on Vico in the *Foreign Review*, 1830. 'Vico's views', says the writer, 'are, upon all occasions, strictly religious and conformable to the Scriptures' (*Foreign Review*, vol. V, p. 382).

[69] Cf. for example, H. P. Adams, *Life and Writings of G. Vico* (1935): 'The central proposition of the new science is that the creative mind which produces the world of institutions is the mind of man.' Croce, *Philosophy of Vico*, p. 121: 'Vico's conception of history thus became truly objective, freed from divine arbitrament.'

[70] If we submit to the fatalism of a deterministic view of history, 'if we think according to a fixed law', 'it is evident our deliverance must proceed wholly from a higher power'. Practically, says Arnold, there is an end of this question [the future of civilization] if the power of our supposed fate goes so far as to make us its willing instruments; I mean if the influences of our time, determined by those of past time, do . . . determine our character. The only question of importance is whether, if our minds be free, our actions can accomplish what we desire, whether we can resist the influences and evil tendencies of the age with success; whether the natural consequences of the misdoings of past generations can be averted now.

[71] 'It is only when applied on the widest scale to the whole human race, that there is the slightest truth in the doctrine of the perfectibility,

or rather of the progressiveness of man' (Hare, *Guesses at Truth* [2nd ed., 2nd series], p. 16).

[72] Goldwin Smith, who shows marked traces of Liberal Anglican influence, recognized the difference between a science and a philosophy of history as used in this study. 'A science of history is one thing, a philosophy of history is another', he said. 'A science of history can rest on nothing short of causation, a philosophy of history rests upon connexion' (*Lectures* [1859-61], pp. 90-1). See below, ch. IV (c).

[73] This review of the pioneers of progress is not found in the 1827 edition. Vico is not included. His theory of history was considered to be purely cyclical: cf. Stanley, *Prize Essay*, Mill, *System of Logic*, Goldwin Smith, *Lectures*.

[74] Cf. Niebuhr, 'Herder was no longer the same man when he ceased to be religious' (Letter to Mme Hensler, 11 Dec. 1812; see *Life and Letters of Niebuhr* [London, 3 vols., 1852]).

[75] *Lectures*: 'This leads us to a view of modern history, which cannot indeed be confidently relied on, but which still impresses the mind with an imagination if not with a conviction of its reality. I mean that modern history appears to be not only *a* step in advance of ancient history, but *the* last step; it appears to bear marks of the fullness of time, as if there would be no future history beyond it' (p. 36). 'We have the full amount of the earth's resources before us, and they seem inadequate to supply life for a third period of human history' (p. 38).

[76] Quinet, *Génie des Religions*, is quoted in support of this view. 'With the appearance of the Persians, says a brilliant French writer... the movement of history begins and humanity throws itself into that restless march of progress which henceforth is never to cease.' A striking passage, Stanley comments, though with some exaggeration. Cf. *Jewish Church*, vol. III, pp. 51-2.

[77] As far as the course of human history is concerned there have been three vast periods, of which two have already passed away. They may be called, in general terms, Primeval History, Classical History and Modern History. Each of these periods has its beginning, middle and end—its ancient and modern stage—but the whole of each is marked by its own characteristics. In the Primeval History we must include all that series of events which begins with the first dawn of civilization in Egypt and Mesopotamia. It is a period of which the Semitic races (taking that word in its most extended sense) were the predominant elements of power and genius... (*Jewish Church*, vol. III, p. 46).

[78] 'This giant age' (*Jewish Church*, vol. III, p. 47); 'The ancient

gigantic monarchies and religions, known to us only through their mighty conquerors and their vast monuments. . . .' (*ibid.* vol. II, p. 578). Cf. Stanley's *Sinai and Palestine*, p. lxix: of the Temple of Ipsambul, he says, 'The whole impression is that gods and men alike belong to an age and world . . . when men were slow to move, slow to think, but when they did move or think, their work was done with the force and violence of giants.'

[79] Cf. Hare, *Contest with Rome*, p. 138: '. . . when the mind of the old world had burnt out, and that of the new modern world was yet in its infancy, and through the centuries [the middle Ages] during which it continued in its nonage. . . .'

[80] 'The momentous epoch, when Christianity may almost be said to have had a second beginning. . . .' (Stanley, *Apostolical Age*, p. 105). Cf. Hare, *Contest with Rome*, p. 138.

[81] There may be nations fit to receive the seed of our civilization, and to produce it 'the same and yet new', for a future period . . . (Arnold, *Lectures*, p. 39).

[82] Whately found an 'insurmountable difficulty' to Lamarck's theory of evolution, in 'the final step from the savage to the civilized man' (*Miscellaneous Lectures and Reviews*, p. 47).

[83] 'Supposing the first men to have been savages, we cannot understand how without some divine interference, the human race could ever have arrived at civilization, so, if we suppose men to have been in such a state as to have had to invent a language, we cannot conceive how mankind, any more than any other animals, should ever have been able to speak at all' (Arnold, *Thucydides*, vol. III, p. vi).

[84] Cf. Hare, 'The agents in the historical development of mankind are rarely more than half-conscious, mostly quite unconscious, of the work they are engaged in. . . . They often suppose themselves to have different objects in view, while God's overruling Providence shapes their ends not seldom directly against their wills' (*The Duty of the Church in Times of Trial*, p. 34).

[85] There is no element of 'priestcraft' in the Liberal Anglican theory of accommodation, as there is in the following remark of Scott: 'that ancient system, which so well accommodated its doctrines to the wants and wishes of a barbarous age' (*The Monastery* [1821], [A. & C. Black, 1860], vol. II, p. 219).

[86] *Christianity*, vol. I: 'The state of mankind seemed imperiously to demand the introduction of a new religion . . . at the present juncture the ancient religions were effete; they belonged to a totally different

state of civilization . . . the general mind was advanced beyond them. . . . Nothing less was required than a religion co-extensive with the empire of Rome, and calculated for the advanced state of intellectual culture' (p. 8). 'The progress of knowledge was fatal to the popular religions of Greece and Rome. . . . Poetry had been religion, religion was becoming mere poetry' (p. 26). 'Philosophy as a substitute for religion was still more manifestly deficient . . . it failed to reach the body of the people whom the progress of civilization was slowly bringing up towards the common level' (p. 34). 'The height to which moral science was carried in Cicero, Seneca, Epictetus and Marcus Antonius, while it made the breach still wider between the popular religion and the advanced state of the human mind, more vividly displayed the want of a faith which would associate itself with the purest and loftiest morality, and remarry as it were, those thoughts and feelings, which connect man with a future state of being, to the practical duties of life' (p. 36).

[87] 'Changes and revolutions in the Church, if they are wide-spreading and lasting, are ever coincident with analogous revolutions in the general history of the human mind. In them we see, as in a clock, the progress of Time's great circle, in them we, as it were, hear the striking of one of its epochal hours' (*Victory of Faith*, p. 67). The frequent apostasy of the Jews was due to the fact that their religion was beyond their state of civilization (Milman's *Gibbon*, vol. II, p. 155 n.).

[88] There are hints in the *Latin Christianity* that Milman was looking forward to a history of Teutonic Christianity. Cf. vol. IV, p. 111: Our history must show . . . the silent growth of Teutonic freedom. Vol. VI, p. 94: The Teutonic constitution of England had slowly . . . developed . . . encroaching on . . . the Latin despotism of the Church. Cf. *Quarterly Review*, vol. 65 (1840), p. 351: It has not been generally observed how completely the Reformation was a Teutonic movement.

[89] The morality of Jesus was 'universal morality, adapted for the whole human race, and for every period of civilization' (*Christianity*, vol. I, p. 201).

[90] '. . . a new childhood, a second imaginative youth. The mythic period of Christianity. . .' (*Latin Christianity*, vol. I, p. 412). Cf. *Christianity*, vol. II, p. 363. Of the religious disputes of the 4th century, Milman says, 'Mankind retrograded to the sterner Jewish character; and in its spirit, as well as in its language, the Old Testament began to dominate over the Gospel of Christ.' Cf. also *Latin Christianity*, vol. VI, p. 400.

[91] 'This new mythic or imaginative period of the world suppressed the development of any strong intellectual energy' (*Christianity*, vol. III, p. 536).

[92] A philosophic vindication of the Papacy and the celibacy of the clergy, as essential preservatives against barbarism, was not then [1843] familiar to the English mind (Bain, *J. S. Mill*, p. 78). Mill had written of his article on Michelet, 'it will make some . . . readers stare'.

[93] 'Even if (though I conceive it impossible) the imagination should entirely wither from the human soul and a severer faith enter into an exclusive alliance with pure reason, Christianity would still have its moral perfection . . .' (*Christianity*, vol. I, appendix III, p. 132).

[94] Milman agreed; 'Mohammedanism, it has been justly said, is but a republication of Judaism' (*Jews* [4th ed.], vol. III, pp. 426-7).

[95] While other histories tell us how nations have arisen, and grown up and spread and flourished and decayed and perished in accordance with that great law to which man and all his works are subject, the history of the Hebrews, on the other hand, foreshows and typifies a higher, spiritual order (Hare, *Mission of the Comforter*, vol. I, p. 335).

[96] Cf. *Guesses at Truth* (3rd ed., 1st series): 'Of Asiatic poetry it is needless to speak: for that even now has hardly emerged from its nonage' (p. 55).

[97] *Quarterly Review*, vol. 95, pp. 49-50. 'The Greek Church . . . has always given tokens of that singular immobility which doubtless is in great part to be traced to its Oriental origin.' Cf. p. 57: 'If the spirit of the original Christianity of Christ . . . is to be found not in the churches which sprang up on its native soil, but in churches more and more remote from those regions in climate, in feeling, in thought, it is because the spirit of the West, the conscience, the energy, the reason of the West, has broken the bonds which still fetter the older and more primitive, but not therefore necessarily the more Christian churches of the East. The Church of Rome is in this respect not only the witness against the exclusive claims of the Byzantine Church, but still more emphatically against her own. The Reformation was but another step in the same direction, to which the movements of Latin Christianity had already pointed the way.'

Cf. Coleridge: 'Europeans and Orientalists may be well represented by two figures standing back to back: the latter looking to the East, that is, backwards; the former looking Westward, or forwards' (*Table Talk*, Jan. 1823).

[98] 'The mind of Greece and Rome is our own, unlike the Asiatic

mind, with which we have no nearer connection or sympathy than that which is derived from our common humanity' (*Miscellaneous Works*, p. 349).

[99] The younger nations are called to take charge of the older races (*American Sermons*, p. 138). We must not look eastward, we must not look backward, if we would know the true strength of human progress and of Christ's religion (*ibid.* p. 101). Only by travelling from its early home has it grown to its full stature (p. 103).

Cf. *Jewish Church*, vol. III, p. 45; *Eastern Church*, p. 185; *Sinai and Palestine*, p. 116: 'that tide of civilisation which has swept far into the remotest West. . . .'

[100] If we look upward from the isthmus which separates the ancient from the modern world we see the 'dissociating principle' at work both in the civil and religious usages of mankind (*Christianity*, vol. I, p. 9).

[101] 'Our future course must be hesitating or mistaken, if we do not know what course has brought us to the point where we are at present' (Arnold, *Lectures*, p. 40).

[102] The scientific observer stands aloof from the object which he submits to his experiments. . . . The progress of society is something in which the student of history has a deep personal concern. He is himself a part of that which he sees. He is carried along by the movement which he scans, and contributes in some measure to modify it by his presence. His actual position and prospects have been determined by the past, and it is only by the light of the past that he can discern their real nature and bearings. But that light would be of no practical avail, it could serve neither as a guide, nor as a beacon, if the movement was the result of mechanical forces, and his own share in it purely passive (Thirlwall, *Remains*, vol. III, pp. 281-2).

[103] Arnold, 'Sermon on Wills', *Sermons*, vol. VI, pp. 325-6: 'In so far as we have another nature than that which we have in common with the brutes, even as far as regarding this world; as we . . . can in no manner get rid of the manifold influences of the generations which have gone before us, neither can our children . . . get rid of the influences of our generation; so it is most natural . . . that the past and present and future should be linked together in a chain . . . that in every age the dead should still, in a manner be present among the living.'

[104] '. . . that sense of reality about the Romans—that living in a manner amongst them, and having them and their life distinctly before our eyes—which appears to me so indispensable to one who would write their history' (Arnold, Letter of 18 Nov. 1836).

[105] 'Antiquarianism' Arnold defined as 'knowledge of the past enjoyed by one who has no lively knowledge of the present' (Lectures, p. 108). The 'lively' provides an interesting glimpse into Arnold's mind.

[106] Cf. Lionel Trilling: It was not on ideals but on the lesson of history that he based his justification of his conception of the State. . . . Arnold saw the past as the dynamic source of the future (Matthew Arnold, p. 52). See Stanley, Life, p. 109.

[107] Cf. Stanley: Just as the qualities fitting to youth are dangerous if continued into manhood, so 'in like manner the preservation of national forms, unchanged amidst the necessary change of all besides, must destroy the life of a nation, either directly by an unnatural rigidity, or indirectly by the re-action which must ensue on the hopeless estrangement of the present from the past' (Prize Essay, p. 28).

[108] Rome, vol. 1, p. 341. All things come best in their season. Political power is most happily exercised by a people when it has not been given to them prematurely, that is, before in the natural progress of things they feel the want of it. This is 'one of the most valuable lessons in history'.

Cf. p. 346: The commons retained and asserted those rights which were the best suited to their actual condition; and thus became gradually fitted to desire and to claim others of a higher character.

Cf. Thucydides, vol. 1. The history of Augsburg to 1548 shows with how little difficulty and danger political change may be effected where 'the effort of the political constitution is neither hurried forwards, nor violently checked' (p. 628).

[109] It was in this connection that Arnold pointed, in 1830, to the negro population of the United States as 'one of the most alarming points in the future prospects of that great and growing people' (Thucydides, vol. 1, p. 634).

[110] There is no evidence, except internal evidence, that Arnold wrote this article. See Quarterly Review, vol. 45 (July, 1831) 'On the Subversion of Ancient Governments.' The ideas correspond closely to the Thucydides, vol. 1, appendix 1 (1830). Arnold had no hatred of the nobility at this time. Cf. Thucydides, vol. 1, appendix III. We must not compare our nobility with that of the Greeks, he said: 'With us, nobility has lost almost all its evil as an element in political society and has become far more powerful in promoting good' (p. 669). These remarks bear the stamp of the Reform Bill years.

[111] See Catholic Claims, p. 9: 'the presumption is always in favour of change' (1829); see also Miscellaneous Works, p. 442: Conservatism

is always wrong because in human affairs nothing will ever stand still (1837). Cf. Letter to Justice Coleridge, 16 Dec. 1835.

[112] *Quarterly Review*, vol. 45, p. 469: 'it belongs to every generation to accelerate or retard its own progress and to render inevitable change gentle and inoffensive or sanguinary and disastrous.'

[113] Arnold is afraid that the Tories will 'stick so tight to the form of the constitution, that the constitution itself will at last be thrown into the fire and a military monarchy succeed' (see Stanley, *Life of Arnold*, vol. II, supplement, p. 36). To attempt to preserve the 'old state of things' is to derange the process of the new birth which must succeed it (Letter of 6 May 1833). Cf. Letter to Susannah Arnold, April, 1831; Letter of 23 Jan. 1840.

[114] Cf. Arnold: 'It is worse than kicking against the pricks to oppose our vain efforts to an eternal and universal law of God's Providence' (*Miscellaneous Works*, p. 116).

[115] Surely Arnold's view was not typical of 'the younger Whigs, soon to be called Liberals', as J. R. M. Butler asserts (*The Great Reform Bill*, p. 259).

[116] This historical diagnosis of the state of the nation is surely more vital in Arnold's conception of the State than the influence of *Organismus-gedanken*, which Klaus Dockhorn emphasizes. Arnold's mind was nothing if not practical. Moreover, his idea of the State was in the tradition of the first English Romantics. The exaltation of the State in a time of warring factions is the heart and centre of Arnold's thought, says L. Trilling (*Matthew Arnold*) but 'Arnold does not ask for a Vichian Caesar'. The State for Arnold is 'sovereign over human life, controlling everything and itself subject to no earthly control'. But cf. Croce's *Vico*, p. 95: For Vico 'the state is the image of God and because "it has all things beneath it, nothing above" . . . therefore "it renders account to God alone and to no one else".' (The quotations, it is only fair to add, are not from the *Scienza Nuova*.) One cannot be dogmatic about 'influences'. In a case like this one can only point to the parallel.

[117] Cf. *Victory of Faith*, p. 300: 'If nations in their youth are apt to err on the side of credulity, they are no less apt to err in their decline on the side of incredulity; which after all is only credulity saying No instead of . . . Yes.'

[118] For Arnold the 'cooling and sobering study' of the past made it 'possible to partake of the activity of the present without catching its feverishness' (*Sermons*, vol. VI [1835], p. 317).

[119] The sin of worshipping the world, instead of God seems to

become huger . . . with the increase of civilization (Hare, *Mission of the Comforter*, vol. 1, p. 121). Religion, which in early ages . . . is the mother of the arts and sciences, is gradually supplanted by her offspring (*ibid.* p. 312).

[120] 'Are we really more enlightened than our ancestors? Or is it merely the flaring up of the candle that has burnt down to the socket and is consuming that socket, as a prelude to its own extinction? Such at least has mostly been the character of those former ages of the world which have prided themselves on being the most enlightened' (*Guesses at Truth* [3rd ed., 1st series], p. 261).

[121] Travelling was the true medicine of the 19th century, the true 'retreat' of our over-heated civilization. *Quarterly Review*, vol. 126 (1869), p. 479.

[122] 'In studying the history of philosophy one can hardly help remarking that the rise and fall of its successive systems have always gone along with the corresponding changes in the character of the people that gave birth to them. . . . Often indeed the current philosophy is merely the reflexion of the reigning vice of an age: as has been the case with a great part of that which has assumed the name of philosophy in England during the last hundred years. Its chief aim has been to palliate and justify, to establish and define that worship of Mammon. . . .' (Hare, *Victory of Faith* [1829], p. 282).

[123] Coleridge, *Constitution of Church and State* (1830), p. 43: 'Civilization is itself but a mixed good, if not far more a corrupting influence, the hectic of disease, not the bloom of health . . . where this civilization is not grounded in *cultivation*, in the harmonious development of those qualities and faculties that characterise our *humanity*.' Cf. p. 50: 'this most valuable of the lessons taught by history . . . that a nation can never be a too cultivated, but may easily be an over-civilised race', 'the permanent *distinction* and the occasional *contrast* between cultivation and civilization.'

[124] Cf. 'The Irony of Sophocles' in *Remains*, vol. III: 'As all things human are subject to dissolution, so and for the same reason it is the moment of their destruction that to the best and noblest of them is the beginning of a higher being, the dawn of a brighter period of action' (p. 7). Cf. Carlyle's 'The Phoenix' in *Sartor Resartus*.

[125] Christopher Dawson, *Spirit of the Oxford Movement*, pp. 40-1. 'Progress' for Newman is but the movement of a dying world sweeping onwards to inevitable destruction.

[126] See John Morley, *Critical Miscellanies*, vol. 1, p. 168; Arnold,

Rome, vol. 1, p. 252: 'Nations, like individuals, have their time of trial; and if this be wasted or misused, their future course is inevitably evil; and the efforts of some few good and wise citizens, like the occasional struggles of conscience in the mind of a single man when he has sinned beyond repentance, are powerless to avert their judgment.' This is the moral of the *French Revolution*.

[127] The period so fascinated Arnold that at one time, Stanley says, he was on the point of sacrificing even his *History of Rome* to a detailed exposition of it.

[128] See Letter of 25 Oct. 1831 (in answer to a question about Irvingism). 'However, whether this be a real sign or no', writes Arnold, 'I believe that the "day of the Lord" is coming, i.e. the termination of one of the great αἰῶνες of the human race; whether the final one or not, that I believe no created being knows or can know. The termination of the Jewish αἰῶν in the first century and of the Roman αἰῶν in the fifth and sixth, were each marked by the same concurrence of calamities, wars . . . all marking the time of one of God's peculiar seasons of visitation. And society in Europe seems going on fast for a similar revolution. . . . But I have not the slightest expectation of what is commonly meant by the Millennium.' Arnold's eschatology is not a naïve millennarianism, as A. W. Benn implies (*English Rationalism in the 19th Century*, vol. 1, p. 334 n.); see also Stanley, *Life*, pp. 363, 501.

[129] 'It is Christianity alone that in the case of nations as well as individuals, possesses the peculiar privilege of restoring the lost and raising the dead' (Stanley, *Prize Essay*, p. 41).

[130] 'Every age has its besetting sins . . . every state of society its diseases to the action of which it is especially liable' (*Guesses at Truth* [1st ed.], vol. 1, p. 214).

[131] Cf. Hare, *Victory of Faith*, p. 83. When nations have begun to sink they have 'scarcely any power to check their descent; unless some happy shock drives them upward, they commonly continue to fall with an ever increasing velocity'.

[132] This explains Arnold's dislike of patriotism: 'that feeling of pride and selfishness which . . . has so long tried to pass itself off for a virtue'. 'Exclusive patriotism', he said, 'should be cast off' (*Thucydides*, vol. 1, p. 638). Cf. Hare, *Mission of the Comforter*, vol. 1, pp. 268, 269. Patriotism which is negative and exclusive is wrong, and blameworthy.

[133] 'That miserable antagonism which later ages have imagined between Religion and Science . . . that unnatural civil war. . .' (*Sermons on Special Occasions*, p. 141).

[134] Cf. Stanley, 'It is but the natural result of the increasing age of the world that it should learn that temperance in theological argument, that better sense of proportion in theological statements which we sometimes see in the increased moderation of the experience of individuals. . .' (*Lectures on the History of the Church of Scotland* [1872], p. 13). Cf. *Jewish Church*, vol. I, p. 195: 'The soothing and widening process which belongs to the old age, not merely of every nation, but of every individual.'

[135] 'Romanizing Fallacies', *Charges* (1845) pp. 88 *et seq.* 'One man became a Romanist because he admired the knights of the middle ages; another because he admired the pictures of Perugino' (p. 91). 'The contrast . . . between the works of the middle ages and those since the Reformation has not the slightest bearing on any controversy or comparison between the present Church of England and the Church of Rome. It has been seen in all nations, in which we know anything of the history of literature and art, that there are certain stages in the life of a nation in which its mind is better fitted for grand and genial conceptions. . . .' The comparison should be between the works of the Reformed and Roman Churches *after* the Reformation (pp. 91-2).

Many of the noblest aspects of medieval life were not Roman, but Teutonic (p. 94). Gothic architecture was not Italian, nor was chivalry. 'Most strange . . . would it seem that the fallacies which were deluding men in Germany forty years ago, should now be deluding so many persons in England' (p. 95).

[136] *Guesses at Truth* (3rd ed., 1st series), pp. 234, 236-7. Critique of the *Broad Stone of Honour:* for the sake of forming an estimate of the worth of any particular period it is necessary to consider that period, says Hare, in all its bearings . . . and in its relative position with reference to the historical development of mankind. The theological controversies of the 19th century are not to be decided by any selection of the ancedotes and apophthegms of the 12th and 13th.

[137] *Quarterly Review*, vol. 50, p. 298 (review of Chateaubriands' *Etudes ou Discours Historiques sur la Chute de l'Empire Romain*): 'His reason is the bond-slave of his fancy and his passions' (p. 297) . . . with us, religion is more an affair of reason (p. 298).

[138] *The Office of the Christian Teacher* (Sermon at Reading): 'The progress of barbarism and the progress of Roman Catholic doctrines were simultaneous. For in the barbarian as in the child, the imagination is the most active and easily excited faculty, the reason is dormant' (p. 21). All the facts of Christianity were made graphic and visible . . .

the truths of religion were embodied in painting and statue, 'everything was as far as possible brought down to the comprehension of the senses' (p. 22). Not only the worship of images but the sacrifice of the mass may be deduced from the increasing desire of governing the public mind through the imagination. In the Gallican Church the fastidiousness of taste arising from a high wrought state of civilization dethroned the imagination which still reigned paramount in Italy and Spain. Hence the masculine minds of Bossuet and Bourdaloue carried the eloquence of the pulpit to a height unprecedented and unrivalled, at least in Roman Catholic countries (p. 23). When Reason awoke at the Reformation it forced the Imagination to withdraw into its proper province (p. 24). This discourse has been a candid enquiry into what I may term the philosophy of preaching (p. 27).

[139] Macaulay put forward this Liberal Anglican argument in the *History of England:* 'Those who hold that the influence of the Church of Rome in the dark ages was, on the whole, beneficial to mankind, may yet with perfect consistency regard the Reformation as an inestimable blessing. The leading strings, which preserve and uphold the infant, would impede the full-grown man. And so the very means by which the human mind is, in one stage of its progress, supported and propelled, may, in another stage, be mere hindrances. There is a season in the life both of an individual and of a society, at which submission and faith, such as at a later period would be justly called servility and credulity, are useful qualities. The child who teachingly and undoubtingly listens to the instructions of his elders is likely to improve rapidly. But the man who should receive with child-like docility every assertion and dogma uttered by another man no wiser than himself would become contemptible. It is the same with communities. The childhood of the European nations was passed under the tutelage of the clergy. The ascendency of the sacerdotal order was long the ascendency which naturally and properly belongs to intellectual superiority. . . . But . . . knowledge gradually spread among laymen. At the commencement of the sixteenth century many of them were in every intellectual attainment fully equal to the most enlightened of their spiritual pastors. Thenceforward that dominion, which, during the dark ages, had been, in spite of many abuses, a legitimate and salutary guardianship, became an unjust and noxious tyranny' (*History of England* [ed. Firth, 1913], vol. I, pp. 39-40).

[140] In the Middle Ages papal dominion 'may be no more than the natural and lawful authority of mature age over childhood, of the

teacher over him who needs to be taught . . . but so soon as the child grew into the man . . . the claim of the Pope to stand in its place became impertinent' (Arnold, *Lectures*, pp. 251-2).

[141] Of the Jesuits, Milman says they 'could not perceive that mankind had outgrown their trammels; and without strength or pliancy to forge new ones, they went on rivetting and hammering at the old broken links' (*Savonarola*, p. 256).

[142] The resolution by which Colenso's book was condemned assumes a paternal authority which rather suits an earlier period in the education of the world (Thirlwall, *Remains*, vol. II, p. 68).

[143] To accuse Michelet of inconsistency in his *Du Pretre, de la Femme, de la Famille*, because of earlier passages in favour of medieval Christianity, Milman pointed out, was absurd. These passages referred to a totally different state of civilization, and were irrelevant in the present controversy. 'We take the opportunity of protesting against the watchful industry with which every attempt to treat the Papacy and the religion of the Middle Ages with fairness and sound philosophy, is seized upon as an extorted concession of Protestant prejudice to the power of truth . . .' (*Savonarola*, p. 378).

[144] Cf. Hare, *The Contest with Rome*, note B. 'Take a sentence or two here and there from this Father, and a couple of expressions from another, add half a canon of this Council, a couple of incidents out of some ecclesiastical historian and an ancedote from a chronicler, two conjectures of some critic, and half a dozen drachms of a schoolman, mix them up in rhetoric *quant. suff.* and shake them well together —and thus we get a theological development.'

[145] A distinction is drawn between the philosopher and the eclectic (cf. *Guesses at Truth*, p. 241). Cf. p. 250: 'that this historical, genetical method [of viewing prior systems of philosophy] is something totally different from Eclecticism, nay, is the direct opposite of it, will not need further proof.'

Cf. *Mission of the Comforter*, vol. I, Preface, p. ix: 'While the revived study of the theology of earlier ages, if carried on critically, with a discernment of that which each age had to effect toward the progressive unfolding of the truth . . . cannot be otherwise than beneficial; on the other hand . . . the merest truisms of our own age are better than the truths of former ages, unless these have been duly appropriated and assimilated to the body of our thoughts.'

[146] Hare described Ward as 'one who is so fond of playing at heels overhead with history' (*Vindication of Luther*, p. 134). Cf. Arnold on

Newman (*Sermons*, vol. IV, introduction, p. viii): 'There are few stranger and sadder sights than to see men judging of whole periods of the history of mankind with the blindness of party spirit.'

[147] See letter to Susannah Arnold, Nov. 1830. A letter in *The Times* had recommended the clergy to preach subordination and obedience. Arnold points out that the Prophets 'in a similar state of society in Judea' were far from preaching subordination. Cf. letter to A. Hare, 24 Dec. 1830; *Sermons*, vol. I, pp. 268 *et seq.*; Stanley, *Apostolical Age*, pp. 264-6, 355.

[148] The young candidate for ordination ought fully to understand the nature of the society which he is to endeavour to influence: 'the relation of its several parts to one another; what may have disordered those relations . . . etc.' (*Sermons*, vol. III, pp. xi *et seq.*).

[149] Leaping from the Apostles to the Reformers as was once done was a great error. We must take into account the process of change in the seventeen intervening centuries.

Cf. letter of 22 Sept. 1839. As regards the application of scripture knowledge, there are two states of the human race which we want to understand thoroughly, says Arnold; the state when the New Testament was written and our own. And our own state is so connected with and dependent on the past that in order to understand it thoroughly we must go backwards into past ages, and thus in fact, we are obliged to go back till we connect our own time with the first century, and in many points with centuries yet more remote.

[150] See Arnold, *Catholic Claims*, p. 102. This attack on the ignorance of the clergy with regard to politics and history caused an outcry. Stanley says that the part of the pamphlet 'in which he denied the competence of the clergy to pronounce upon historical questions, created an impression against him in the great body of his profession, which, perhaps, was never wholly removed' (Stanley, *Life*, p. 135).

[151] Cf. Whately, Bampton Lectures (1822): 'it should be remembered that, practically speaking, all truth is relative.'

Stanley, *Essay on the Theology of the 19th Century* (1865). 'That there is such a thing as the Theology of a particular age is obvious' (*Essays chiefly on Church and State*, p. 452).

Stanley attacks Macaulay's belief in the changelessness of theology (*Addresses and Sermons*, pp. 62-3). 'There are times when ancient truths become modern falsehoods' (*Jewish Church*, vol. II, p. 521). 'As there is a varying theology of the 6th, 13th and 18th centuries, as there is a separate theology of Greek and Latin and German Christendom. . . .' (*American Sermons*, p. 231). The Medieval schoolmen are described as 'the extinct species of a dead theology' (*Sermons on Special Occasions*, p. 229). 'What in one station of life, or one age of the world, is a grace, in another station or age is a deformity' (*Sermons . . . in Canterbury Cathedral*, p. 260).

Hare, *Guesses at Truth* (2nd ed., 2nd series): 'The forms, the colouring, the vegetation change, as we pass from one zone of time to another: nor, would it require a very nice discrimination to distinguish, on reading any theological work, to what age of Christianity it belongs' (p. 25). Every age has its own peculiar forms of moral and intellectual life (p. 166).

Milman, *Christianity*, vol. 1. Each state of social culture has its characteristic theology, self-adapted to the intellectual and moral condition of the people and coloured in some degree by the habits of life (p. 11).

[152] Arnold, letter of 4 Nov. 1835: 'My own firm belief is that every difference of opinion amongst Christians is either remediable by time and mutual fairness, or else is indifferent: and this, I believe, would be greatly furthered, if we would get rid entirely of the false traditional standard of interpretation, and interpret Scripture solely by itself.' An historical approach to the Bible would help to heal the division between sects.

[153] 'The religion of Christendom has, besides its other transcendent marks of superiority, this broad distinction from all other religions, that it is essentially historical. Of the three great manifestations of God to man . . . "God in History" will to a large part of mankind be the most persuasive' (Stanley, *Sermons on Special Occasions*, p. 156).

[154] 'I have used the language of the Law . . . because I was afraid that you could not profitably understand any other' (*Sermons*, vol. II, p. 99).

[155] R. L. Archer, *Secondary Education in the 19th Century*, p. 50. Archer talks of Arnold's 'discovery': 'no one discovered it [the use of the Sixth Form to transmit the headmaster's influence] before and everyone used it afterwards' (p. 68).

[156] L. Trilling describes Arnold's Rugby as a fine example of Vico's Second Age [that is, the Age of Heroes]. By this arrangement [the praepostors of the Sixth Form with their powers of flogging] Arnold sought, successfully, to channel bullying strength into a feudal protective nobility (*Matthew Arnold*, p. 63).

[157] *Miscellaneous Works*, p. 360: 'It is our wisdom and our duty to

cultivate their faculties each in its season, first the memory and imagination and then the judgment.' These are Coleridge's words; see *Literary Remains*, vol. I, pp. 198-9; Arnold had read this work.

[158] Contrast the Edgeworths, who, like Locke, distrusted the creative imagination and banned all such things as fairy tales. 'Why', asks Maria Edgeworth, 'should the mind be filled with fantastic visions instead of useful knowledge?' See Adamson, *English Education*, p. 98.

[159] In Stanley's school note-books, which are to be seen at Rugby School, there are constant parallels such as that between the mutilation of the Hermae and the Popish Plot, and the following entry: 'The Plataeans had done for Greece what Rome did once for Christendom, i.e. preserving it from its common enemy—the Thebans had done for it what the Protestants did—preserving it from its internal enemy—Marathon was the Crusades . . . Coronea the Reformation.'

[160] Herodotus should be rendered in the style and language of the chroniclers; Thucydides in that of Bacon or Hooker, while Demosthenes, Cicero, Caesar and Tacitus require a style completely modern—the perfection of English such as we now speak and write it. Cf. letter of 20 Dec. 1837: 'If I were to translate Herodotus it were absurd to do it in my common English because he and I do not belong to analogous periods of Greek and English literature. I should try to translate him in English of that period of our national cultivation which corresponds to the period of Greek cultivation at which he wrote.'

[161] See R. L. Archer, *Secondary Education*, p. 57. At Rugby the history of Greece and Rome was more studied than that of France and England. Arnold was not the first to introduce modern history into the public schools (Adamson, *English Education*, p. 59).

There is at Rugby School (in MS.) an article, headed 'Thoughts on the Advancement of Academical education in England' (London, 1826), which appears to be an unpublished review in which Arnold criticizes the prevailing classical education. Most people complete this education, Arnold wrote, without anything more than the most superficial acquaintance with the history of ancient nations and in entire ignorance of the state of opinion amongst them, of the progress of the arts, of all the most important points in their physical and moral condition. There is an examination of Sixth Form syllabuses at Eton, Winchester and Westminster. Arnold argues that for most minds the aesthetic value of the poetry which is studied is slight, therefore why not concentrate on the historians, where there are other values which to understandings of the ordinary stamp are absolutely essential? The editor of a historian is more useful than the editor of a poet. He suggests a school museum, a collection of coins, etc. to illustrate classical history. (There is a portrait in *Tom Browne's School Days* of 'the Doctor' chiselling a model of 'one of Nicias' galleys'; see Everyman ed., p. 115). In this respect Arnold is one step in advance of the critics of classical education in the *Edinburgh Review* (see vol. xv, p. 47: 'scholars have come to value not the filbert, but the shell, not what may be read in Greek but Greek itself' [1809]), who maintained, however, that the poets and orators of classical literature are of 'infinitely greater value' than its philosophy, 'for as society advances men think more accurately . . . and imagine more tamely'. They are arguing against verbal scholarship for more aesthetic content, Arnold is arguing against both for historical content.

[162] Arnold, *Sermons*, vol. vi, p. 244: 'Our classical reading is on the whole conducted wisely . . . we study it in its beginning, middle and end.'

[163] The Gower St. College was anti-Christian, inasmuch as it meddled with moral subjects—having lectures in History—and yet did not require its professors to be Christians (Letter of 28 Nov. 1837) Adamson, *English Education*, p. 94.

[164] Oxford and London Universities, Arnold wrote, were 'as bad as one another in their opposite ways, and perpetuating their badness by remaining distinct, instead of mixing' (Letter of 20 May 1835).

[165] Cf. Thirlwall's sermon preached on the occasion of the laying of the foundation stone of the Welsh Educational Institute, 1849: 'Above all I would say that the education afforded by such an institution as this should be *practical*. And by this I mean neither to include nor to exclude that which often passes under the name, as if alone entitled to it; the knowledge which is applicable to the supply of the material wants of society. I could not admit that the sciences which are connected with this object, are either eminently practical or eminently progressive, unless I believed that historical knowledge has no bearing upon action, or that it admits of no enlargement from future observation and discoveries. But when I speak of *practical* education, I am speaking of that quality without which no education deserves the name, and which involves the highest end of all learning' (*Remains*, vol. iii, p. 351).

Cf. Adamson on Arnold, in *English Education*, p. 68. Because of his conviction that the true aim of education was religious and moral, Arnold found the chief value of a classical training in its application to the everyday affairs of English life. It is not an accident that so many of his pupils became workers for social and political reforms. Here again knowledge, learning, scholarship were instruments, not ends.

[166] Cf. Thirlwall, *Remains*, vol. III, p. 379: 'This simple description marks its place in the present, and its relation to the past and the future. Unless it answered to this description, it would not be a real living thing, and would have no right to take up room in God's world, and no power to occupy it long.'

[167] See *Life and Letters of Macaulay* (G. O. Trevelyan). Macaulay writes, 'What the Greek and Latin were to the contemporaries of More and Ascham, our tongue is to the people of India' (p. 291).

[168] Cf. Arnold: Because the early age of an individual bears a great resemblance to the early age of a nation, the characters of the Old Testament are often more suited in a Christian country for the instruction of the young than for those of more advanced years (*Sermons*, vol. IV, pp. 93-4).

[169] Cf. Milman: 'The great principle of education by the State—education on perfectly equable terms to all classes of the community' (*Quarterly Review*, vol. 78, p. 417).

Cf. *Connop Thirlwall* by J. C. Thirlwall, p. 149. In his own diocese Thirlwall fostered the cause of middle and lower class education, on the ground that training so valuable should not be the exclusive property of a privileged class.

[170] Arnold applied the Romantic theory of the development of poetry to the breaking down of cultural class barriers. He wrote a preface to a collection of poems for the poorer classes (1831) in which he was at pains to point out that poetry, the most natural thing in the world, has been regarded as the most artificial, the exclusive possession of the rich. This, he said, was owing to a real honest ignorance as to 'the natural history of poetry'. Poetry is simply the expression of feelings, of the feelings predominant in any given age (*Miscellaneous Works*, pp. 253-4).

Cf. Stanley. The principles of the science of history illustrated by the Old Testament would make for a wider understanding of the Bible and of history generally. 'The difficulty which uneducated ... classes of men find in rightly judging, or even rightly conceiving, of a state of morals and religion different from their own is one of the main obstacles to a general diffusion of comprehensive and tolerant views of past history. What we want is some common ground on which the poor and unlearned can witness the application of such views no less than the highly educated. Such a ground is furnished by many parts of the sacred narrative; but by none so much as the Book of Judges. If we urge that the Middle Ages must be judged by another standard than our own . . . to half the world we shall be saying words without meaning. But if we can show that the very same variation of judgment is allowed and enforced [in Judges] we shall . . . have a chance of being heard' (*Jewish Church*, vol. 1, pp. 308 *et seq.*).

A general education, said Stanley, would unite citizens more closely than ever by a common bond; 'because its social movements would be invested with that moral interest which alone can prevent them from sinking into party politics.' Education was not so much the result, as the very soul, of civilization itself (*Prize Essay*, pp. 22-3).

See *Connop Thirlwall*, pp. 147-9. Hook's famous pamphlet 'on the means of rendering more efficient the education of the people' (reviewed by Milman in the *Quarterly Review*, 1846), designed to test public feeling, was in the form of a letter to Thirlwall. See Adamson, *English Education*, p. 141; *Connop Thirlwall*, p. 148. His biographer talks of Thirlwall's advanced philosophy of education, 'undoubtedly influenced by Rousseau and Pestalozzi'. Thirlwall need not, however, have gone so far for his philosophy of education—though foreign theories of education were receiving attention in England at this time (see Adamson) —because it is simply the application of the Liberal Anglican 'science of history', as in the case of Arnold and Milman.

[171] He praises Elphinstone (*History of India*) for not affecting 'that display of philosophical indifference, too common among modern writers, which makes justice, purity, humanity merely the result of a certain stage of civilization' (*Quarterly Review*, vol. 68 [1841], p. 380).

[172] 'I think Conservatism far worse than Toryism, if by Toryism be meant a fondness for monarchical or even despotic government; for despotism may often further the advance of a nation, and a good dictatorship may be a very excellent thing' (Arnold, 16 Dec. 1835). 'Different states of society require governments more or less despotic. . .' (27 Jan. 1838).

Milman: 'There are periods in human history when despotism, temporal or spiritual, seems necessary or inevitable for the maintenance of social order' (*Savonarola and other Essays*, p. 364).

[173] Shall it then be inferred with the author, from this theory of progressive refinement, as developed in Jewish history, that Christianity is the religion of civilized . . . man and by consequence . . . that the uncivilized and unenlightened offer little hopes of conversion? (Fausset's *Jewish History*, etc., p. 37).

[174] Arnold wrote to a missionary in India that the different notions of right and wrong encountered there would incline one to think that truth was subjective, 'one truth for Europe and another for India', were it not for the existence of a moral sense common to all men (see letter of 10 April 1842).

[175] *Two General Lectures on Modern History delivered on Inauguration*, H. H. Vaughan (1849): The whole character of Modern History is due to the fact that while nations perish, society lives on (p. 17). Through the greatest revolutions [the Germanic Invasions] was preserved the continuance of society (p. 19). The idea of society 'carries us to the limits of History as an isolated branch of knowledge' (p. 20). Historical experience has not disclosed any very close analogy between the lives of of individuals and of nations. There is no law to be collected by observation prescribing certain periods for development, maturity, and decay. There are not even any constant conditions and symptoms of such states in the history of different nations, as there are unfailing indications of them in the progress of individual life. The analogy between the life of individuals and of nations is 'slight and fallacious' (pp. 14-15). I would define history 'as a disclosure of the critical changes in the condition of society' (p. 5). It may be observed that I have spoken of society, that is, a social unity, rather than of a nation, or a national unity (p. 12).

'A truth in the principle of which we must acquiesce . . . that the same general condition of society can hardly be exemplified in different nations'. It appears therefore that history can rarely reach a universal or even a highly general form (p. 41). The changes of history are not recurrent, nor periodic, but critical (p. 29).

Vaughan 'approaches the region of general and universal truth' thus: the historical judgment, he says is a judgment by peers; the many are . . . impanelled and indirectly questioned to pronounce on the one. Through the poetry of all ages we must estimate the poetry of one. This applies to art, finance, military organization, social economy; the many comment on the few and all on each (pp. 47-8). Historical understanding demands this comparative knowledge. Thus we are borne into the general truths of science past the particular statements of history. This seems to correspond to the 'chemical method' of Macaulay.

[176] Goldwin Smith, *Lectures:* History cannot be made into a science because it is made up of human actions which are free (p. 56). Is history then a chaos, asks Goldwin Smith, because it has no necessary law? Is there no philosophy of history because there is no science? (p. 70). For Goldwin Smith the philosophy of history deals with two 'grand facts':

the division of nations ('nationality is an ordinance of nature and a natural bond') and the succession of ages. The moral, intellectual, and material progress of the race is natural (being caused by the action of desires and faculties implanted in the nature of man, cf. Hare) but is not like any progress caused by a necessary law. It is a progress of effort (p. 73). The idea of progress, properly considered, makes for humility (cf. Arnold) (p. 74). Progress is the advance of the moral character of the race (pp. 76-7). The moral and spiritual experience of man as well as his knowledge grows from age to age; progress is not intellectual only. If the end and key of history is the formation of character by effort, the end and key of history are the same with the end and key of the life of man (p. 79). There follows a critique of Comte's Law of the three Stages (p. 83) (see also pp. 57-9). The religious theory of the world covers all the facts; the physical view, the physical facts alone (p. 87). The philosophy of history springs from the realization of the facts of the moral unity of the human race (p. 91). Effort is the law, if law it can be called, of history (p. 95). History is a series of struggles to elevate the character of humanity in all its aspects frequently followed by a relapse. Those who espouse the theory of necessary development as the key to history are driven to strange consequences, e.g. asserting the torpid sensualism of the Roman Empire to be an advance upon the narrow virtue of the Republic (p. 95). Nevertheless, the elevation of the moral type gained by the previous effort is gained for ever (p. 96).

Moral effort and reaction constitute the rhythm of history for Goldwin Smith. For Goldwin Smith, too, there is an historical and an absolute morality. It is folly to force on backward nations the laws of the most forward, but that which is good for all may be given to all, pure morality and true religion. We cannot at once give a constitution to the Hindu, but we may at once, in spite of the necessary development of civilization through which all nations pass, teach him the virtue and the unity of God (pp. 61-2). If the Churches of Hildebrand, Luther and Calvin are passing away, above them rises that Church of pure religion and virtue (p. 92). Sustained progress has not been universal, but confined to Christian nations (p. 123). Christianity alone is compatible with true progress, it cannot conflict with science and the progress of knowledge (p. 153).

This summary of Goldwin Smith's historical thought, as revealed in his lectures, shows the close connection between it and the Liberal Anglican philosophy of history. Goldwin Smith went to Oxford in 1841; so that he probably heard Arnold, and may have known Stanley.

[177] According to Michael Oakeshott, for example, historical experience is not scientific, nor philosophical, nor practical. The science of history, the philosophy of history, and practical history, are examples of *ignoratio elenchi*. (See *Experience and its Modes*.)

[178] See, for example, Shotwell, *The History of History* (1939). The great historians of antiquity were writers of modern history. Herodotus, Thucydides, Polybius, Tacitus were interested in what had happened because of what was happening (p. 325). The study of the past 'for its own sake' reflects the professionalism of the late 19th century, and Oakeshott's philosophy reflects this professionalism. Cf. *Experience and its Modes*, p. 158: 'The worlds of history and of practice are different . . . modifications of experience, and taken as worlds and by themselves, there can be no relation or commerce between them.'

[179] Coleridge arguing against 'the historical method of investigation', in which 'the author professes to find out the truth by collecting the facts of the case and tracing them backwards', said 'what can be more striking, in illustration of the utter inadequacy of this line of investigation for arriving at the real truth, than the political treatises and constitutional histories which we have in every library? A Whig proves his case convincingly . . . then comes an old Tory and ferrets up a hamperful of conflicting documents and notices, which proves his case *per contra*. A takes this class of facts; B takes that class: each proves something true, neither proves *the* truth; or anything like *the* truth; that is the whole truth' (*Table Talk* [1833], p. 219).

[180] 'Arnold's liberalism, religious and political, was the liberalism of one whose soul was possessed by a vision of Christian unity' (Storr, *Development of English Theology*, p. 106).

[181] Cf. Hare: 'The difficulties which stand in the way of an impartial objective history, such as shall do justice to all men in a spirit of love . . . are much greater, inasmuch as our feelings are far otherwise affected by human interests and actions . . . than by anything in inanimate nature' (*The Means of Unity*, note A, p. 55).

[182] Cf. Hare: The historical method in philosophy will only make us conceited and presumptuous if we sit in judgment on the great thinkers of the past. But the attentive, scrutinizing contemplation of them is a corrective to such attitudes of mind, because 'the very process of endeavouring faithfully and carefully to enter into the minds of others, as it can only be effected by passing out of ourselves, out of our habitual prepossessions and predilections, is a discipline both of love and humility' (*Guesses at Truth* [2nd ed., 2nd series], p. 251).

History properly studied is an emancipation from narrow, clinging prejudices, because it reveals the diversity of forms under which the same Spirit manifests Himself (Hare on 'Impartiality as a principle of Ecclesiastical History', *The Means of Unity*, p. 12).

[183] 'My sole object is truth—truth uttered in charity' (Milman, *Latin Christianity*, vol. IV, preface, p. iii). Cf. Lecky on Whately: 'It was . . . one of his first principles that there is no more fatal obstacle to the discovery of truth than the deflecting influence of party and system. . . .' (*Historical Essays*, 1910, pp. 84–5).

[184] 'In the representation of character, Poetry portrays men in their composite individuality, mixed up of good and evil, as they are in real life: whereas historians too often anatomize men; and then, being unable to descry the workings of life, which has passed away, busy themselves in tracing the more perceptible operations of disease. Hence it comes that they give us such false representations of human character: one of their chief defects is, that they have seldom enough of the poet in them' (Hare, *Guesses at Truth* [3rd ed., 1st series], p. 394).

[185] Alexander was 'answerable, as a man, even to posterity, for all the evil he wrought, which did not essentially belong to his vocation as a conqueror' (Thirlwall, *Greece*, vol. VI, p. 294). Nevertheless it was Plutarch's 'great failing', according to Thirlwall, that 'he makes the truth of history subordinate to its moral uses, just as a history is sometimes written for the purpose of inculcating certain political tenets' (*ibid.* vol. II, p. 398).

According to Gooch (*History and Historians*, p. 320), the fundamental principle of Arnold's conception of history was that it was a divine process, and that man was a moral being accountable for his actions. The moral test is never absent in the volumes on Rome, says Gooch, and it appears with added emphasis in his lectures. This represents only one side of the picture. The relativism of Arnold's historical thought has been noticed already. Perhaps the following remarks of Milman's will make the Liberal Anglican position clear:—The disputes about Charlemagne's virtues, Milman says, arise from the opposite principles of judgment adopted by different writers. Few great men will stand the test of 'the high and abstract standards of justice, humanity and religion'; where, on the other hand, allowance is made for the opinions and genius of their age, they assume the honours of which they have been despoiled. The verdict founded on such different principles cannot be the same. It is well, perhaps, that there should be writers of both these classes: it is well that the crimes, the 'barbarous glories' of antiquity should be weighed in the balance of more enlightened reason and purer Christianity, 'that so posterity may be disenchanted from its misplaced admiration'. Yet unless due regard is paid to the predominant character of each age of civilization, neither will the leading men who have formed or been formed by each period, be fairly or justly estimated, nor will the true philosophy, derived from considering human nature in every state of moral probation be deduced from the lessons of history (*Quarterly Review*, vol. 48 [1832], pp. 427-8).

Arnold himself said, 'I have tried to be strictly impartial in my judgments of men and parties, without being indifferent to those principles which were involved more or less purely in their defeat or triumph. I have desired neither to be so possessed with the mixed character of all things human, as to doubt the existence of abstract truth; nor so to dote on any abstract truth as to think that its presence in the human mind is incompatible with any evil, its absence incompatible with any good' (*Rome*, vol. 1, preface, p. xii).

Goldwin Smith's words, 'there is a historical and an absolute morality' (*Lectures*, p. 61), sums up the Liberal Anglican position (Goldwin Smith regretted that Caesar was becoming an 'object of adoration', *ibid.* p. 161). Arnold wrote in 1842, 'I have always believed in the existence of a moral sense amongst all men, in spite of the tremendous differences in the notions of different ages and countries as to right and wrong' (Letter of 10 April).

[186] 'Justice and impartiality of judgment to friend and foe he deemed one of the first moral duties of an historian, and Dean Church was not wrong in ascribing to him a quite unusual combination of the strongest feeling about right and wrong with the largest equity. . . . While he was constitutionally extremely averse to the moral casuistry which confuses the boundaries of right and wrong, he had too sound a grasp of the evolution of history to fall into the common error of judging the acts of one age by the standards of another' (Lecky, *Historical Essays*, p. 242).

Prescott said of Milman that, throughout the *Latin Christianity*, he shows that enlightened charity which is the most precious of Christian graces as, unhappily, it is the rarest (see *Life of Milman*, p. 189). All observers are agreed as to the strength of this common characteristic of the Liberal Anglicans.

[187] For Mill, history, in contrast with the physical sciences, discloses a law, not of repetition, but of continuous progressive development. Mill is careful to guard himself against making any assumption

in this definition as to the moral value of one stage in history when compared with another. Progress in the moral sense he does not affirm; he affirms merely the technical law, that the curve which describes the course of history never returns upon itself (Robert Mackintosh, *From Comte to Benjamin Kidd* [1899], p. 39). Cf. Mill, *System of Logic*, bk. VI, ch. X, sec. 3.

[188] The connection between the historical movement proper and the Romantics is the historical philosophy of mind, and this is not noticed by Cobban. For the history of history it is 'the nucleus of romanticism'.

[189] 'If we try to sum up Coleridge's view of political society we shall . . . find the root and essence of it in the idealistic principle which may be said to be the sum of all his thinking, that the whole is more than the sum of its parts' (J. H. Muirhead, *Coleridge as Philosopher*, p. 193).

[190] It is a common opinion with these exoteric philosophers that the invention of printing was the chief cause of the Reformation, that the invention of the compass brought about the discovery of America, and that the vast changes in the military and political state of Europe, since the middle ages, have been wrought by the invention of gunpowder. It would be almost as rational to say that the cock's crowing makes the sun rise (*Guesses at Truth* [3rd ed., 1st series], p. 85).

[191] Letter of 18 Nov. 1835: 'The "*Idea*" of my life, to which I think every thought of my mind more or less tends, is the perfecting the "idea" of the Edward the Sixth Reformers—the constructing a truly national and Christian Church. . . .'

[192] 'There is yet another ground for the affirmation of its reality; that, as the fundamental idea, it is at the same time, the final criterion by which all particular frames of government must be tried' (*Constitution of Church and State*, pp. 12-13).

[193] Cf. Stanley's article in *Quarterly Review*, vol. 86 (1850), p. 387. The reader will learn to recognize not merely a distinct character, but a distinct type of character in the eminent men of the several periods, whom before we regarded much as we usually regard the fixed stars, etc.

For examples of this aspect of Grote's *History of Greece*, see Everyman ed. vol. III, pp. 213, 238 ('the Greek mind was of a progressive character', not stationary like that of the Orientals), 366; vol. V, pp. 336-7; vol. VII, p. 85 (the Argeians about 420 B.C. challenged Sparta to a judicial combat, 'nevertheless, such was the alteration which the Greek mind had undergone during the interval, that it now appeared a perfect absurdity'), p. 163.

[194] For Macaulay, see Taine, *English Literature*, vol. II, p. 416: 'He practises in his style the philosophy of Bacon and Locke. With him, as well as with them, the origin of every idea is a sensation.' Macaulay in his arguments 'must appeal to the reader's personal observation, set out from his experience, compare the unknown objects presented to him with the known objects which he sees every day, place past events beside contemporary events'. G. M. Young says, 'under his Romantic ornament Macaulay is through and through Augustan' (*Victorian England*, p. 8).

Cf. Otto Jespersen: The omission of the relative pronoun, which Dr Johnson terms 'a colloquial barbarism', according to Thum is found only twice in the whole of Macaulay's *History* (*Growth and Structure of the English Language*, p. 119).

[195] Cf. Carlyle's 'Essay on History': 'The inward condition of Life . . . so far as men are not mere digesting-machines, is the same in no two ages' (*Essays*, Everyman ed., p. 82).

[196] 'In estimating . . . the probability of the original composition and conservation of [the *Iliad* and *Odyssey*] in the mind alone (without written records) we must entirely detach ourselves from our busy and complicated state of society' (Milman, *Quarterly Review*, vol. 78, p. 140).

[197] *Mission of the Comforter* (3rd ed.), note G, pp. 206-7: In most cases, Hare says, when criticizing the writers of former ages we are apt to take our own point of view and to quarrel with them for not seeing things exactly as we see them. 'Whereas it is plain that we cannot understand any writer duly, unless we try to place ourselves in his point of view, and to look at things from his position in the world. . . . It is true, this is difficult, because we are so penned in by our circumstances, and hidebound by our habitual thoughts and feelings. It is true too that, in order to exercise judgment, we need a position as well as a comparative standard . . . that each age is to be judged . . . according to the worthiness of [its special object]. This standard however is not to be an abstraction from the notions of our own age: for if it were, the accidents and prejudices of our age would much distort it . . . to gain a just standard, we must correct that which is accidental and partial in each age by the opposite bearings of other ages: not indeed eclectically, so as to get a mere negative result, but seeking by a philosophical analysis after the living principles which manifest themselves thus diversely.'

[198] This is (though not in intention) a criticism of Macaulay. Hare attacked 'that stiff imperious self-will . . . one of the chief diseases of the English character . . . prone to demand that all mankind shall dress

themselves after our pattern'. 'A few years back we used', he said, 'to fancy that the forms of our Constitution were the panacea for all political evils; and we imposed them upon countries wholly unfit to receive them' (*Means of Unity*, note H, p. 99).

[199] Cf. *Christianity*, vol. III, p. 474: 'History itself could only reflect the proceedings of the Christian world, as they appeared to that world.'

Milman disagreed with Grote that the poetic myths of Greece were entirely creative. 'We believe', he said, 'that it is altogether contrary to the genius of this kind of poetry to be *creative*. To the young imaginative age of man, it is in the place of history—it is history' (*Quarterly Review*, vol. 78, p. 125).

[200] Whether the Germans were indebted to Vico or not, their approach to philology is Vichian. See R. Flint, *Vico*, p. 191: Philology as defined by Boeckh is the systematic knowledge of what has been known; the view taken by Vico is substantially the same (*la cognizione delle lingue e de' fatti de' popoli*). See also Croce, *Philosophy of Vico*, p.274.

For the influence of the German movement on the Liberal Anglicans see Dockhorn, *op. cit.* The Liberal Anglicans, he says, were acquainted with 'das Prinzip der ganzheitlichen Erhellung, die nicht dem Wort des Textes, sondern dem gesamten Sinnzusammenhang des Werkes und darüber hinaus der Zeit, in der es entstanden ist' (p. 29). He shows how the same principle was applied by Schleiermacher to Biblical criticism, and adopted by Thirlwall (who translated the critical essay on the Gospel of St Luke in 1825). An example not mentioned by Dockhorn, which illustrates the historical (Vichian) approach, is provided by Stanley, who, in 1848, was planning a work on the New Testament. This was to consist of two parts, each preceded by a preface and the second preface was to discuss 'the subjective mind of the Apostolic Age' (Prothero, *Life*, vol. I, p. 407). The influence of the philosophy of language is also discussed by Dockhorn. It is clearly seen in two essays written by Hare:

(*a*) *Guesses at Truth* (1st ed.), vol. II, pp. 201-14, in which he says, for instance, that peculiarities of language always correspond with and indicate something peculiar and idiomatic in national character. 'Every language must be the print of the national mind. No thought can be taken up permanently into that mind, but it will stamp its image in words' (p. 203). He goes on to discuss the relation between national character and the use of consonants (the objective element) and vowels (the subjective).

(*b*) *Ibid.* (3rd ed., 1st series), pp. 289 *et seq.* The theme of this essay is that language, being the expression of the national mind, grows and changes with the development of the nation. He discusses the 'three genial and generative periods in the history of language' (p. 306). Elsewhere he says, 'Languages are the barometers of thought and character. . . . Every age has a language of its own' (p. 216).

[201] See Taine, *English Literature*, vol. ii, pp. 249-52, for a review of this 'historical poetry'. 'A genuine historian', Taine says, 'is not sure that his own civilization is perfect, and lives as gladly out of his country as in it [contrast Macaulay]. Judge whether Englishmen can succeed in this style. In their eyes there is only one rational civilization, which is their own; every other morality is inferior, every other religion is extravagant. Amidst such want of reason, how can they reproduce different moralities and religions? Sympathy alone can restore extinguished or foreign manners and sympathy here is forbidden.'

[202] *Ivanhoe* was the first of the novels in which Scott crosses the border of his country and of his world of experience. The underlying theory of this new departure, and of his historical reconstruction in general, is set forth in the dedicatory epistle. Scott is at pains to point out that 'the passions . . . are generally the same in all ranks and conditions, all countries and ages; and it follows, as a matter of course, that the opinions, habits of thinking, and actions, however influenced by the peculiar state of society, must still, upon the whole, bear a strong resemblance to each other. Our ancestors were not more distinct from us, surely, than Jews are from Christians; they had "eyes, hands, organs, dimensions, senses, affections, passions" . . . as ourselves. The tenor, therefore, of their affections and feelings, must have borne the same general proportion to our own' (A. & C. Black, 1860, pp. xxxvi *et seq.*).

For Carlyle's critique, see *Scottish Miscellanies* (Everyman ed.), p. 100. Cf. also L. M. Young, *Thomas Carlyle and the Art of History*, pp. 42-3.

Cf. Taine, *English Literature*, vol. ii, pp. 254 *et seq.*: 'All these pictures of a distant age are false. Costumes, scenery, externals alone are exact. Actions, speech, sentiments, all the rest is civilised . . . arranged in modern guise. . . . How should he discover, or dare exhibit the structure of barbarous souls? This structure is too difficult to discover, and too little pleasing to show.' Every two centuries, says Taine, the mind of man ('the source of passions, the degree of reflection') changes. 'Walter Scott pauses on the threshold of the soul, and in the vestibule of history. . . . After all his characters, to whatever age he transports them, are his neighbours.'

Bagehot said of Scott: 'Above all minds, his had the Baconian propensity to work upon "stuff".' Cf. *Literary Studies* (Everyman ed.), vol. II, p. 154.

Cf. Beers, *History of English Romanticism in the 19th Century:* Scott could not enter into the spiritualities of the Middle Ages (pp. 39-40). His apprehension of the spirit of chivalry, though less imperfect than his apprehension of the spirit of medieval Catholicism, was but partial (pp. 42-3).

Ruskin said of him, 'Scott was entirely incapable of entering into the spirit of any classical scene. He was strictly a Goth and a Scot and his sphere of sensation may be almost exactly limited by the growth of heather' (Quoted in Beers, *op. cit.* p. 6 n.).

Heine compared Scott's works to the romances of Fouqué—'It is . . . shallow; brilliant superficiality. . .' 'this mannerism of portraying not the inner nature of men and things, but merely the outward garb and appearance' (Quoted in Beers, *op. cit.* p. 36).

For Scott as a Rationalist, see Benn's *History of English Rationalism in the 19th Century*, vol. I, pp. 309-13.

Of *Ivanhoe*, Buchan says, 'Scott was not depicting a life in whose soul he shared, as he could share in the ancient world of the Border ballads. . . . Medieval England was to him primarily a costume play.' He could not 'think himself consciously into the medieval mind'. We find ourselves in a 'bright bustling world; very modern except for the odd clothes. . . .' (*Sir Walter Scott*, p. 199). Again, 'Scott's strength did not lie in reading the mind of the remote past, but in chronicling its deeds' (p. 273).

Cf. Legouis and Cazamian, *History of English Literature:* 'Scott loses his force as he wanders from the solid ground of contemporary reality, and from those features of it which are of durable enough nature to be looked upon as ancient; it is through the present that he interprets and reconstructs the past' (p. 1024).

In view of the evidence of these authorities and of Scott himself, it is impossible to accept the statement of G. M. Trevelyan (*History and Fiction*, 1921): 'It was Sir Walter who first showed us how not only clothes and weapons, but thought and morals vary according to the period, the province, the class, the man.'

[203] Of Hume, Hare said 'few men have been more poorly endowed with the historical spirit, or less capable of understanding or sympathizing with any unseen form of human nature' (*Guesses at Truth* [2nd ed., 2nd series], p. 53).

[204] 'In historical matters the power of seeing differences cannot be

too highly prized. The tendency of ordinary men is to invest every age with the attributes of their own time' (Stanley, *Christian Institutions. Essays chiefly on ecclesiastical Subjects*, preface, p. 6).

[205] Whately's *Historic Doubts* (1819) is an attack on this criterion of rational experience. Cf. also his edition of Bacon's Essays (1856). 'In former times men knew by experience that the earth stands still. . . . Experience taught the King of Bantam that water can never become solid', etc. Whately, who rejected the Rationalist uniformity of experience, rejected also the theory of Hutton and Lyell, of geological uniformitarianism. See *Lectures on the Scripture Revelation concerning Good and Evil Angels*, pp. 37-8.

[206] Cf. also Goldwin Smith: 'Historical analogy as an interpreter of present events has its limits, the King of Siam may be about to see the water freeze' (*Lectures*, p. 121); Arnold, *Quarterly Review*, vol. 32, p. 78.

[207] Dockhorn quotes this in illustration of the influence of 'Historismus' and also the following remark of Arnold to Bunsen: 'How heartily do I sympathize in your feeling as to the union of philological, historical and philosophical research, all to minister to divine truth' (Letter of 10 Feb. 1835).

[208] 'The immeasurable importance of literature for our understanding of mental life and history lies here, in the fact that only in speech does the inner life of man find its complete, exhaustive, and objectively intelligible expression. Therefore the art of understanding has its centre in the exegesis or interpretation of the remains of human existence which are contained in writing' (Dilthey, quoted in *Wilhelm Dilthey: an Introduction* [H. A. Hodges], p. 127).

Dilthey is only stating here, in so many words, the principle which the German philologists had practised. Cf. also H. P. Adams, *The Life and Writings of Giambattista Vico*. For Vico, 'since words represent ideas or things, philology embraces the whole history of articulate man, the manners, traditions, laws, politics and disciplines of tribes and peoples' (p. 121).

[209] See Stanley, *Life*, ch. 1: Letter from Justice Coleridge, who was still under the sway of the older scholarly ideal. The letter is dated 1843, but refers to Arnold's years at Oriel, 1815-19. Arnold, says Coleridge, did not leave the college with scholarship proportioned to his abilities because he was too interested in the philosophers and historians, and because of the distinction 'which he then made, erroneous as I think, and certainly extreme in degree, between words and things, as he termed it'. This was before Arnold read Niebuhr.

[210] Cf. O. Müller, 'die Philologie darauf ausgehe, die Periode der Bildung des Menschen-geschlechtes, mit der sie sich beschäftige, ebenso in ihrer gesetzmässigen Entwicklung wie in ihren individuellen Gestaltungen in anschaulicher Vorstellung aufzufassen' (Quoted in Dockhorn, *Der Deutsche Historismus in England*, p. 28). Dockhorn deals with the influence of this conception of philology on the Liberal Anglicans.

[211] Was Colonel Leake more than an antiquarian? Curtius, the friend and pupil of Müller, said of him: 'He devoted his life to the rediscovery of the Old World, which has its history quite as much as the discovery of the New World, and for which Leake was the true Columbus.' 'He occupies in the history of science, indeed we may say of modern civilization, an important position.' See Merz, *History of European Thought in the 19th Century*, vol. III, p. 153 n. 2.

[212] '. . . in every country, where there are national legends, they are always deeply and vividly impressed with a feeling of the magnificance or the loveliness in the midst of which they have arisen. Indeed they are often little else than the expression and outpouring of those feelings: and such primitive poetical legends will hardly be found, except in the bosom of a beautiful country, growing up in it, and pendent from it, almost like fruit from a tree. The powerful influence exercised by natural objects in giving shape and life to those forms in which the Imagination embodies the ideas of superhuman power, is finely illustrated by Wordsworth in one of the noblest passages of *The Excursion*, in which he casts a glance over the workings of this principle in the mythologies of the Persians, the Babylonians, the Chaldeans and the Greeks; showing with what plastic power the imaginative love of Nature wedded and harmonized the dim conceptions of the mysteries which lie behind the curtain of the senses, with the objects by which it happened to be surrounded, incarnating the invisible in the visible and impregnating the visible with the invisible. The same principle is of universal application. You may perceive how it has operated in the traditions of the Highlands, of the Rhine, of Bohemia, of Sweden and Norway, in short of every country where poetry has been indigenous. As the poetry of the Asiatic nations may be termed the poetry of the sun, so the Edda is the poetry of ice' (Hare, *Guesses at Truth* [3rd ed., 1st series], pp. 52–3).

[213] The picturesque, poetical, romantic details which mark the peculiar physiognomy and complexion of every period, belong to the completeness of history, but, said Thirlwall, 'we must beware of supposing that the exhibition of them is either a measure or an indispensable

condition of the highest excellence in historical composition' (*Remains*, 1861, vol. III, p. 278).

[214] See Hallam's *Middle Ages*, vol. III, p. 301 (the note O was added in 1848). The fashion of the 18th century, says Hallam, was to exaggerate the crimes and follies of medieval ages; 'perhaps I have fallen into it a little too much; in the present, we seem more in danger of extenuating them.' He criticizes Digby's interpretation—'the general effect is that of a mirage'—and S. R. Maitland's.

[215] 'Latin Christianity . . . had an irresistible tendency to monarchy. . . . Hence our history obtains that unity which impresses itself upon the attention and presents the vicissitudes of centuries as a vast, continuous, harmonious whole' (*Latin Christianity*, vol. I, pp. 18-19). 'The sentence of Polybius which describes the unity, and the plan of his History . . . might be adopted by the historian of the Rise and Progress of Christian Rome' (*ibid.* preface, p. iii).

[216] 'The range of the history of the Church is as wide as the range of the world which it was designed to penetrate, as the whole body which its name includes.' It is the 'distinguishing excellence' of Milman's work that 'it embraces within its vast circumference the whole story of medieval Europe' ('The Province of Ecclesiastical History' in Stanley's *Eastern Church*, pp. xxxiii, xxxiv).

[217] 'It is by a strong effort of vivid *imagination* (a faculty whose importance in the study of history is seldom thought of) that we can so . . . transport ourselves in idea . . . to [e.g. the time of the Reformation] as to forget for the moment all our actual knowledge of the results —to put ourselves completely in the place of the persons living in those times and to enter fully into all their feelings' (Whately in 1830 [*Errors of Romanism*, pp. 149-51]).

Cf. also Whately's edition of Bacon's *Essays*, pp. 458-60. It is a mistake to suppose, he says, that the imagination necessarily tends to pervert the truth of history and to mislead the judgment. On the contrary, our view of any transaction will necessarily be imperfect, generally incorrect, unless we have before the mind a lively idea of the scenes in which the events took place, the habits of thought and of feeling of the actors, and all the circumstances connected with the transaction; unless, in short, we can in a considerable degree transport ourselves out of our own age and country and persons and imagine ourselves the agents or spectators. We are liable, of course, says Whately, to false impressions, but false impressions are much more likely to take possession of those whose imagination is feeble or uncultivated. They are apt to imagine the things, persons, times, countries, etc. which they read of, as much less different from what they see around them, than is really the case. The practical importance, he says, of such an exercise of imagination to a full and clear and, consequently, profitable view of the transactions related in history, can hardly be over-estimated. From not putting ourselves in the place of the persons living in past times and entering fully into all their feelings, we are apt to forget how probable many things might appear, which we know did not take place; and to regard as perfectly chimerical, expectations which we know were not realized, but which, had we lived in those times, we should doubtless have entertained, and to imagine that there was no danger of those evils which were, in fact, escaped. It is typical of Liberal Anglican thought that Whately should stress the practical importance of the use of the historical imagination. It is the practical aspect which is emphasized in the *Errors of Romanism*. Lack of allowance for the prejudices of past ages, which no longer exist precisely in the same form among ourselves, impedes the 'full and clear and consequently profitable view of the transactions related'.

See also Hare on 'The Poet and the Historian', *Guesses at Truth* (1st ed., 3rd series), pp. 367 *et seq.*

[218] See in this connection, Sanders on Coleridge: 'Guided by a "philosophic tact for what is truly important in facts", the real student of history often took into consideration out-of-the-way facts which a reader without the genuine historic sense would ignore. In his own writings, Coleridge delighted to quote from writers and refer to facts which he knew were not generally known' (Sanders, *Coleridge and the Broad Church Movement*, p. 55).

[219] It is Collingwood's criticism of Spengler that he sees the 'dominant' and misses the 'recessive' factors in a historical period. See *Antiquity* (1927), 'The Theory of Cycles'.

[220] Arnold's historical stages are bound together by the dynamic of the nation's social progress, whereas the 'stages of society' of, for example, Condorcet, are not linked by any inner logical cohesion. This conception of 'turning into', of becoming, according to Collingwood, is the fundamental idea of all history (*op. cit.*). 'Where there is no strain there is no history.' See *Metaphysics* (1940), pp. 74-6. It is a characteristic of the thought of Vico. H. P. Adams says, 'Vico had a very subtle sense of the complex influences by which one phase of society gives place to another. We should search in vain for a clear line between periods. In a short work like the present it is quite impossible to convey that feeling

of immense respect for his imaginative realization of the character of change in human affairs which grows upon the careful reader of his volumes. Nowhere more than in him do we feel the truth of the maxim that all times are transitional' (*The Life and Writings of Giambattista Vico*, p. 129).

[221] J. S. Mill, *Dissertations and Discussions*, vol. II, p. 130: The 'shadow of the coming' of a new era of philosophical history rested for an instant on the lamented Dr Arnold at the close of his career (p. 120). Mill obviously did not know of the 'Social Progress of States'; he calls Arnold's lectures 'the earliest of his systematic meditations on *general* history'.

[222] 'There are ... passages in which the author's sympathy with his subject, and desire to represent faithfully a state of feeling and society different from our own, has led to what may, perhaps, be justly deemed an unnecessary semblance of indifference to the loftier aspirations and instincts of humanity which an historian in the 19th century of the Christian era would naturally be expected to commend, at least by implication, to his readers.' 'We may lament, for example, the absence of more direct allusions to that good Providence, which Niebuhr delighted to recognize...' (*Quarterly Review*, vol. 86, p. 394).

[223] Cf. Hare: 'in the intellectual world also the process of Nature is not by fits and starts but gradually...' (*Guesses at Truth* [2nd ed., 2nd series], p. 79). 'All human improvement must be gradual ... the law of continuity cannot be infringed ...' (*Victory of Faith*, p. 215). 'The changes in the moral are usually wrought as imperceptibly as those in the physical world' (Milman, *Christianity*, vol. II, p. 48).

[224] This essential difference between natural and historical evolution is not always made clear. Randall, to take one instance, does not recognize it. 'The romantic conception of growth and expansion and development as the fundamental thing in human experience ... naturally coalesced with the rationalistic conception of progress, as typified by Condorcet in France and Lessing in Germany' (*Making of the Modern Mind* [1940], p. 422). And of the growth of critical history, he says, 'More and more this historical research adopted genuinely scientific principles: that is, it assumed that the laws and relationships observed and experimentally verified to-day have been operating in the same manner at every stage in the past development, and that the past is to be explained by a consistent appeal to such laws and such laws alone' (*ibid.* p. 465). But the historical movement proper, based on the romantic philosophy of mind, assumed, and can assume, no such thing.

[225] See Macaulay, 'On History': 'No past event has any intrinsic importance. The knowledge of it is valuable only as it leads us to form just calculations with respect to the future' (*Critical and Miscellaneous Essays*, p. 189). 'The instruction derived from [social history] would be of a vivid and practical character. . . . An intimate knowledge of the domestic history of nations is . . . absolutely necessary to the prognosis of political events. A narrative defective in this respect, is as useless as a medical treatise, which should pass by all the symptoms attendant on the early stage of a disease, and mention only what occurs when the patient is beyond the reach of remedies' (p. 195). Scott, therefore, is of indirect value (in his novels) to practical history. The practical historian must 'mingle with the crowd'.

[226] See Peardon, *Transition in English Historical Writing*, ch. II. For instance, Peardon quotes Priestley as saying, 'It would be endless to point out every useful object of attention to a reader of history as there is no branch of useful knowledge which history will not furnish materials for illustrating and extending.'

Grote wrote in his journal in 1822, 'Read some very interesting matter in the first volume of Goguet respecting the early arts, agriculture, baking, brewing, oil, drinks and clothes. This is far the best part of Goguet which I have yet seen' (*Personal Life of Grote* (H. Grote, 1873), p. 48).

[227] 'A man will scarcely err in his judgment concerning the sum total of any future national event . . . if he have a philosophic tact for what is truly important in facts and in most instances, therefore, for such facts as the DIGNITY OF HISTORY has excluded from the volumes of our modern compilers, by the courtesy of the age entitled historians' (Quoted in Sanders, *Coleridge and the Broad Church Movement*, p. 55).

[228] Whately's edition of Bacon's *Essays*, pp. 456-8. Histories are to the political economist what geological collections, collections, that is, of specimens of the commonest strata and not of rarities, are to the geologist. They should deal not with what is remarkable, but with the normal business of everyday life. 'An injudicious reader of history is liable to be misled by the circumstance that historians . . . occupy themselves principally (as is natural) with the relation of whatever is *remarkable*.' A full report of the business talk in the markets and shops of Athens and Piraeus on a single day would probably throw more light on the state of things in Greece at that time, in all that political economy is most concerned with, than all the histories that are extant together.

[229] Cf. Hume, 'Inquiry concerning the Human Understanding',

section VIII, *Essays* (1809), vol. II, p. 86: 'Would you know the sentiments, inclinations and course of life of the Greeks and Romans? Study
well the temper and actions of the French and English. You cannot be
mistaken in transferring to the former most of the observations which
you made with regard to the latter. Mankind are so much the same in
all times and places that history informs us of nothing new or strange in
this particular.'

[230] Compare, for instance, Hume: 'If we would explode any forgery
in history, we cannot make use of a more convincing argument, than to
prove that the actions ascribed to any person are directly contrary to
the course of nature . . . so readily and universally do we acknowledge a
uniformity in human motives and actions as well as in the operations of
the body'; and Hutton: In the interpretation of Nature 'no powers are
to be employed that are not natural to the globe, no action to be admitted
of except those of which we know the principle and no extraordinary
events to be alleged in order to explain a common appearance . . . nor
are we to proceed in feigning causes when those seem insufficient which
occur in our experience' (quoted in Geikie, *The Founders of Geology*,
1905, p. 315). Edinburgh, where Hutton worked, was the citadel of
Rationalist history. There is, in fact, a distinct chain of ideas from Hume
to Hutton, Lyell and Darwin, and this is the truth of the saying that the
scientists owe the idea of evolution to historians. But between natural
evolution and history proper there is and can be no connection.

[231] Thus Freeman says: 'Looking then at the history of man, *at all
events as the history of Aryan man in Europe*, as one unbroken whole . . .'
[my italics] (*Unity of History*, p. 21).

[232] Carlyle, *Essays* (Everyman ed.), p. 86. The difference between
the artist and the artisan in history is that the artist informs and
ennobles the humblest department with an idea of the whole, and
habitually knows that only in the whole is the partial to be truly discerned, the latter labours mechanically without eye for the whole.

[233] *Sartor Resartus* (Everyman ed.), p. 86: The Systole and Diastole
of Faith and Denial, etc.

History for Carlyle is a world of organisms, growing and decaying,
'a world-wide jungle, at once growing and dying. Under the green
foliage and blossoming fruit-trees of to-day, there lie, rotting slower or
faster the forests of all other Years and Days', etc. (*Cromwell*, introduction, p. 6).

[234] Cf. letter to Carlyle (Jan. 1840): 'My true reason for addressing
you is, because I believe you sympathize with me on that most

important subject, the welfare of the poorer classes, and because I know, from your History of the French Revolution, that you understand the real nature and magnitude of the evil. . . .'

Cf. L. M. Young, *Carlyle and the Art of History*. Carlyle 'turned to the past for the sake of the present . . . a critical discontent with his own age . . . possibly the primary motive animating his writing' (p. 93). The historian's task according to Carlyle is 'to interpret the value of past experience in terms of present needs' (p. 115). Carlyle's 'ultimate concern is with the problems of the present and how the experience of the past can best be made to serve in solving them' (p. 68).

[235] 'He impatiently dismissed as futile the "blarney about history" which emanated from Germany and the pens of Hegel, Schelling and Schlegel . . .' (Young, *Carlyle and the Art of History*, p. 57).

Thirlwall, like Schopenhauer, regarded Hegel as 'one of the most impudent of all literary quacks', his work as 'arrant nonsense', and his influence as a fantastic phenomenon deserving a study in itself (see letter to Whewell, 1849). See *Letters: Literary and Theological*, pp. 194-7.

[236] Abbot Samson emerges 'In most antiquarian quaint costume, not of garments alone [Cf. Carlyle's critique of Scott] but of thought, word, action, outlook, and position' (*Past and Present* [Everyman], p. 87).

[237] Cf. e.g. *Life of Sterling* (World Classics), p. 40: 'a world all rocking and plunging, like that old Roman one when the measure of its iniquities was full'; *Sartor Resartus*, p. 175: 'The aspect of a deceased or expiring Society fronts us everywhere'; *Cromwell*, vol. II, p. 45: 'late decadent generations, fast hastening towards radical change or final perdition'.

Critics of Carlyle, for example, Crane Brinton, who complain of his lack of constructive remedies, do not sufficiently emphasize the historicism which dominated his thought. He gave the world 200 years in which to work back to the sanity and wholeness, to the Belief and Loyalty, characteristic of the Middle Ages, to pass through the Mechanical ages of Flunkeyism to the Dynamical age of Heroism (*French Revolution* [Everyman], vol. I, p. 107). 'From this present date . . . two centuries . . . hardly less; before Democracy go through its due . . . stages of *Quack*ocracy; and a pestilential World be burnt up, and have begun to grow green and young again' (*Sartor Resartus*, p. 178). 'Two centuries of convulsion', etc. (*Cromwell*, vol. I, p. 351).

[238] L. M. Young, *Carlyle and the Art of History*, p. 73. Cf. *French Revolution*, vol. II, p. 383: 'Aristocracy of Feudal Parchment has passed away with a mighty rushing; and now by a natural course we arrive at

Aristocracy of the Moneybag. It is the course through which all European societies are, at this hour, travelling. Apparently a still baser sort of Aristocracy? An infinitely baser; the basest yet known.' This coincides with Arnold's theory of social progress and with his general outlook.

BIBLIOGRAPHY

The following editions were used:

THOMAS ARNOLD.

A. P. Stanley, *Life and Correspondence of Thomas Arnold*. 2 vols. London, 1844. ditto. London, 1910.

History of Rome. 3 vols. London, 1838–40.

Thucydides. 3 vols. Oxford, 1830–5.

Introductory Lectures on Modern History. Oxford, 1842.

Miscellaneous Works. London, 1845.

Sermons. vols. I–III. London, 1829–34.

vols. IV–VI. London, 1841–5.

Arnold's Travelling Journals. London, 1852.

The Christian Duty of Granting the claims of the Roman Catholics. Oxford, 1829.

J. C. HARE.

The Contest with Rome. London, 1852.

The Duty of the Church in Times of Trial. London, 1848.

The Means of Unity. London, 1847.

Sermons preacht in Herstmonceux Church. 2 vols. London—Cambridge, 1841–9.

Guesses at Truth, 1st ed. 2 vols. London, 1827.

2nd ed., 2nd series. London, 1848.

3rd ed., 1st series. London, 1847.

Vindication of Luther, 2nd ed. London, 1855.

Vindication of Niebuhr's History of Rome. Cambridge, 1829.

Charges, 1843–6. Cambridge, 1856.

Essays and Tales of John Sterling, ed. Hare, 2 vols. London, 1848.

Victory of Faith and other Sermons. London, 1840.

Mission of the Comforter and other sermons. 2 vols. London, 1846.

Mission of the Comforter with notes, 3rd ed. London, 1876.

H. H. MILMAN.

Arthur Milman, *Henry Hart Milman*. London, 1900.

History of the Jews. 3 vols. London, 1829.

History of the Jews, 4th ed. 3 vols. London, 1866.

History of Christianity. 3 vols. London, 1840.

History of Latin Christianity. 6 vols. London, 1854.

Gibbon: Decline and Fall with notes, etc. London, 1872.

The Works of Horatius Flaccus etc. London, 1849.

Savonarola, Erasmus and other essays. London, 1870.

The Office of the Christian Teacher. Oxford, 1826.

A. P. STANLEY.

R. E. Prothero, *Life and Correspondence of Arthur Penrhyn Stanley.* 2 vols. London, 1893.

Lectures on the History of the Jewish Church. 3 vols. London, 1863-76.

Lectures on the History of the Eastern Church. London, 1861.

Addresses and Sermons. London, 1877.

Sermons on Special Occasions. London, 1882.

Sermons preached mostly in Canterbury Cathedral. London, 1859.

Corinthians, with critical notes. 2 vols. London, 1855.

Sinai and Palestine in connection with their history. London, 1856.

Whether States, like individuals . . . inevitably tend to decay. (Prize Essay). Oxford, 1840.

Essays chiefly on questions of Church and State. London, 1870.

Sermons and Essays on the Apostolical Age, 2nd ed. Oxford, 1852.

Lectures on the History of the Church of Scotland. London, 1872.

Christian Institutions: Essays chiefly on ecclesiastical subjects. London, 1881.

Addresses and Sermons delivered during a visit to the United States, etc. London, 1883.

CONNOP THIRLWALL.

John Connop Thirlwall, *Connop Thirlwall: Historian and Theologian.* London, 1936.

History of Greece. 8 vols. London, 1835-44.

Letters: Literary and Theological, ed. Perowne and Stokes. London, 1881.

Remains: Literary and Theological, ed. Perowne. 3 vols. London, 1877.

RICHARD WHATELY.

Jane Whately, *Life and Correspondence of Richard Whately.* 2 vols. London, 1866.

Miscellaneous Lectures and Reviews. London, 1861.

Bacon's Essays: with annotations. London, 1856.

Lectures on the Scripture Revelation respecting Good and Evil Angels: by a Country Pastor. London, 1851.

The use and abuse of Party Feeling in matters of Religion (Bampton Lectures, 1822). Oxford, 1822.

The Errors of Romanism traced to their origin in human nature. London, 1830.

Historic Doubts relative to Napoleon Buonaparte. London, 1819.

Introductory Lectures on Political Economy. London, 1831.

Remains of the late Edward Copleston. London, 1854.

MISCELLANEOUS.

Dr Fausset, *Jewish History vindicated from the unscriptural view of it.* Oxford, 1830.

H. Hallam, *View of the State of Europe during the Middle Ages.* 3 vols. London, 1855.

H. H. Vaughan, *Two General Lectures on Modern History, etc.* Oxford, 1849.

Goldwin Smith, *Lectures on the Study of History*, 2nd ed. London, 1865.

INDEX